Edexcel GCE History

Poverty, Public Health and the Growth of Government in Britain 1830–75

Rosemary Rees

Series editors: Martin Collier   Rosemary Rees

Unit 2 Student Book

WITHDRAWN

OXFORD AND CHERWELL VALLEY COLLEGE

042743

A PEARSON COMPANY

Published by Pearson Education Limited, a company incorporated in England and Wales, having its registered office at Edinburgh Gate, Harlow, Essex, CM20 2JE. Registered company number: 872828
www.pearsonschoolsandfecolleges.co.uk

Edexcel is a registered trademark of Edexcel Limited

Text © Pearson Education Limited 2011

First published 2011

13 12 11

10 9 8 7 6 5 4 3 2

British Library Cataloguing in Publication Data
A catalogue record for this book is available from the British Library

ISBN 978 1 84690 5032

Copyright notice

All rights reserved. No part of this publication may be reproduced in any form or by any means (including photocopying or storing it in any medium by electronic means and whether or not transiently or incidentally to some other use of this publication) without the written permission of the copyright owner, except in accordance with the provisions of the Copyright, Designs and Patents Act 1988 or under the terms of a licence issued by the Copyright Licensing Agency, Saffron House, 6–10 Kirby Street, London EC1N 8TS (www.cla.co.uk). Applications for the copyright owner's written permission should be addressed to the publisher.

Edited by Jane Anson and Rhian McKay
Designed by Florence Production Ltd, Stoodleigh, Devon
Typeset by Florence Production Ltd, Stoodleigh, Devon
Cover photo/illustration © **Alamy Images:** Mary Evans Picture Library
Printed in Malaysia, CTP-KHL

Acknowledgements

The author and publisher would like to thank the following individuals and organisations for permission to reproduce:

Photographs (Key: b – bottom; c – centre; l – left; r – right; t – top)
Alamy Images: INTERFOTO 156, Mary Evans Picture Library 108, 145, World History Archive 70, 129; **Bridgeman Art Library Ltd:** Manchester Art Gallery vii, Private Collection 2, 91b, Royal Holloway, University of London iii; **Corbis:** Hulton-Deutsch Collection 116; **Mary Evans Picture Library:** 42, 91t, 98, 114; **Getty Images:** Hulton Archive 8, 48, 56, 136, 144, Science & Society Picture Library 117, 151, 157, Time & Life Pictures 23; **Norfolk Public Record Office:** 6, 7, 11; **Peter Higginbotham/workhouses.org.uk:** 37; **Punch Cartoon Library:** 142; **TopFoto:** Corporation of London / HIP 55, Punch Limited 149; **Wellcome Library, London:** 104, 155

Tables
Table in unit 6, Source C from *The Forging of the Modern State 1783–1870*, Longman (Evans, E. J., 1983) copyright © Pearson Education Ltd.

Text
Extracts in units 7, Source C, 8, Source E, F, 10, Source C from *Endangered Lives: Public Health in Victorian Britain*, JM Dent & Sons (Wohl, A.S., 1983). Reproduced by permission of The Orion Publishing Group, London.

Every effort has been made to contact copyright holders of material reproduced in this book. Any omissions will be rectified in subsequent printings if notice is given to the publishers.

Disclaimer

This material has been published on behalf of Edexcel and offers high-quality support for the delivery of Edexcel qualifications.

This does not mean that the material is essential to achieve any Edexcel qualification, nor does it mean that it is the only suitable material available to support any Edexcel qualification. Edexcel material will not be used verbatim in setting any Edexcel examination or assessment. Any resource lists produced by Edexcel shall include this and other appropriate resources.

Copies of official specifications for all Edexcel qualifications may be found on the Edexcel website: www.edexcel.com

Oxford & Cherwell Valley College
Library
Acc. No. 042743
Class: 941.081 REE
Location BKN
Date 01.13
Oxford

Contents

References

Many books and articles have been written on poverty and public health that explore the gradual involvement of local and central government throughout the nineteenth century. The following titles are recommended as being particularly useful. The titles have been divided into sections to make it easier for you to select which you want to use for wider reading.

Poverty and the Poor Laws, 1830–75

Brundage, A. *The Making of the New Poor Law* (Hutchinson 1978)

Crompton, F. *Workhouse Children* (Sutton 1997)

Crowther, M. A. *The Workhouse System, 1834–1929* (University of Georgia Press 1982)

Englander, D. *Poverty and Poor Law Reform in 19th Century Britain, 1834–1914* (Longman 1998)

Finer, S. E. *The Life and Times of Sir Edwin Chadwick* (Methuen 1952)

Horn, P. *The Victorian Town Child* (Sutton 1997)

Longmate, N. *The Workhouse* (Temple Smith 1974)

Midwinter, E. *Victorian Social Reform* (Longman 1968)

Marshall, J. D. *The Old Poor Law 1795–1834* (Macmillan 1968)

Rose, M. E. *English Poor Law, 1780–1930* (David and Charles 1971)

Ward, J. T. (ed.) *Popular Movements 1830–50* (Macmillan 1970)

Wood, P. *Poverty and the Workhouse in Victorian Britain* (Sutton 1991)

Social Policy

Evans, E. J. *Social Policy 1830–1914* (Routledge 1978)

Fraser, D. *The Evolution of the British Welfare State* (Macmillan 2nd edition 1984)

Henriques, U. R. Q. *Before the Welfare State* (Longman 1979)

Midwinter, E. *The Development of Social Welfare in Britain* (OUP 1994)

Public Health 1830–75

Flinn, M. *Public Health Reform in Britain* (New York 1968)

Halliday, S. *The Great Stink of London* (Sutton 1999)

Longmate, N. *King Cholera* (Hamish Hamilton 1966)

Longmate, N. *Alive and Well: Medicine and Public Health 1830–the present day* (Hamish Hamilton 1970)

Midwinter, E. *Victorian Social Reform* (Longman 1968)

Rodger, Richard *Housing in Urban Britain 1780–1914* (Cambridge 1989)

Ward, J.T. (ed.) *Popular Movements 1830–50* (Macmillan 1970)

Wohl, A.S. *Endangered Lives: public health in Victorian Britain* (Dent 1983)

Local studies

Boot, H. M. 'Unemployment and Poor Law Relief in Manchester 1845–59' in *Social History* 15 (1990)

Boyson, R. 'The New Poor Law in North-East Lancashire 1834–71' in *Transactions of the Lancashire and Cheshire Antiquarian Society* 70 (1960)

Crompton, F. *Workhouse Children: Infant and Child Paupers under the Worcestershire Poor Law, 1780–1871* (Sutton 1997)

Fraser, D. 'Poor Law Politics in Leeds' in *Publication of the Thoresby Society* 53 (1970)

Hastings, P. R. *Poverty and the Poor Law in the North Riding of Yorkshire 1780–1837* (University of York Borthwick Institute of Historical Research 1982)

White, G. *In and Out of the Workhouse: The Coming of the New Poor Law to Cambridgeshire and Huntingdonshire* (Ely 1978)

Source books and collections of documents

Chadwick, E. *Report on the Sanitary Condition of the Labouring Population of Great Britain 1842* (reprinted Edinburgh 1965 ed. M. Flinn)

Checkland, S. G. and E. O. A. *The Poor Law Report of 1834* (Penguin 1974)

Jenkins, J. with Evans, E. *Victorian Social Life* (John Murray 2002)

Thompson, E. P. and Yeo, E. (eds) *The Unknown Mayhew: Selections from the Morning Chronicle 1849–50* (Merlin Press 1971)

Webb, S. and B. *English Poor Law History* (reprinted Cass 1973)

Personal accounts and contemporary fiction

Dickens, Charles
Hard Times (many publishers)
Oliver Twist (many publishers)

Gaskell, Elizabeth
Mary Barton (Penguin 1970)

Cobbett, William
Rural Rides (Penguin 2005)

Introduction

The nature of the problem

What does the phrase 'the poor' conjure up? Men and women, ragged clothes clutched around them, desperation in their eyes, queuing outside a workhouse? Barefooted crossing sweepers, flower sellers and boot boys holding out their grimy hands for a few pence to keep themselves from starvation on the streets of Britain's nineteenth-century towns? A dispossessed farm labourer and his family, pathetic possessions piled on a handcart, trudging the muddy lanes of the nineteenth-century countryside, looking for work? Barefooted girls with matted hair and dirty dresses, playing hopscotch on the pavement outside their slum homes? All of these images would be correct for some of the time between 1830 and 1875 and in some towns, cities and villages. None of them would be correct for all of the time and all places in Britain. What links them is that all the people described here were desperately poor: they lived close to the edge. Any crisis, like unemployment or sickness of the main breadwinner, easily pushed the whole family into destitution. How was 'respectable' nineteenth-century society to deal with these people? Was state intervention the answer?

Source A

Applicants for Admission to a Casual Ward, painted by Sir Luke Fildes in 1874. A 'casual ward' was usually attached to a workhouse and gave very basic temporary overnight accommodation to the destitute.

Definitions

Proletariat

Originally the name given to the lowest class of citizen in ancient Rome. By the nineteenth century it had come to mean the lowest class in any community and was usually used derogatively. The term usually referred to wage-earners with little or no property of their own, who depended for their income on the sale of their labour.

Overseer of the poor

Each year, every parish appointed one or two overseers of the poor who were approved by the local magistrates. These people were usually churchwardens or landowners. Overseers were responsible for administering poor relief in their parish. They levied a poor rate and supervised its distribution. Under the 1834 Poor Law Amendment Act, boards of guardians took over the work of the overseers and, where overseers did remain, their job was usually one of simply assessing and collecting the poor rate.

Who were the poor?

In the nineteenth century, administrators, legislators, investigative journalists and social scientists used words and phrases like 'working class', 'lower orders', '**proletariat**' and 'labouring poor' to define a group of people of whose existence they were well aware but who somehow evaded precise definition.

In 1849 Henry Mayhew, an investigative journalist working for the *Morning Chronicle*, began a series called *London Labour and the London Poor*, which captured the imagination of the reading public. Although this series was primarily concerned with London, Mayhew did place his findings for London in a wider national context. The point about Mayhew was that he visited the homes and workplaces of the poor and wrote about what he saw and heard and smelled and felt. He was also interested in classification. He divided the 'labouring poor', whose lives he was investigating, into three categories: 'Those who will work, those who cannot work and those who will not work'.

- **'Those who will work':** These were the able-bodied poor, who undertook an enormous range and variety of jobs. The elite of this group, Mayhew found, were the skilled artisans. These ranged from the cabinet-makers and jewellers of London to the machine-tool engineers and textile-mill overlookers in the midlands and the north. They were manual workers, but they had specific skills which they could sell. Similarly, there were craftsmen like masons and bricklayers, mule-spinners, weavers and ironworkers who, when the demand was there, could command a reasonable wage. Finally, there was the largest group of all: the labourers. In an age only just becoming mechanised, most of the lifting and blasting, reaping, mowing, carrying, sweeping and scrubbing had to be done by hand. This was casual work and readily available when times were good, but virtually nonexistent in times of slump.

- **'Those who cannot work':** Some of the able-bodied poor could not work because there simply was no work for them to do. In bad weather, house-painters and bricklayers could not work. A failed cotton crop in the USA meant that mill-workers in England were laid off. The skilled artisans could, possibly, have been able to save some money against bad times. But, in an age when there was no redundancy money and no unemployment benefit, most of the labouring poor had to do the best they could. Pawnbrokers flourished and corner shops gave credit but, when these possibilities were exhausted, many took to begging or were forced to ask the **overseers of the poor** for help. Labouring work brought with it its own dangers, from working with unfenced machinery to living in cramped, wet conditions. Many labourers could not work because of smashed limbs, cracked skulls, broken backs, ripped scalps and diseases like pneumonia, tuberculosis, bronchitis and arthritis. The elderly, with neither the strength nor the health to work, also fell into this group. In an age with no state or occupational pensions, the childless elderly faced a desperate old age.

- **'Those who will not work':** In every society and at all times there are people who choose not to work. It was no different in Mayhew's time. Beggars and vagrants (Mayhew noted they were nearly always men and boys) were a common sight. Mayhew calculated that there were between 40,000 and 100,000 destitute men and boys tramping the roads and begging where they could.

William Booth, who founded the Salvation Army in 1865, defined poverty and the poor slightly differently from Mayhew. He thought of three concentric 'circles of poverty'. At the centre were those people who existed by living a life of crime; in the second circle were people who lived by vice; and in the outer, larger circle were the 'starving and homeless, but honest, poor'. Beyond Booth's outer circle were all those skilled workers in permanent employment, who could usually put a little money aside for emergencies and for their old age. But even these people could be hit by problems and disasters beyond their control. Hand-loom weavers, for example, once the elite of the textile industry, were forced into destitution by the introduction of mechanisation.

Who were the paupers?

To be poor was not necessarily to be a **pauper**, but all paupers were, by definition, poor. Paupers were all those people who could not support themselves and their families at a level generally acceptable to society, and so were given **relief**. This relief could be 'outdoor' and came in the form of food, clothing or grants of money from the pauper's **parish**, enabling the pauper to stay in his or her own home and be supported there. Relief could, on the other hand, be 'indoor', whereby paupers were given support only if they entered a parish poorhouse or workhouse. Whether or not individuals received indoor or outdoor relief depended very much on their own circumstances: whether, for example, they were forced to ask for relief because they were old and infirm, sick or simply unable to find work, and on the attitude of parish officials to the giving of relief and to those who received it.

Why were people poor?

Thousands of families drifted in and out of pauperism. The death of the main wage-earner could plunge a whole family into long-term pauperism, from which it could only be retrieved by, say, remarriage or the older children becoming wage-earners. In a similar way, for a family existing at or around subsistence level with little or no money put aside for emergencies, the illness of the main wage-earner, or more generalised crises like an economic depression, could force a family to ask for short-term relief. It was, indeed, the volatile nature of the economy itself that created poverty for many thousands of people. A rapidly increasing population, coupled with an economy that was moving fast from a pre-mechanical one to an industrialised one, created huge fluctuations in wages over which people had no control.

Discussion point

Do you find Henry Mayhew's attempt to classify the poor more or less convincing than that of William Booth?

Definitions

Pauper
A person in receipt of poor relief.

Relief
Support given to paupers to enable them to maintain a basic standard of living. This relief could be 'outdoor' (in their own homes) or 'indoor' (in a workhouse or poorhouse).

Parish
Originally an area served by a vicar and a parish church. However, acts of Parliament from the sixteenth century used the parish as an area for secular administration.

This was because many old skills were no longer needed and new ones were being demanded; poor harvests and uncertainties over overseas supplies added to the problem, as did the mobility of the population. In short, the labour market was, at times, chaotic and this in itself created poverty.

Why was there such an interest in categorising the poor?

Many nineteenth-century social writers and reformers regarded poverty as being both inevitable and necessary. For most of the nineteenth century, a distinction was drawn between poverty, which was seen as the lot of most people, and **pauperism**. Poverty was necessary because it was only through fear of **indigence** that people would work. Indigence was the inability of individuals to support themselves. It was this desire to force the poor to stand on their own feet and participate in a healthy economy that drove much of the thinking behind legislation for and about the poor. It is important to realise that the Poor Laws had nothing to do with trying to bring about the end of poverty. They had everything to do with preventing the 'indigent' from starving while at the same time forcing the poor to work rather than become indigent and dependent on the authorities for support.

Definitions

Pauperism

The situation when the poor could no longer feed and clothe themselves, even at subsistence level, and had to turn to the authorities for help.

Indigence

A frequently used nineteenth-century term meaning a person's inability to support themselves, and so they became **indigent**.

Source B

Poverty is a most necessary and indispensable ingredient in society, without which nations and communities could not exist in a state of civilisation. It is the lot of man – the source of wealth, since without poverty there would be no labour, and without labour there could be no riches, no refinement, no comfort and no benefit to those who may be possessed of wealth. The natural source of subsistence is the work of the individual. While that remains with him, he is called 'poor'. When it fails in whole or in part, he becomes indigent.

From Patrick Colquhoun, *On Destitution*, published in 1806. Colquhoun was a friend of Jeremy Bentham (see page 19), whose thinking influenced nineteenth-century social policy.

In the nineteenth century, social commentators and legislators were greatly concerned with establishing and quantifying the links between poverty and what they saw as morality. The 'deserving poor' were those who were poor through no fault of their own and were therefore deemed worthy of help and support. The 'undeserving poor' were those whose poverty was the result of some sort of perceived moral failure, like drunkenness or prostitution. While they would be kept from starvation, any help directed toward this group would have to contain within it elements of both punishment and improvement. One of the main reasons, then, for trying to categorise the poor in the nineteenth century was to determine those who were deserving of help and those who were not.

Source C

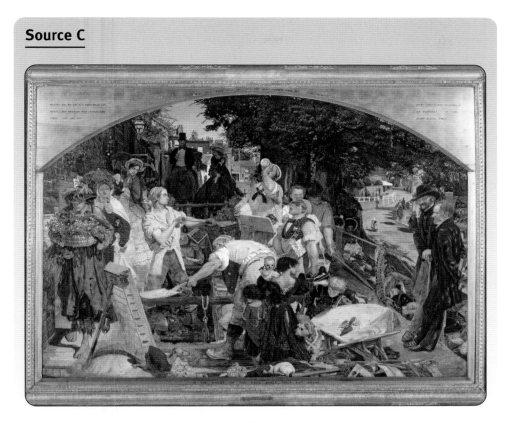

Work, painted by Ford Maddox Brown in 1865.

The great fear, of course, was that if too much help was provided for the undeserving poor, they would see no reason to look for work. Worse, the deserving poor might see the attractions of an idle life with adequate support and be attracted into immoral, jobless living. The army of the undeserving poor would grow, and fewer and fewer poor people would lead responsible, independent lives.

Some kind of balance was required. A system was needed that would adequately support the genuinely needy while at the same time deterring those unable, unwilling or just plain work-shy from using it as a permanent solution to their needs.

The experience of poverty: what was it like to be poor?

Wages, by themselves, are not good indicators of poverty. It all depends on what the wage would buy. Luckily for us, prices remained pretty steady between the 1830s and the 1880s, so it is possible to make sensible comparisons between the expenditure of poor families and what they had to eat. Remember that diet, among other things, was (and still is) a good indicator of general health.

Source D

In many of the cottages, the beds stood on the ground floor which was damp three parts of the year; scarcely one had a fireplace in the bedroom, and one had a single pane of glass stuck in the mud wall as its only window, with a large heap of wet and dirty potatoes in one corner. Persons living in such cottages are generally very poor, very dirty, and usually in rags, living almost wholly on bread and potatoes, scarcely ever tasting meat, and consequently highly susceptible of disease and very unable to contend with it.

From a report written by John Fox, Medical Officer of the Cerne Poor Law Union, Dorset, in 1842.

Definition

Laissez-faire

Literally, 'let be' or 'leave alone'. The belief that the government should involve itself as little as possible in the affairs of its people. In the context of poverty, this did not mean that the poor should be neglected, simply that it was not the government's responsibility to look after them.

In the early 1860s, Dr Edward Smith conducted the first national food survey on behalf of the Medical Officer of the Privy Council (Sir John Simon) and this was published in 1863. His enquiry covered some 370 families of 'the poorer labouring classes' and included farm-labourers and certain badly paid domestic trades like silk-weavers and needlewomen. Smith based his conclusions on the nutritional value of the food that was eaten, not on the wage going into a house. He found that bread was the principal food consumed (12.5lbs per adult per week) followed by potatoes (6lbs per adult per week). Comparatively little milk, cheese and eggs were consumed, even by farm-labourers and their families. It may have been that farmers preferred to sell their dairy products in bulk to nearby towns rather than in small amounts to local workers.

Translated into modern terms, Smith calculated that the minimum subsistence level for an adult was roughly 2,760 kilocalories and 70 grams of protein a day. Modern nutritionists suggest that the calorific intake was sufficiently low to affect growth and physical output. Most labourers spent their days in a state of chronic tiredness bordering on exhaustion, whilst the protein intake was certainly inadequate for pregnant and nursing mothers, as well as for growing children and adolescents. The bulk of the energy-providing foods went to the adult male, who was the main wage-earner, leaving the rest of the family without.

What was the connection between poverty and public health?

Poverty and pauperism affected the most vulnerable members of society: those who had few saleable skills and less education, who were at the mercy of market forces, the vagaries of employers, and their own health. A poor diet, lack of sufficient clean clothing or even a change of clothing at all, and crowded, often dilapidated and dirty accommodation created conditions in which disease flourished.

Poor families were, inevitably, prone to infection. Influenza, measles and scarlet fever were all killers among the poor in the nineteenth century. Diphtheria, tuberculosis and typhus were common. However, to try to improve the health of the community, particularly the health of the poor, posed huge problems. There had to be appropriate technical skill and knowledge of sanitary engineering, and there had to be appropriate medical knowledge about the causes of disease. Above all, there had to be the willingness of the public, local authorities and Parliament to legislate and conform to that legislation. This latter was going to be particularly tricky where the well-to-do had paid for their own private arrangements for sewage removal and a clean water supply, and were going to be asked to pay again to help the poor have similar arrangements for free.

The creation of appropriate support for the poor, and the provision of public health that would inevitably favour the poorer members of society, was to be no easy task in a Britain wedded, in the early years of this period, to the doctrine of *laissez-faire*.

Source E

6 Cottage Place, Kenton Street, London

Pays 3s a week rent; owes £1 13s. Does cleaning and brush-making; earned nothing this week; last week 3s; the week before 5s 8d.

Expenditure: Dec 15 1839

Sunday:	bought on Saturday night, potatoes 1½d, bacon 2d, candle ½d, tea and sugar 2d, soap 1½d, coals 2d, loaf 8½d.
Monday:	tea and sugar 2d, butter 1½d, candle ½d
Tuesday:	coals 2d
Wednesday:	tea and sugar 2d, candle ½d, wood ½d, potatoes 1d
Thursday:	coals 1d
Friday and Saturday:	no expenditure

Had five 4lb loaves from the parish this week.

> From S. R. Bosanquet, *The Rights of the Poor and Christian almsgiving vindicated*, published in 1841. In the book the author gave many fully authenticated examples of the budgets and diets of the poor. Here he is writing about the budget of Elizabeth Whiting, a forty-year-old widow with four young children.

Source F

DEVON	(Case 135)
Breakfast and supper	Tea-kettle broth*, bread and treacle.
Dinner	Pudding**, vegetables and fresh meat.
	(Case 163)
Breakfast	Wife has tea, bread and butter; husband has tea-kettle broth with dripping or butter added, and with or without milk, also bread, treacle or cheese.
Dinner	Fried bacon and vegetables or bacon pie with potatoes and bread.
Supper	Tea, or milk and water, with bread, cheese and butter.
LINCOLNSHIRE	(Case 248)
Breakfast	Milk gruel, or bread and water or tea and bread.
Dinner	Meat for husband only; others, vegetables.
Tea and supper	Bread and potatoes.
CUMBERLAND	(Case 301)
Breakfast	Husband has oatmeal and milk porridge; others have tea, bread, butter and cheese.
Dinner	Meat and potatoes daily, bread, cheese and milk.
Supper	Boiled milk, tea, bread, butter and cheese.

*Tea-kettle broth = bread, hot water, salt and milk. **Pudding = flour, salt and water.

> From the first national food survey, conducted by Dr Edward Smith on behalf of the medical officer of the Privy Council and published in 1863. These are examples of the daily meals eaten by families in Smith's sample.

Definition

Woolcombers

Woolcombers combed fleeces to straighten the fibres and remove lanolin from the wool. This entailed heating huge iron combs in open fires and pulling the hot combs through the fleeces, which were hung up close to the fire. Most woolcombers lived and worked in the same dwellings and were desperately poor.

Source G

NELSON COURT

A great many **woolcombers** reside in this court. It is a perfect nuisance. There are a number of cellars in it utterly unfit for human dwellings. No drainage whatsoever. The Visitors [those compiling the Report] cannot find words to express their horror of the filth, stench and misery which abounds in this locality, and were unable to bear the overpowering effluvia [smell] which emanates from a common sewer which runs from the Unitarian Chapel beneath the houses. Were this to be fully described, the Committee might subject themselves to the charge of exaggeration.

HOLGATE COURT

A miserable hole, surrounded by buildings on all sides. This place resembles a deep pit – no chance of ventilation; a number of men and women work in the cellars near charcoal fires. Seven feet below the surface.

From the *Report of the Sanatory Committee*, appointed by the Bradford Woolcombers Protection Society in 1845 to enquire into the living and working conditions of the Bradford Woolcombers.

The main focus of this book is on the changing policy towards the relief of poverty in Britain from 1830 to 1875, on the development of public health policies in these years and on their impact on the health of the people. The theme which links the issues is how and why governments responded to pressure for change, and the ways in which this period saw a growth in the responsibilities assumed by the state.

SKILLS BUILDER

1 Look at Sources A and C.

   How would you account for the differences in the way poor people are portrayed?

2 How far does Source B challenge the portrayal of poor people shown in Sources A and C?

3 What are the inherent problems in categorising the poor as 'deserving' or 'undeserving'?

4 How far do Sources D, E and F show that the state had to help the poor?

5 To what extent do Sources D and G demonstrate the link between poverty and public health?

6 What, in your view, posed the greater problem: providing for the poor or the provision of public health? Explain your answer.

1 How effective was the old Poor Law?

What is this unit about?

This unit focuses on the importance of the Elizabethan Poor Law and on the ways in which it was used and adapted for over three hundred years until 1834. It considers the basic philosophy on which the Poor Law was based and how this was interpreted in practice throughout the following centuries. In particular, it focuses on the importance of settlement and on the problems posed to the authorities by the able-bodied poor. Those who were fit for work and yet could not, or would not, find it were very difficult to cope with. To give them too much aid would discourage them from finding work, yet to give them too little would mean they would starve. Different solutions to this problem were found by different authorities with varying degrees of success.

Key questions

- Why did the able-bodied pauper present a greater problem to the authorities than those who could not work?
- Why was settlement so important?
- What different solutions were found to the 'problem' of the able-bodied poor?

Timeline

1601 **Elizabethan Poor Law**
Parishes become the administrative unit for raising money for poor relief and for giving such relief; repression and punishment were abandoned in favour of assistance.

1662 **Settlement Law**
On asking for relief, individuals could be returned to the parish of their birth to receive it.

1667 **Settlement Law**
Strangers could be denied entry to a parish unless they produced a Settlement Certificate stating that their parish of origin would take them back if they needed relief.

1722 **Knatchbull's Act**
Parishes could buy buildings to use as workhouses and could make entry to a workhouse a condition of obtaining relief.

1782 **Gilbert's Act**
Parishes could combine to build a workhouse and so share the cost of relief, but these were only to be used for the **impotent poor**.

1795 **Speenhamland system**
Relief given to able-bodied poor by linking it to the price of bread. Widely used in south and east of England. Labour Rate and Roundsman system also used.

Definition

Impotent poor
People, such as the sick, disabled and old, who could not look after themselves.

| 1824 | Select Committee on Labourers' Wages publish their Report. |
| 1828 | Select Committee on the Employment or Relief of Able-bodied Persons, Report IV published. |

The 'old Poor Law' was not one law but a collection of laws that Parliament had passed between the end of the sixteenth century and the end of the eighteenth century. These were, in turn, based on medieval and early-Tudor Poor Laws. Overlying central legislation was a host of local rules and regulations agreed by different parishes throughout the country. This ragbag of laws, rules and regulations was driven by the assumption that the Elizabethan Poor Law provided the philosophical and practical basis for providing assistance to the needy. Indeed, there were no new ideas in Poor Law legislation between 1601 and 1834.

SKILLS BUILDER

1 What can you learn from Source A about Elizabethan treatment of beggars?

2 What can you learn from Source A about Elizabethan attitudes to the poor?

Source A

A sixteenth-century Elizabethan woodcut showing the treatment of beggars.

Definition

Vagrancy

Roaming from place to place with no settled home, work or obvious means of support.

How did medieval and early-Tudor law treat the poor?

The medieval laws sought to prevent a specific type of activity by the destitute: **vagrancy**. Vagrants were labourers wandering the countryside in search of work, begging and stealing when they couldn't, or wouldn't, find it. Images of bands of the disaffected unemployed, roaming between isolated villages, hamlets and farmsteads, struck fear into the hearts of otherwise worthy citizens who regarded them as a threat to law and order. Thus, vagrancy, itself usually a product of poverty, was punished with whippings and the stocks.

The early Tudors adopted a slightly more constructive approach. In 1536, parishes were authorised to collect money in order to support the impotent poor and so reduced the number of those obliged to beg. While the motivation for this approach can be seen as humanitarian, it was also prompted by a concern for social stability. The old, sick and disabled, and orphaned and abandoned children would be cared for. The able-bodied poor should be set to work. This, however, was where the problems began. These people were clearly able to work and yet were not, for a variety of reasons, doing so. Early-Tudor legislation took a hard line: the able-bodied poor were treated as vagrants and were punished as such with beatings, whippings and imprisonment. If they wanted any sort of help, they had to work for it. In 1576 local Justices of the Peace (JPs) were instructed to provide materials with which the able-bodied poor could work in return for relief. This was to be the basis of state assistance to the able-bodied poor for centuries to come.

This was the legal basis of help for the poor, but was not the only help that was available to them. Christian churches and monasteries up and down the land gave extensive charity to the poor in terms of food and clothing and, occasionally, shelter. And, of course, philanthropic individuals did what they could, too.

What was the Elizabethan Poor Law?

The Elizabethan Poor Law of 1601, sometimes referred to as the 43rd Elizabeth, was an important step away from earlier Tudor and medieval Poor Laws. These had tried to control the poor and destitute by punishment. The Elizabethan Poor Law abandoned the more obvious sorts of repression in favour of 'assistance' and 'correction'. The impotent poor – the sick, old, infirm and mentally ill – were to be looked after in poorhouses or almshouses. The able-bodied poor who wanted relief were to be set to work in a 'workhouse' while they continued to live at home. Those who refused work and continued a life of begging and general vagrancy were to be punished in a 'house of correction'. Pauper children were to be apprenticed to a trade so that they could support themselves when they grew up. It all seemed so simple and straightforward. But was it?

Discussion point

Why were vagrants such a problem to the authorities?

SKILLS BUILDER

Read Source B carefully.

What principles were laid down in the Elizabethan Poor Law for:

a the administration of poor relief

b the financing of poor relief

c the giving of poor relief?

Source B

I. The Overseers of the Poor, with the consent of two or more Justices of the Peace, shall:

   (i) set to work the children of parents thought unable to keep and maintain their children and bind any such children to be apprentices

   (ii) set to work all such persons, married or unmarried, who have no way of making a living

   (iii) raise sums of money from every inhabitant and landowner to buy flax, hemp, wool, iron, thread, and other necessary stuff to set the poor to work, and to support the lame, blind and impotent not able to work.

II. Places of habitation [workhouses] may be provided for poor impotent people at the general expense of the parish.

III. All begging is forbidden.

IV. Justices of the Peace for every county shall rate every parish to such a sum as they think correct. This tax shall be assessed annually. If any person refuses or neglects to pay any of the money so taxed, it shall be lawful for the churchwardens and constables to sell that person's goods or send that person to prison.

Adapted from the Elizabethan Poor Law, 1601.

Definition

Poor rate

A tax on property levied at parish level and used to provide relief for the parish poor.

Discussion point

Did the advantages of using the parish as an administrative unit for poor relief outweigh the disadvantages?

Reliance on the parish

The basis of the administration of the Elizabethan Poor Law lay in the parish as a unit of government with unpaid, non-professional administrators. It was not until the mid to late eighteenth century that rapidly growing towns began to employ paid officials. Each parish was to administer relief to its own poor. Local magistrates appointed local overseers, who were empowered to levy a **poor rate** on property in the parish and use the money for the relief of the parish poor.

By embedding the administration of the Poor Law in the 1,500 or so parishes in England and Wales, the Elizabethan legislators had intended to ensure that local needs would be met appropriately. However, they had also laid the foundations for the immense diversity in practice – and therefore in fairness and in effectiveness – that was to be found throughout the country by the beginning of the nineteenth century.

It can be argued that, because the administration of relief was based on an administrative unit as small as a parish, greater humanity and sensitivity could be shown to the poor and needy, because those seeking relief and those dispensing it would be known to each other. Local people would be better able to distinguish the deserving from the undeserving poor. On the other hand, the opportunities for tyrannical behaviour on the part of local overseers, and for the settling of old scores and the perpetuating of grievances, were manifold. It was not surprising, too, that local class relationships and the habit of deference to one's 'betters' tended to prevail. Furthermore, any local crisis such as a poor harvest could place an almost intolerable burden on locally raised finances. With no general pooling of resources, consistent treatment of paupers was impossible.

The importance of settlement

Each parish in England and Wales was to be responsible for its 'own' poor. But this in itself created problems with a population that was becoming increasingly mobile. Was a parish to be responsible for all the individuals who had been born within its boundaries, no matter how far they had travelled since? Or was a parish to be responsible for those who were currently living and/or working there, no matter how brief their sojourn, nor where they had been born? What happened to married couples who needed relief but who were born in different parishes and, maybe, had children born in several different parishes, too? From where would a family such as this claim relief?

The Elizabethan Poor Law stated that a person claiming relief had to be returned to the place of his or her birth in order to receive it. Alternatively, if the place of birth was not known, they would be sent to a place where they had lived for a year or more, or to the last parish through which the person had passed without getting into trouble. This gave rise to an immense amount of squabbling, prevaricating and litigation between parish overseers, anxious to keep their own poor rate as low as possible, as they struggled to stop paupers from becoming a charge on their particular parish. Local **vestry minutes** frequently recorded the fortunes of pauper families as they were shunted back and forth across parish boundaries.

The Settlement Law of 1662 tried to clarify matters. After this date, legal settlement was by birth, marriage, apprenticeship or inheritance. So, for any individual claiming relief, the responsible parish could be the one in which that person was born, married, served an apprenticeship or inherited property. Strangers staying in a parish could be removed, if they were not working, within 40 days and if the overseers considered they were likely to end up claiming poor relief. In practice, most strangers were left alone until they tried to claim relief. Then, removals were common.

Settlement legislation was tightened up in 1697, when strangers could be barred from entering a parish and finding work there unless they could produce a settlement certificate issued by their home parish, stating that they would be taken back and given relief there should they become needy.

The Settlement Laws were designed to control a migrant population and at the same time ensure that the burden of providing for the poor did not overwhelm some parishes. However, they were never applied consistently over time or from place to place. Hated and evaded by the poor and manipulated by administrators, they did not stop a mobile population creating the growing cities of the late-eighteenth and early-nineteenth centuries.

Definition

Vestry minutes

A vestry is a room in an Anglican church where meetings are held. Vestry minutes would therefore be a written account of such meetings – in this case, meetings of churchwardens or overseers of the poor.

Source C

Sir

I have sent you my examination in a letter. But you have sent me no word about it as to whether you mean to relieve me or not. But if you don't relieve me, I shall send my wife and five children home to your parish anyway. I have enquired into the law and you can't take only the two of my children into the House [workhouse] which are above seven years old for you can't take the others away from her until they are seven years old. So if you don't think it proper to relieve me I shall sell my things to pay my debts. Then I shall go to sea or for a soldier. So then you will have to keep them all. It seems to me that you mean to drive me to it for I can't maintain them with my pay. And if you will get me a house to live in and find me work at my trade I will come home. And then I must have things to put in, for I am sure that I shan't have any money to buy goods with. So I will be glad if you will send me an answer about it.

From
Yours truly, Robt Fitch
(Brasted, Kent)

A letter sent by Robert Fitch to the Overseers of Royston, Hertfordshire, early in the nineteenth century. The exact year is not known, but the letter is dated 21 February.

Source D

The examination of a 'rogue and vagabond' removed to North Elmham in 1791.
The accompanying order removed Mary back to North Elmham, but made no
mention of her illegitimate daughters.

Source E

An order for the removal of William Pyman and his family from Watton, Norfolk, to Clerkenwell, London, in 1819. The order was suspended for three months to allow Mrs Pyman to give birth to their fifth child. When the order was eventually carried out, the overseers of Clerkenwell were ordered to pay the costs incurred by its suspension.

Discussion point

Look again at Sources D and E. What, if any, was the significance in having printed forms so that the overseers had simply to fill in the blank spaces?

SKILLS BUILDER

1 What can you learn from Sources D and E about the ways in which the Settlement Laws worked?

2 What was Robert Fitch's problem (Source C)?

3 How far does Source C challenge the view of Settlement given in Sources D and E?

4 How far would you agree with the view that, given a mobile population, the Settlement Laws were unworkable? Use Sources C, D and E in your answer.

Definition

Workhouse test

Any able-bodied poor person applying for relief should be required to enter a workhouse where their life would be regulated and their conditions less comfortable than those outside. This was itself a self-selecting test of destitution. Only the genuinely needy (and, some would say, desperate) would accept relief on these terms.

Poorhouses, workhouses and houses of correction

The initial division of institutions for the giving of relief into 'poorhouses' for the impotent poor, 'workhouses' for the able-bodied poor and 'houses of correction' for the idle, never really worked in practice. It simply was not cost-effective for each parish to provide for paupers in this way, although some parishes tried a variety of experimental approaches. The city of Bristol, for example, gained a private act of Parliament in 1696 which allowed the city parishes to combine to create a 'manufactory', where the profits made from the paupers' work were ploughed back into the system for their maintenance. The aim was to make poor relief self-supporting.

Knatchbull's Act of 1722 allowed parish officers to buy buildings to be used as workhouses by able-bodied paupers. Under this act, parishes could, but did not have to, apply the **workhouse test** – making admission to their workhouse a condition of gaining relief. The workhouse was thus gradually becoming both a place of work for paupers and a place of deterrence. By 1776 there were some 2,000 workhouses throughout England and Wales providing around 90,000 places. Even so, outdoor relief, whereby paupers remained in their own homes, remained the most common way of giving them help.

Source F

The parish workhouse of St James, London, 1809.

Source G

In 1826, and for some years previous, the workhouse was in every part of it, a scene of filth, wretchedness and indecency, which baffles all description, without regulations of any kind. Imagine, too, paupers who for weeks, months and years together, breakfasted, dined and supped, without any order or regularity; who had neither knife, fork or plate; they were to be seen in groups with their hot puddings and meat in their hands, literally gnawing it. Imagine 600 persons indiscriminately lodged, crowded into rooms seldom or never ventilated, the beds and bedding swarming with vermin; single and married, old and young, all mixed without regard to decency.

From an article written by Isaac Wiseman and published in the *Norwich Mercury* on 7 March 1829.

SKILLS BUILDER

1 What, by the beginning of the nineteenth century, were workhouses used for?

2 How far does Source G challenge the view of workhouses given by Source F?

Source H

A meeting of the magistrates for the county [Berkshire] was held about Easter 1795, when the following plans were submitted to their consideration: 1st, that the magistrates should fix the lowest price to be given for labour, as they were empowered to do . . .; and secondly, that they should act with uniformity, in the relief of the impotent and infirm poor, by a Table of universal practice . . . The first plan was rejected . . . but the second was adopted, and the Table [below] was published as the rule for the information of magistrates and overseers.

Income should be	For a man	For a single woman	For a man and his wife	With one child	With two children
When the gallon loaf* is 1s 0d	3s 0d	2s 0d	4s 6d	6s 0d	7s 0d
When the gallon loaf is 1s 1d	3s 3d	2s 1d	4s 10d	6s 5d	8s 0d
When the gallon loaf is 1s 2d	3s 6d	2s 2d	5s 2d	6s 10d	8s 6d
When the gallon loaf is 1s 3d	3s 9d	2s 3d	5s 6d	7s 3d	9s 0d
When the gallon loaf is 1s 4d	4s 0d	2s 4d	5s 10d	7s 8d	9s 6d
When the gallon loaf is 1s 5d	4s 0d	2s 5d	5s 11d	7s 10d	9s 9d
When the gallon loaf is 1s 6d	4s 3d	2s 6d	6s 3d	8s 3d	10s 3d
When the gallon loaf is 1s 7d	4s 3d	2s 7d	6s 4d	8s 5d	10s 6d
When the gallon loaf is 1s 8d	4s 6d	2s 8d	6s 8d	8s 10d	11s 0d
When the gallon loaf is 1s 9d	4s 6d	2s 9d	6s 9d	9s 0d	11s 3d
When the gallon loaf is 1s 10d	4s 9d	2s 10d	7s 1d	9s 5d	11s 9d

*Loaf weighing 8lb 11oz (just over 4kg)

From F. M. Eden, *The State of the Poor*, published in 1797.

In an attempt to combat the financial burden of relieving the poor in their own homes, Gilbert's Act was passed in 1782. It allowed small groups of parishes to join together, if the majority of ratepayers wished it, for the purpose of supporting a poorhouse, and in doing so enabled the cost of maintaining the poorhouse to be shared between the parishes concerned. By 1834 over 900 parishes had joined together in some 67 unions, most of which employed a paid relieving officer. However, Section 29 of the act stated that no one was to be sent to the poorhouse except children, the aged or the infirm. The overseers were required to find work for the able-bodied poor who needed relief.

Outdoor relief

Parishes thus continued to provide outdoor relief for their able-bodied poor, largely because it was easy to administer and could be applied flexibly. Families might, for example, have sudden and urgent calls upon their funds at a time when the principal breadwinner was ill; **cyclical unemployment** might cause only short-term distress and long-term provision of relief in a poorhouse or a workhouse would not be appropriate.

Inevitably, different parishes worked out different systems of outdoor relief. These were geared to a pre-industrial economy and were, more or less, effective. However, from about 1750, industrialisation and a growing, mobile population began to test to the limits the ingenuity of magistrates and vestries in devising effective ways of meeting the needs of the able-bodied poor. In the last years of the eighteenth century, a series of bad harvests coupled with the stresses and strains of the **Napoleonic Wars** brought the Poor Law almost to breaking point. Central government could not, or would not, provide any answers and it was the parishes themselves that had to find solutions to the crisis.

What different solutions did the parishes develop?

Parishes adopted, developed and amended over time several different ways of providing relief to the poor outside workhouses and poorhouses. All attempted to supplement the wages paid by employers; all were open to abuse by employers and paupers.

The Speenhamland system

One of the most widely used systems was the Speenhamland system, which was introduced in 1795 by magistrates at Speenhamland in Berkshire. It was a way of providing relief by subsidising low wages and, as such, it was not new. What was different about it was that it established a formal relationship between the price of bread and the number of dependants in a family.

Definitions

Cyclical unemployment

Unemployment that would only be short term and was related to trade cycles. For example, the failure of one season's cotton crop in the USA could mean unemployment for workers in Manchester's cotton mills, but a good crop next time would lead to full employment.

Napoleonic Wars

A series of wars fought by different combinations of European states against revolutionary France and the armies led by Napoleon. The wars were fought during 1792–7, 1798–1801, 1805–7 and 1813–14. British involvement was during 1793–1802 and 1803–1815. The wars ended with the Battle of Waterloo on 18 June 1815, when the forces of Prussia under Blucher, and Britain under Wellington, defeated the armies of Napoleon.

Source I

The allowance system used by the parish of Winfarthing, Norfolk.

Parishes did not always give relief in cash. Newton Valance (Hampshire), for example, made up the wages of the parish poor by giving them flour. Some parishes took each child into consideration, while others did not increase the relief given until there were more than a certain number of children in a family.

The Speenhamland system and its variations were widely adopted in the south and east of Britain at the beginning of the nineteenth century. It was rarely, if ever, used in the north. However, the system was never given legal backing, although some politicians tried, and it was often abandoned or modified out of all recognition as overseers struggled to cope with changing economic conditions, particularly after 1815.

Discussion point

Which was fairer: a flat-rate system of relief, or one based on the variables of bread prices and family size?

The Labour Rate

The Labour Rate was a different way of providing relief. Overseers did not directly top up low pay. Instead, they levied a parish rate to cover the relief of the able-bodied poor, as usual, and then set a wage for each unemployed labourer. Ratepayers who employed these labourers, and paid them at the rate set by the parish, were exempt from paying poor rates into the general fund. The popularity of this system is not clear, but it does seem that, by 1832, about one parish in five was operating some sort of Labour Rate.

Source J

A Plan to Regulate the Employment of the Labouring Poor as acted upon in the Parish of Oundle

(Since the first edition of this little pamphlet was published in February last, experience has fully proved the usefulness of the plan proposed; and it is now adopted in most of the neighbouring villages, sanctioned with the approval of the Magistrates of the county.)

The Plan is as follows:

A separate rate for the above purpose, distinct from all other rates, is made upon the parish. This rate is regularly collected and published as 'A Rate for the Relief of the Poor'. The payment of it, of course, may be legally enforced in cases where any of the occupiers have neglected to employ a sufficient number of men or boys at the wages fixed upon them to excuse them paying the poor rate.

The principle of the Plan is this, that every occupier who is liable to be assessed shall pay a labourer's wages according to his assessment. This leaves him the choice as to whom to pay it. He may pay either the labourer himself if he chooses to employ one, or to the overseer, to whom the labourer must ultimately apply for support.

From the evidence of Thomas Bowyer, a maltster and corn factor, given to the Select Committee on Labourers' Wages and published in their Report in 1824.

Source K

In the parish of Ash, there is a regular meeting every Thursday, and the paupers that are out of employment are put up for auction.

What do they fetch? That will depend on the character of the man; the best will fetch the full pay of twelve shillings per week. If a person bids eight or ten, then the wage is made up by the poor rates.

From the Select Committee on the Employment or Relief of Able-bodied Persons, Report IV, published in 1828. This is part of the evidence of Henry Boyce, who was an overseer in Kent.

The Roundsman system

The Roundsman system was a common variant on the Labour Rate. Here, able-bodied pauper labourers were sent round the parish until they found a parish ratepayer to employ them. The ratepayer paid the pauper a wage agreed with the overseer and the parish overseer made up the rest from the poor rate. Locals often called this a 'billet' or 'ticket' system. This was because the overseer would sign a 'ticket' for the pauper to take to a potential employer, authorising the pauper to work under the parish relief system. When the work was completed, the pauper would return the 'ticket' to the overseer, signed by the employer to show that the work had been done and a wage paid. The overseer would then make up the difference from the poor rates. In some parishes this would be based on the price of bread and the size of a pauper's family; in other parishes, a flat rate would be paid.

Source L

Q Will you state exactly what the system is that is called the System of Roundsman?

A It is sending in rotation to each of the occupiers in the parish those unemployed labourers (who have Settlement in the parish) to work for such farmers, and to have their wages paid, in whole or in part, out of the poor rates.

Q When a part is to be paid by the farmer, is that sum fixed by the Parish?

A Yes.

Q Are those men, called Roundsmen, considered good labourers?

A Quite otherwise; they become Roundsmen, perhaps, in consequence of their not being so well liked as other labourers; and by being employed as Roundsmen, they become still worse, by the lazy habits they thus acquire.

From the evidence of the Reverend Phillip Hunt, a Bedford JP, given to the Select Committee on Labourers' Wages and published in their Report, 1824.

SKILLS BUILDER

1 Reflect on the three main systems of giving outdoor relief to the able-bodied poor: Speenhamland, the Labour Rate and the Roundsman system. What did they have in common? What were their main differences?

2 Read Source L. The Reverend Hunt clearly thinks that paupers working as Roundsmen were abusing the system. How do you think it was possible for them to do this?

3 Now consider all three systems. How would it have been possible for each system to be abused by (a) the overseers and (b) the paupers? Set up a debate in which 'overseers' defend their own system.

Source M

The labourers here look as if they were half-starved. For my own part, I really am ashamed to ride a fat horse, to have a full belly, and to have a clean shirt upon my back, while I look at these wretched countrymen of mine; while I actually see them reeling with weakness; when I see their poor faces present me with nothing but skin and bone. I am ashamed to look at these poor souls, and to reflect that they are my countrymen.

From William Cobbett, *Rural Rides*, published in 1830. Here he is commenting on what he saw as he rode towards Warminster, Wiltshire, on 31 August 1826.

Discussion point

Does Source M prove that, by the 1820s, outdoor relief wasn't working?

The old Poor Law certainly did not provide a nationwide system of consistent relief for the poor. Practice differed from parish to parish and from county to county. In many places there was a genuine attempt to vary provision to meet local needs. In many parishes the care for the sick and elderly was woefully inadequate, and the level of support given to labourers barely kept them from starvation. But what all these interpretations and modifications of the Elizabethan Poor Law had in common was that they were genuine attempts to deal with the worst effects of poverty. It reflected a tradition by which the more powerful sections of society took on responsibility for the welfare of the most vulnerable. Indeed, the old Poor Law was regarded by the poor themselves as an essential safety net – a safety net that they had a right to access and from which they had a right to benefit.

Unit summary

What have you learned in this unit?

You have learned that the Elizabethan Poor Law of 1601 provided the basic principles underpinning the provision of relief for the poor for over two hundred years, by which the deserving poor were supported and the able-bodied poor had to work as a condition of receiving relief. The parish was the administrative unit used to deliver relief under national Poor Law legislation. Parishes took responsibility for providing relief for their 'own' poor, and settlement became a serious issue for paupers and parishes alike. By the beginning of the nineteenth century, the able-bodied poor were provided for by way of outdoor relief, and the sick, old, infirm and disabled were generally looked after in poorhouses and workhouses. Three main types of outdoor relief were in use: Speenhamland, the Labour Rate and the Roundsman system, and these varied from parish to parish. They were all open to abuse and the old Poor Law was not delivering effective, consistent relief throughout the country.

What skills have you used in this unit?

You have worked with a range of contemporary source material, cross-referencing between sources in order to analyse the ways in which the old Poor Laws were working. You have begun to develop your empathetic skills by using the source material in support or challenge of hypotheses.

Exam style question

This is the sort of question you will find appearing on exam papers as an (a) question.

Study Sources F, L and M.

How far do Sources F, L and M suggest that the old Poor Law was not effective in helping the able-bodied paupers?

Exam tips

Tips for answering (a) questions:

- Don't see these as an opportunity to display your own knowledge. All (a) questions focus on the analysis, cross-referencing and evaluation of source material. Your own knowledge won't be credited by the examiner and you will waste valuable time writing it out.
- Do remember that the only knowledge you should introduce will be to put the sources into context.
- Don't describe (or even write out or rewrite) the sources. The examiner will have a copy and doing this will waste your time.
- Do draw inferences from the sources to show how they could suggest that the old Poor Law was not effective in helping able-bodied paupers.
- Do reach a supported judgment about 'How far' the sources suggest the old Poor Law was not effective in helping able-bodied paupers.

Remember, there is an Exam zone section at the end of this book (see pages 161–66) to help you further.

Now plan an answer to the question above and write a response.

RESEARCH TOPIC

William Cobbett (1763–1835)

William Cobbett was the author of *Rural Rides*, published in 1830, part of which is reproduced in Source M.

1 Who was William Cobbett?
2 How has he contributed to our understanding of the rural poor in the early years of the nineteenth century?

The old Poor Law attacked: why was change necessary?

What is this unit about?

By the beginning of the nineteenth century, many people were coming to believe that the Poor Law was ceasing to cope with the growing and very different demands placed upon it by a mobile and increasingly industrialised population. This belief was overshadowed, and possibly exaggerated, by the pressures placed on the Poor Law by the Napoleonic Wars. Indeed, many of the attacks on the Poor Law were made against systems of relief that were introduced and applied as emergency measures during this time of war and blockade. However, the belief that reform was necessary was bolstered by the views of economists and political theorists who urged different 'solutions' to the problem of the poor. Reform was supported, too, by all those who viewed with delight the prospect of lower poor rates. Governments, aware of the growing pressures for change, instituted a series of enquiries, the most influential of which was the 1832 Royal Commission of Enquiry into the Operation of the Poor Laws. It was the report from this commission that resulted in the 1834 Poor Law Amendment Act.

This unit focuses on the reasons why the old Poor Law was attacked, on the nature of the criticism that was levelled against it and on the motives of those making the criticism. It considers the theoretical, philosophical and practical reasons why change was considered necessary. The unit then moves to a consideration of the commission, the reasons why it was set up and the ways in which it carried out its work. Finally, the recommendations of that commission are addressed and analysed.

Key questions

- On what basis was the old Poor Law attacked?
- Why did the Royal Commission of Enquiry into the Operation of the Poor Laws make the recommendations it did?

Timeline

1815

Ending of the wars with France
Allied forces defeat Napoleon; returning soldiers and discharged sailors, and the return to a peacetime economy, put pressure on the Poor Laws.

Parliament passes the Corn Laws
Import of foreign corn forbidden until price of British corn reached 80 shillings a quarter. Farmers protected but price of bread kept high. Radical protests and riots.

1817

Habeas Corpus suspended
People could be imprisoned indefinitely without trial.

Report of Select Committee on the Poor Laws
Poor Laws condemned as being the creators of poverty.

— 1819   **Six Acts passed**
Confirmation of the government's policy of repression in the face of protest.

— 1830–1   **Swing Riots**
Series of riots by agricultural labourers mainly in south and east England.
The government fears rebellion.

— 1832   **Royal Commission of Enquiry into the Operation of the Poor Laws**
Recommends the ending of outdoor relief; relief should only be obtained in a workhouse.

Source A

The labouring poor seem always to live from hand to mouth. They seldom think of the future. Even when they have an opportunity of saving, they seldom exercise it; but all that is beyond their present needs goes, generally speaking, to the ale-house. The poor laws of England may therefore be said to reduce both the power and the will to save, and thus to weaken one of the strongest incentives to stop drinking and to work hard and consequently to find happiness.

I feel little doubt in my own mind that, if the poor laws had never existed, though there might have been a few more instances of very severe distress, happiness amongst the common people would have been much greater than it is at present.

From Reverend T. R. Malthus, *An Essay on the Principle of Population*, published in 1798.

SKILLS BUILDER

What was Malthus' attitude to (a) the poor and (b) the Poor Laws?

Theories, ideas and opinions

Philosophers, commentators, political theorists and economists all had views that they made known. Ideas and theories, like those outlined below, which influence the ways in which contemporaries act are sometimes described as '**prevailing ideologies**'.

Definition

Prevailing ideologies
Ideas and theories that are current at the time and which influence contemporaries in their thoughts and actions.

Ideology

Thomas Malthus (1766–1834)

Thomas Malthus was an economist specialising in demography – the study of population. He argued that population had an inbuilt tendency to rise and outstrip all available food supplies. The Poor Law made the situation worse because the poor would have more and more children so that they could claim more and more relief. He favoured the abolition of the Poor Law altogether. The poor would then keep their families small because there would be no financial advantage in them having a lot of children; wages would rise because the poor rate would no longer be levied and employers could afford to pay more; everyone would prosper.

Ideologies

David Ricardo (1772–1823)

A political economist, David Ricardo reached the same conclusions as Malthus about the Poor Law, but by a slightly different route. In his *On the Principles of Political Economy and Taxation* (1817) he put forward the idea of an 'iron law of wages', believing that there was a 'wages fund' from which money for wages and poor relief was paid. It therefore followed that, the more was paid out in poor relief, the less was available for wages. Because less money was available for wages, more and more people were being drawn into pauperism, thus draining the wage fund still more. The only way to break out of this cycle was to abolish the Poor Law altogether.

Not all theorists favoured abolition!

Tom Paine (1737–1809)

Tom Paine was a writer and republican who criticised the Poor Law because it was so inadequate. He proposed a property tax on the very rich to be used for a variety of support systems for the poor, among these being family allowances and old-age pensions. He, like others, had a problem with the able-bodied poor and implied that they had to go into workhouses before they could receive relief.

Robert Owen (1771–1858)

Robert Owen was a radical factory owner who blamed the capitalist economic system and abuse of the factory system for creating poverty. At his New Lanark site, which consisted of a huge cotton-spinning mill and a mill-workers' village, he tried to put his ideas into practice by building a new sort of community. No adult was allowed to work for more than ten and a half hours per day, and sick pay was provided when illness or accident prevented a person from working. Children had to be educated in the New Lanark school until they were ten years old, and only then could they work in his mills; corporal punishment of children and adults was forbidden. To the surprise of Owen's fellow mill-owners, his mills ran at a profit. A large store at New Lanark sold goods to Owen's workers at cost price. This, again, was part of Owen's concept of a fair community. He suggested that, if workers were employed in co-operative communities, everyone would share in the profits of whatever organisation they worked for. In this way, the harder they worked the greater would be their income, and they would have no need for poor relief. Care would only need to be taken of the impotent poor.

Discussion point

How sensible is Thomas Malthus' solution, bearing in mind what you know about the workings of the old Poor Law?

Source B

If I was to propose a solution, it should be, in the first place, the total abolition of all the present parish laws. This would at any rate give liberty and freedom of action to the peasantry of England, which they can hardly be said to possess at present. They would be able to settle where there was plenty of work and high wages. Being now in better circumstances, and seeing no likelihood of parish assistance, the labourer would join organisations that would provide for him and his family at times of sickness.

For cases of extreme distress, county workhouses might be established, supported by rates upon the whole kingdom. The food should be hard, and those that were able, obliged to work. They should not be considered as comfortable institutions to be used in all cases of difficulty, but merely as places where severe distress might be reduced.

From Reverend T. R. Malthus, *An Essay on the Principle of Population*, published in 1798.

Source C

Any plan for improving the lot of the poor should combine ways of preventing their children from acquiring bad habits and to give them good ones – to provide useful training and instruction for them – to provide proper work for the adults – to direct their work and expenditure so as to produce the greatest benefit to themselves and to society; and to place them under such circumstances as shall remove them from unnecessary temptations.

These advantages cannot be given either to individuals or to families. They can only be effectively introduced in establishments containing a population of from 500 to 1500 people.

From Robert Owen, *Report to the Committee of the Association for the Relief of the Manufacturing and Labouring Poor*, March 1817.

Discussion point

Who was more likely to have more correct ideas about poverty and the poor – Thomas Malthus, who was a professor of history and political economy, or Robert Owen, who was a mill-owner?

Ideologies

Jeremy Bentham (1748–1832)

Jeremy Bentham was a philosopher and lawyer who developed the theory of **utilitarianism**. Any society should, he argued, be so organised as to enable the greatest amount of happiness to be delivered to the greatest number of its people. He believed that this could be achieved if wages and prices found their true level in a free market and all state institutions, like the Poor Law, were centrally controlled to agreed standards. All responsibility for the poor should be given to a profit-making private company. He wanted all outdoor relief to be abolished. The poor would only get help if they entered an 'industry house' where conditions inside would be so bad that only the genuinely destitute paupers would be helped.

Edwin Chadwick (1800–90)

The most fervent of Bentham's disciples, Edwin Chadwick was his secretary in the years before his death in 1832. Chadwick developed Bentham's ideas in that he believed the able-bodied poor (a problem for all Poor Law reformers) should be kept in workhouses in conditions that were worse than those of the poorest 'free' labourer outside. In this way, only the genuinely desperate would ask for relief. The others would seek and find work outside the workhouse. This, combined with a centralised, controlling authority would reduce the poor rate, give relief only to the genuinely needy and ensure that the economy flourished by allowing wages and prices to find their true levels.

Definition

Utilitarianism

A theory that society should be organised so as to secure the greatest happiness for the greatest number of people. Actions and institutions should be judged according to whether or not they added to this sum total of happiness. Utilitarianism underpinned the reforms of the first half of the nineteenth century, in particular the Poor Law Amendment Act of 1834 and sanitary reform. Jeremy Bentham was one of the thinkers who developed this theory and it had a profound influence on his secretary, Edwin Chadwick.

As well as theorists and philosophers, there were others who observed the situation and who made their views known.

Source D

Much of the disorderly conduct of the lower orders is doubtless owing to the habits generated by the existing system of the poor laws. Without a fundamental change, it is clear that the moral character of that peasantry which has been described as 'its country's pride' must be entirely destroyed.

From *The Times*, 30 May 1816.

Source F

The labouring people of England inherit, from their fathers, the habit of regarding parish relief as their right. Those who want poor law reform ought to have known something of the habit of the people's mind in this respect. The labouring people talk of losing their parish as a rich man talks of losing his estate.

From William Cobbett, *Two-Penny Trash*, published in December 1830.

Source E

My heart fails within me when I see in the poor, no marks of deference to the rich, in the ignorant none of the submission to the wise, in the labourer none of the attachment to his employer. When I hear no more the sound of the shuttle in the cottage, nor the merry song in the fields; when I see boys lured to sin through the cheapness of drunkenness, and girls growing up to womanhood in ignorance of the simplest household cares; when I am told, in a whisper, of evils of which pauperism is the parent.

From Reverend T. Thorp, *Individual Vice, Social Sin*, published in 1832.

SKILLS BUILDER

Read Sources D, E and F. How far do the sources agree about the problems created by the operation of the old Poor Law?

What were the pressures for change?

The impact of the wars with France

The ending of the wars with France (1793–1815) led to greater demands for poor relief.

- The harvests of 1813 and 1814 were good in England and on the continent. The ending of the blockade meant that cheap foreign corn could again be imported from Europe, which forced the English farmers to keep their prices low. They had wartime taxes to pay as well as large increases in the poor rate. Some, too, had interest to pay on loans to cover the cost of enclosure. Many went bankrupt, which meant unemployment for their labourers. Farmers who survived were forced to reduce the wages they paid to their workers. Those whom they employed were pushed closer to pauperism. The already creaking Poor Law was close to collapse.

- In 1815 the government tried to improve the situation. Persuaded by Parliament to do so, it introduced Corn Laws to protect British farmers. The new Corn Laws would not allow the import of foreign corn until the price of British corn reached 80 shillings a quarter. In this way the government hoped to hold the price of corn steady and so keep the price of bread steady, too. Since the landowners' profits would not fluctuate wildly, wages would also remain stable. That was the theory.
In practice, many people resented the Corn Laws, which they believed kept the price of bread artificially high. There were riots and outbreaks of violence up and down the country.

Source G

	Yearly average price per imperial quarter	Peak price	Year
1780–89	46s 1d	54s 3d	1783
1790–99	57s 7d	78s 7d	1796
1800–09	84s 8d	119s 6d	1801
1810–19	91s 5d	126s 6d	1812
1820–29	59s 10d	68s 6d	1825
1830–39	56s 9d	70s 8d	1839

Average wheat prices 1780–1839.

SKILLS BUILDER

How could Source G be used to explain:

a that the government was right to introduce the Corn Laws

b the high level of unrest amongst the poor

c why so many more people claimed poor relief in the years after the Napoleonic Wars ended in 1815?

- Post-war distress meant that more people than ever before claimed relief and, to the horror of some observers, began to regard relief as a right. The crisis years were 1817–1819, when the problems experienced by returning soldiers and sailors, the continuing dislocation of trade, appalling weather and poor harvests resulted in expenditure on poor relief reaching an hitherto unimaginable £8 million per year, somewhere between 12 and 13 shillings per head of population.

- The situation was exacerbated by continuing radical protests, which forced the government to suspend **Habeas Corpus** in 1817, and introduce the **Six Acts** two years later, confirmation of its policy of repression and the curtailing of individual liberties in the face of protest.

In the midst of all this, the 1817 Report of the Select Committee on the Poor Laws comprehensively condemned the evils of the Poor Law as being themselves the creators of poverty. While abolition might have seemed to some commentators to be the only way forward, no sensible government could go down that road at a time when distress was at its height and society seemed to many to be so unstable.

The impact of the increasing cost of providing poor relief

Traditionally, as you have seen, parishes looked after their own poor. The money to do this was raised by a rate on property, and was obviously limited. Years of, for example, bad harvests when many more people than

Definitions

Habeas Corpus

Literally, 'you have the body'. In 1679 the Habeas Corpus Act was passed by Parliament to prevent people being imprisoned in secret and without trial. It was suspended in 1817 (and in other times of crisis), which meant that people could be imprisoned without trial for an indefinite period.

Six Acts, 1819

The Six Acts together prohibited meetings of more than 50 people, increased stamp duties on newspapers, made the publication of blasphemous and seditious material a transportable offence, forbade military training by civilians, limited the right of an accused person to adjourn his or her trial to prepare a defence and gave magistrates powers to search private houses for arms.

Question

Why did peace in 1815 lead to more people claiming poor relief? List the reasons in order of priority and explain your thinking behind this.

usual would be claiming poor relief, could prove disastrous for a particular parish. The situation was worsened by having a mobile population, with hundreds of people crowding into parishes in industrialising areas and claiming poor relief that the parishes could hardly afford to pay. However, whether a parish was urban, rural or somewhere in between, the overall cost to the nation of poor relief was rising.

Source H

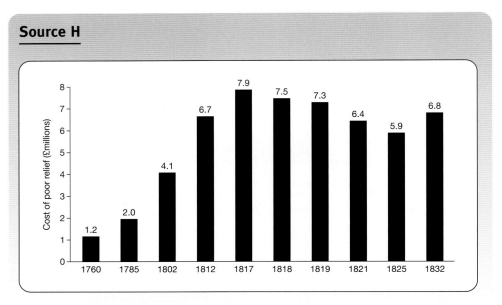

The cost of poor relief, 1760–1832.

SKILLS BUILDER

1 What is the connection between Sources G and H?

2 Does this mean that the government was wrong to bring in the Corn Laws?

The impact of agricultural unrest

Urban protest was matched by rural discontent that came to a head in 1830. In over 20 counties, mainly in southern and eastern England, the rural poor burned hayricks and barns, smashed the hated threshing machines and intimidated their employers, poor law overseers and magistrates. What did the rioters want? They wanted a halt to the reductions in their wages that created paupers out of them, and they wanted the removal of the steam-powered threshing machines that deprived them of autumn and winter employment. Petitions and threats signed 'Captain Swing' gave the impression of an organised revolt under one leader. In fact, there was no such leader and no organised revolt, but it was enough for the authorities to think that there was, and to believe they had to face up to a very real threat of revolution. The Home Secretary, Lord Melbourne, ordered that the rioters should be dealt with harshly. A revolution had just happened in France and he couldn't risk one breaking out in Britain. Afraid that local magistrates would be sympathetic and too lenient, a special commission of three judges was appointed to try the rioters. Although no deaths had happened as a result of the Swing Riots, 19 rioters were hanged, over 400 were sentenced to transportation to Australia, 644 sentenced to imprisonment, seven were fined, one was whipped and 800 were either acquitted or bound over to keep the peace.

Source I

A contemporary cartoon, commenting on the Swing Riots of 1830.

Source J

I can understand how it came about that these poor labourers, poor spiritless slaves as they had been made by long years of extremist poverty and systematic oppression, rose at last against their hard masters and smashed the agricultural machines, and burnt ricks and broke into houses to destroy and plunder their contents. It was a desperate, a mad adventure but oppression had made them mad; the introduction of the threshing machines was but the last straw. It was not merely the fact that the wages of a strong man were only seven shillings a week at most, a sum barely sufficient to keep him from starvation and rags, but it was customary, especially on the small farms, to get rid of the men after harvest and leave them to exist the best way they could during the bitter winter months. Thus every village, as a rule, had its dozen or twenty or more men thrown out each year. The misery of these out-of-work labourers was extreme. They would go to the woods and gather logs of dead wood, which they would try to sell in the villages; but there were few who could afford to buy them; and at night they would skulk about the fields to rob a swede or two to satisfy the cravings of hunger.

From W. H. Hudson, *A Shepherd's Life*, published in 1910.

Source K

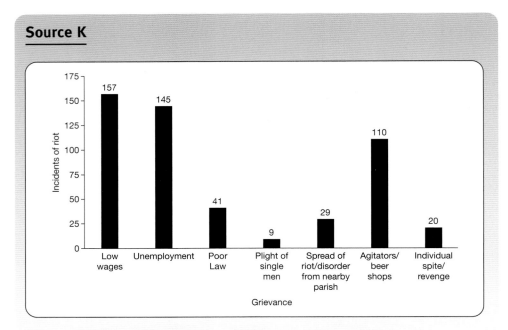

The causes of the Swing Riots, compiled from the *Report of the Royal Commission on the Poor Law* published in 1834.

SKILLS BUILDER

1 Look carefully at the cartoon, Source I. What does the cartoonist think the rioters wanted?

   In your judgement, is the cartoonist in sympathy with the rioters or not?

2 Read Source J. What does the author believe were the causes of the 1830 Swing Riots?

3 Study Sources I, J and K. How far does Source K support Sources I and J about the causes of the Swing Riots?

Definition

Whigs

One of the two main political parties in Britain between the late seventeenth and mid-nineteenth centuries, they were traditionally associated with political, religious and social reform. By the middle of the nineteenth century, Whigs had been absorbed into the new Liberal Party.

Why did the government take action in 1832?

There had been enquiries, investigations, comments and reports on the Poor Law since the end of the eighteenth century. Why, then, did matters come to a head in the early 1830s? The general election of 1831 brought about a change of government, with the reforming **Whigs** having a clear, and probably absolute, majority in the House of Commons. This, combined with a general consensus among the propertied classes that something had to be done about the escalating costs of maintaining the poor, pushed a willing government into action.

In February 1832, the Whig government set up a Royal Commission of Enquiry into the Operation of the Poor Laws. This decision was prompted by long-term concerns and immediate problems.

Long-term concerns

- The increasing cost of poor relief.
- The growing belief that those administering the Poor Law were corrupt, or, at the very least, had a tendency to exploit the laws for their own benefit. Contracts for supplying food, beer, clothing and maintaining the fabric of the workhouse, for example, usually went to local traders who were frequently either members of the local select vestry or closely related to them.
- Fears that the commonly applied systems of relief, such as Speenhamland, that related the amount of relief given to the price of bread and the size of a claimant's family, were actually encouraging large families and perpetuating a cycle of poverty. Similarly, systems such as the Roundsman did nothing to encourage labourers to search for work, since the labourers grew to believe that the parish would supply all their needs.

Immediate problems

- The Swing Riots that hit the agricultural counties in the late 1820s and early 1830s.
- Fear that unrest would turn to revolution. France was again embroiled in revolution in 1830 and there was genuine concern among the powerful and influential that this could spark off something similar in Britain.

How did the commission of enquiry set about its work?

The commission of enquiry consisted, ultimately, of nine commissioners, the most influential of whom were Nassau Senior and Edwin Chadwick. Nassau Senior was Professor of Political Economy at Oxford University and deeply disapproved of the allowance system, and Edwin Chadwick was a committed **Benthamite**. It was not very likely that a survey of the old Poor Laws, and any recommendations for their amendment, would be impartial. The 26 assistant commissioners, who put in the legwork actually collecting and collating evidence, knew what they were supposed to find. Indeed, Nassau Senior had written the main sections of the report before all the evidence was submitted, let alone analysed. Thus, the 'evidence', when it had been collected, was used selectively to support conclusions the commissioners had already reached.

The data was collected in two ways. First, the commissioners devised three different questionnaires. Two were sent to parishes in rural areas and the third to parishes in towns. Around ten per cent of the parishes replied: there was no compulsion to do so. But from this first trawl came an immense amount of information that was difficult to analyse. So difficult, in fact, that assistant commissioners were sent out to 'ascertain the state of the poor by personal enquiry among them, and the administration of the Poor Law by being present at the vestries and at the sessions of the magistrates'. The assistant commissioners were hardworking and unpaid.

> **Question**
>
> What, in your view, was the most important reason behind the government's decision to set up, in 1832, a Royal Commission of Enquiry into the Operation of the Poor Laws?

> **Definition**
>
> **Benthamite**
> A follower of the teachings of Jeremy Bentham (see page 19).

Between them they visited around 3,000 places, about one-fifth of the Poor Law districts. All the information they collected was published by the commissioners in 13 volumes of appendices to their report. They were confident that the evidence would support their conclusions.

Of course, the procedures used by the commissioners and their assistants did not have the sophistication of modern enquiries; many questions were badly phrased and tended to elicit the desired response; many of the interviews were similarly skewed, as witnesses were led along predetermined paths. Nevertheless, this survey was the first of its kind and it would be totally unrealistic and wrong to expect a more systematic and sophisticated approach to have been taken. Furthermore, the enquiry was not intended to be impartial. Its function was to focus specifically on how the old Poor Laws worked with a view to reforming them. The maintenance of the status quo was not an option.

What did the assistant commissioners find?

Unsurprisingly, the assistant commissioners found what they were looking for. It would be best to let them speak for themselves.

Source L

As a body, I found the annual overseers wholly incompetent to discharge the duties of their office. This was either because of the demands of their private occupations, or from a lack of experience and skill, or both. Their object is to get through the year with as little unpopularity and trouble as possible. Their successors, therefore, complain of demands left unsettled, and rates uncollected, either from carelessness or a desire to gain popularity from having called for fewer assessments than usual.

From the report of Assistant Commissioner S. Walcott, North Wales, in the *Report of the Royal Commission on the Poor Laws,* published in 1834.

Source M

In many parishes, especially in Oxfordshire, I have seen the Roundsman and Ticket system adopted as being the best means of giving the pauper the income which the parish has determined to be his due. This scheme recommends itself peculiarly to the selfishness and shortsighted jealousy of the farmers, amongst whom every man's eye is on his neighbour, lest by any means his portion of the burden should be heavier than theirs. Many a farmer has dismissed labourers from profitable employment, in order, as he imagined, to make others assist in maintaining them.

From the First Annual Report of the Poor Law Commissioners, published in 1835.

Source N

Four men were working together near a farmhouse. Upon questioning them as to the wages they were earning, one among them who informed us he was thirty years old and unmarried, complained much of the lowness of his wages, and added 'that if he was married and had a parcel of children, he should be better off as he should either have work given him by the parish or receive allowances from the parish for his children'.

From the *Main Recommendations of the Poor Law Commissioners of 1834,* published by HMSO in 1905.

Source O

It appears that in this parish [Cholesbury, Buckinghamshire] the population, which has been almost stationary since 1801, has steadily climbed. The poor rates were then only £10 10s and just one person received poor relief. In 1832 it was proceeding at the rate of £367 per year and then relief suddenly stopped because of the impossibility of continuing to collect the poor rate.

From the *Main Recommendations of the Poor Law Commissioners of 1834*, published by HMSO in 1905.

What did the royal commission's report recommend?

Published in early 1834, the first part of the report attacked the old Poor Law, citing examples of corrupt practices and demoralised paupers. The second part contained the commissioners' conclusions and recommendations. Throughout, the reader is led inexorably to one conclusion: that the old Poor Law was itself the cause of poverty. At the core of the commissioners' analysis was their unshaken belief in the need to keep the distinction between poverty, which was part of the natural order of things, and indigence – the inability to earn enough to live on – which was not. The commissioners, too, had no problem with the impotent poor – those who could not work. They clearly had to be cared for in an appropriate way. Their problem, as generations before them found, and generations after were to find, was with the able-bodied poor who either could not, or would not, earn sufficient to keep themselves from grinding poverty.

The commissioners recommended radical changes, designed to save money and improve efficiency:

- Separate workhouses should be provided for the aged and infirm, children, able-bodied females and able-bodied males. They deemed at least four classes necessary:
  - the aged and really impotent
  - the children
  - the able-bodied females
  - the able-bodied males.
- Parishes should group into unions for the purpose of providing these workhouses.
- All relief outside workhouses should stop, and conditions inside work-houses should be such that no one would readily choose to enter them:
  - *All relief whatever to able-bodied persons or to their families, otherwise than in well-regulated workhouses* [places where they may be set to work according to the spirit and intention of the 43rd Elizabeth] *shall be declared unlawful.*
  - *The first and essential of all conditions is that his* [the pauper's] *situation on the whole shall not be made really or apparently so eligible as the situation of the independent labourer of the lowest class.*
- A new, central authority should be established with powers to make and enforce regulations concerning the workhouse system.

SKILLS BUILDER

1 Read Sources L, M, N and O. What are the main criticisms made here about the workings of the old Poor Law?

2 How far do these criticisms relate to the prevailing ideologies of the time? (See pages 17–19.)

Question

How far did the recommendations of the royal commission's report meet the concerns of those who wanted the old Poor Law reformed?

Unit summary

What have you learned in this unit?

You have learned that there was a range of contemporary ideas about the old Poor Laws and the impact these were having on poverty and paupers, and that the dominant belief was that, if the Poor Laws were not to be abolished, then at the very least they needed changing. You have understood that there were various different pressures on the government such that, by 1832, they set up a Royal Commission of Enquiry into the Operation of the Poor Laws. This commission knew what it was going to recommend before the data to support its recommendations had been collected and collated. It recommended the ending of outdoor relief and that relief could only be obtained inside a workhouse, where conditions were to be so spartan that only the desperate would seek relief.

What skills have you used in this unit?

You have worked with a range of different types of source material, including data. You have cross-referenced between them and drawn inferences. You have used your understanding of the context from which the sources were drawn to prioritise reasons why the government acted as it did.

Biography

Edwin Chadwick (1800–90)

Born near Manchester and moving to London when a child, as a young man Chadwick entered the legal profession. Supplementing his income with journalism, he wrote about contemporary social conditions, in particular the state of the poor, as well as political issues. His writing brought him to the attention of the utilitarian philosopher, Jeremy Bentham, and Chadwick went to work for him as his secretary. Chadwick became greatly influenced by Bentham's philosophical ideas.

Chadwick was a major contributor to the report resulting from the Royal Commission of Enquiry into the Poor Laws (1832–4). Working as an assistant commissioner, he was a tireless, 'hands-on' investigator who insisted on seeing for himself the effects of poverty and the operation of the Poor Laws. The final report of the committee was greatly influenced by Chadwick and led directly to the Poor Law Amendment Act of 1834. As a result of the act, a central Poor Law Commission was set up, with Chadwick as its secretary and with the power to issue orders to reform poor relief.

Chadwick, appreciating that poverty and ill-health were closely connected, began to press for public health reform. In 1842 he published his three-volume *Survey into the Sanitary Condition of the Labouring Classes in Great Britain* that eventually led to the Public Health Act of 1848.

A difficult man to work with, Chadwick was pensioned off from public service in 1854 but continued to campaign for sanitary and social reform until his death. His main motivation was the desire for efficiency and hatred of waste.

Source P

A change occurred in public opinion, especially within the owners of property, in favour of a major overhaul of the poor law system. The chief reason for this was the impact of the Captain Swing Riots. In 1830–31 a great rising of the labourers took place and grievances over the poor law soon began to surface. In Sussex there were repeated arson attacks against the property of the overseers of the poor. In Hampshire, workhouses were destroyed by mobs.

The Whig leaders were worried about social stability. Savage punishments were given to rioters by the government. Government ministers and many MPs were determined that the anarchy of 1830–31 should never recur. The labourers may have been subdued by the courts, but there was further disciplinary work to be done. And that required major reform of the poor laws.

From A. Brundage, *The English Poor Laws 1700–1930*, published in 2002.

Source Q

While the present laws are in force, the cost of the fund for the maintenance of the poor will increase. The nature of the problem points out the remedy. By reducing the scope of the poor laws, by impressing upon the poor the value of independence, by teaching them that they must look to their own exertions for support, we shall have a healthier state.

From David Ricardo, *On the Principles of Political Economy and Taxation*, published in 1819.

Exam style question

This is the sort of question you might find appearing on exam papers as a (b) question.

Study Sources P and Q and use your own knowledge.

Do you agree that the Poor Laws were reformed in 1834 mainly in order to reduce the cost of poor relief?

Explain your answer, using Sources P and Q and your own knowledge.

Exam tips

Tips for answering (b) questions:

- Do be clear about the question focus. What is being claimed? In this case, what is being claimed is that the Poor Laws were reformed mainly in order to reduce the cost of poor relief.
- Analyse the sources to establish points that support and points that challenge the view given in the question. Remember to look for implications as well as what is actually stated.
- Develop each point by reference to your own wider knowledge, using it to reinforce and/or develop the points derived from the sources.
- Combine the points into arguments for and against the stated view.
- Evaluate the conflicting arguments.
- Present a judgment as to the validity of the stated view.
- And, above all, plan your answer.

RESEARCH TOPIC

Edwin Chadwick, as you have read in this section, played a major part in recommending reform of the poor laws.

How far can the influence of the doctrine of utilitarianism be seen in what he did?

3 Implementing the Poor Law Amendment Act

What is this unit about?

The royal commission took two years to compile data and write its report. That the main recommendations of the report became law in less than a year is a measure of the strong all-party acceptance of its recommendations. Indeed, the Poor Law Amendment bill passed through all its stages in the Commons and the Lords, with never more than 50 votes being cast against it, and gained royal assent in August 1834.

This unit looks at what happened next. It focuses on the terms of the Poor Law Amendment Act, the establishment of the central Poor Law Commission to implement and administer the act and the ways in which the commission did this. The unit then addresses reactions to the implementation of the act and to the support and opposition this engendered among different social and economic groups. Finally, the nature of Poor Law policy in the years to 1847 is considered.

Key questions

- How successfully did the Poor Law Commission exercise its powers?
- Why was there opposition to the implementation of the Poor Law Amendment Act?

Timeline

1834	**Parliament passes the Poor Law Amendment Act** Poor Law Commission established to implement and administer the act.
1830s	**Commission issues orders to individual poor law unions, prohibiting outdoor relief**
1835	**Commissioners begin work in southern England**
1836	**General Prohibitory Order forbidding outdoor relief**
1837	**Commission begins work in industrialised north** Protests, riots and the formation of the anti-Poor Law movement.
1838	**General Prohibitory Order set aside for unions in Lancashire and the West Riding of Yorkshire**
1842	**Labour Test Orders state that outdoor relief can only be given in return for some form of parish work and may not be given wholly in cash**
1844	**General Outdoor Relief Prohibitory Order** This applied to all unions and forbade outdoor relief to the able-bodied poor.

Source A

We cannot but regret the unseemly and noisy interruption offered by a few misguided individuals to the proceedings of the Board of Guardians on Monday. It exhibits a strange lack of sense as well as of decency. We say nothing of the impertinence of two or three hundred people, not one third of them ratepayers, taking upon themselves to assert that their opinions are those of the ratepayers, of whom there are many thousands in the Bradford Union. But unseemly as was the interruption while the Board was sitting, the attack on Mr Power [an assistant commissioner] in the street was infinitely more disgraceful. We are glad to be able to say that very few of the working-men of Bradford were implicated in this outrage. The perpetrators were principally from the surrounding townships. As far as our information extends, there is a growing feeling among the operatives in the town in favour of the new Poor Law. We are quite confident that, after six months fair trial, they will acknowledge it to be the best measure for the poor which has been enacted in modern times.

From a newspaper, the *Bradford Observer*, Thursday 2 November 1837.

SKILLS BUILDER

Source A is part of a report on what became known as the 'Bradford Riots'.

Bradford is a city in what was then the West Riding of Yorkshire and was the centre of the woollen industry in the north of England.

1 Summarise:

  a what happened on Monday 30 October in Bradford

  b the attitude of the *Bradford Observer* to the new Poor Law.

2 What further questions would you want to ask about this source before you could be sure about the ways in which the Poor Law Amendment Act was received in the north of England?

Why was there hardly any opposition in Parliament to the Poor Law Amendment bill?

Clearly, there were riots in Bradford when the Poor Law guardians, helped by an assistant commissioner, tried to implement the new Poor Law. Why? Why, in contrast, was there hardly any opposition to the Poor Law bill when it came before Parliament?

Why, indeed, should there be any opposition? The **Tories**, who might have stood out against it as an encroachment on traditional paternalism, were in a minority in the Commons and were overwhelmed by the arguments of the Whigs, seduced as they were by utilitarian arguments. Leading Whigs like Brougham, Althorp, Russell and Landsowne were receptive to ideas of change.

Definition

Tories
One of the two main political parties in Britain between the late seventeenth and mid-nineteenth centuries, they were traditionally associated with the belief that the Crown and the Anglican Church were the mainstays of political, religious and social order. The Tory groupings of the 1830s resulted in the emergence of the Conservative Party.

Indeed, several of them had helped create the climate of change. Brougham, for example, had contributed to the *Edinburgh Review*, which throughout the 1820s published a stream of articles on social problems of the day. Thus, it was not surprising that old-stagers – radicals like William Cobbett, who argued that the poor had a right to relief and that the object of the bill was to 'rob the poor man and enrich the landowner' – were barely listened to. Most of those who argued against the bill were not concerned with its underpinning philosophy. They were more worried by the centralisation involved, and the increased opportunities for patronage this would provide. But theirs were voices in the wilderness.

The bill reflected closely the recommendations of the report of the Poor Law Commission and the report itself, its supporters argued, was based on a mass of carefully collected evidence. What was more, the bill did exactly what MPs and the Lords wanted: it reduced the cost of providing for the poor by providing for them efficiently. Significantly, what opposition there was to the bill in the Commons came from MPs in the industrial west-midlands and north-west of England.

What were the main terms of the 1834 Poor Law Amendment Act?

The purpose of the act was radically to reform the system of poor relief in England and Wales, making it cost-effective and efficient. To this end, it laid down that:

- a central authority should be set up to supervise the implementation and regulate the administration of the Poor Law
- parishes were to be grouped together to form Poor Law unions in order to provide relief efficiently
- each Poor Law union was to establish a workhouse in which inmates would live in conditions that were worse than those of the poorest independent labourer
- outdoor relief for the able-bodied poor was to be discouraged but, significantly, was not abolished.

However, the actual programme of reform was not laid down by Parliament. Parliament simply set down the administrative arrangements through which the three commissioners were to implement and, indeed, interpret the act.

Question

Read Source B and use your own knowledge to explain why the government did not abolish outdoor relief.

Source B

And whereas difficulty may arise in case any universal remedy is attempted to be applied in the matter of outdoor relief for the able-bodied, be it further enacted that it shall be lawful for the said commissioners to declare to what extent and for what period the relief to be given to able-bodied persons or to their families may be administered out of the workhouse.

From W. C. Glen, *The Statutes in Force Relating to the Poor*, published in 1857.

What was the Poor Law Amendment Act really all about?

There are many different interpretations of the Poor Law Amendment Act and they rest, as interpretations frequently do, on the political and ideological stance of the individual making the interpretation. Modern historians generally hold to one of the three main interpretations:

- **The Marxist view** is a straightforward one. Its proponents maintain that the act was nothing more than naked class exploitation by the newly enfranchised (1832) middle classes. In holding down the poor rate by making harsh and unacceptable workhouses the way to obtain relief, the poor were forced to work for lower wages. Thus, workers were forced to accept the capitalist principles of the market economy.

- **The traditionalist view** is equally straightforward. It maintains that the act in fact emphasised continuity more than change by reinforcing the traditional social and economic powers of the landowners and property-owning elite. Faced with unrest in the countryside and towns, the traditionally powerful enforced a new Poor Law system that reasserted their authority. The old system had broken down and the property-owning elite were the ones best placed to put it right.

- **The revisionist view** attempts to synthesise the two previous viewpoints. It maintains the traditionalist view that, by the act, the land- and property-owning classes had reasserted their dominance, but makes a nod towards Marxism by maintaining that this dominance was asserted in favour of the new capitalist classes.

Question

With which view do you agree, and why?

The Poor Law Commission

How was the commission set up?

A central Poor Law Commission was established to administer the Poor Law Amendment Act throughout the country. The commission worked in Somerset House, London; there were three commissioners:

- Thomas Frankland Lewis, the chairman of the commission, who had been a Tory MP
- George Nicholls, who had been an overseer under the old Poor Law
- John Shaw Lefevre, who was a lawyer.

Edwin Chadwick, who had been the driving force behind the report of the Royal Commission of Enquiry into the Operation of the Poor Laws, hoped to be a commissioner. Indeed, it has been argued that the recommendations of the report and the subsequent act were less than specific because Chadwick had expected to be implementing them himself, along the utilitarian lines he wanted. He was, instead, made secretary to the commission where, bitterly disappointed and clashing frequently with the commissioners, he used his influence to the full for 14 years.

The commissioners were originally assisted by nine assistants (the number varied over time), whose job it was to make sure that decisions made centrally were implemented at local level in the parishes.

Definitions

Radicals

Radicals are people who seek a fundamental change in political structures. In nineteenth-century Britain, radicals looked for reform within the existing constitutional framework: they did not look to overthrow the existing system, simply to change it legally and legitimately. There was never a single radical party. Radicals grouped differently under different causes: free speech, factory reform and free trade, for example.

Bashaw

A haughty, proud, imperious man; a grandee.

Question

What were the strengths, and what were the weaknesses, of the Poor Law Commission?

What power did the commission have?

The commission was independent of Parliament, which was at once its great strength and its great weakness. Independence meant that the commission had no spokesman in Parliament to defend it against the criticisms levelled against it by MPs, **radicals**, parish officials and the poor. Outside Parliament – in the press, books and journals, songs and broadsides – the commissioners were lampooned as the 'Three **Bashaws** of Somerset House' and as the 'Pinch-pauper Triumvirate'. Out in the parishes, the commissioners and assistant commissioners were almost universally hated.

The commission had a powerful constitutional position because it had been established by Parliament, but it did not have the direct power that many people assumed it could wield. The commissioners could issue directives, draw up regulations and monitor their implementation, but in reality there was no mechanism for making recalcitrant parishes do what they were told. The commission did, however, have a considerable range of negative powers at its disposal. It could, for example, veto appointments it thought unsuitable; refuse to allow certain types of building; set dietaries for the workhouses; centralise accounting procedures; and generally make life very difficult for those parishes that opposed it.

First steps: putting parishes together and building workhouses

The first task of the assistant commissioners was to establish unions of parishes so that each union could set up its own workhouse. They were working under pressure: pressure to implement the Poor Law Amendment Act as quickly as possible and so reduce the cost of poor relief, and pressure because the new unions were to be used as the administrative units for the civil registration of births, deaths and marriages, due to be introduced in 1837.

In theory, a union should comprise about 30 parishes, one town and about 10,000 people. This, the commissioners believed, was the optimum unit for maintaining a reasonable-sized workhouse and giving effective poor relief as efficiently as possible. The assistant commissioners went out into the parishes, held public meetings and canvassed local opinion. They quickly found that reality differed from theory.

One of the first problems to present itself was that many parishes were already amalgamated under Gilbert's Act of 1782. Most of them refused to reamalgamate into different Poor Law unions. So did those parishes that had set up their own select vestries under the Sturges-Bourne Act of 1819. By the middle of the century, 20 of the 50 most populous unions in Britain were dispensing poor relief, not under the aegis of the Poor Law Amendment Act, but under other, older acts.

Even when the assistant commissioners persuaded parishes to combine into unions, they had no powers to insist the new unions built a workhouse, although they could insist that alterations were made to an existing one. Assistant commissioners, grown skilled in the art of negotiation, managed to persuade most unions to indulge in purpose-built workhouses. But an obdurate **Board of Guardians** could delay the implementation of the Poor Law Amendment Act almost indefinitely. In Todmorden (Lancashire), for example, the guardians demolished the old workhouse and were not persuaded to build a new one until 1877. But, given the imperatives of the time, the assistant commissioners did a reasonable job of work. By 1840, 14,000 English parishes with a population of around 12 million people had been incorporated into Poor Law unions.

Source C

Our domestic revolution is going on in the most peaceful and prosperous way. The Poor Law Act is covering England and Wales with a network of small aristocracies, in which the Guardians are chosen by the occupiers and ratepayers. By this time all Kent has been split into 21 Poor Law Unions, Sussex into certain others; in short, the old parochial authorities have been suspended in half the country already, and will be superseded in the rest by the end of the year. Fifteen Assistant Commissioners, with £1,000 a year to invigorate their exertions, are in constant motion to effect these operations, and ten more are to be added to them.

From a letter written by Nassau Senior to George Villiers on 1 December 1835. George Villiers was a member of the government at the time.

Source D

Your orders and rules being calculated to make visits to the beer-shop less frequent, and to stop the improper use of parish influence and parish funds, have here, as elsewhere, excited opposition amongst those parties who benefited by former abuses. The leaders of the opposition are to be found amongst the former overseers (gentlemen accustomed to accept the office for £15 a year and leave it with a well-filled purse); the little shop-keeper at whose house the poor received their relief and so were able to pay off old debts and make new ones from which the pauper was never free; the beer-shop keeper at whose house a great part of the relief was spent; and the little farmer or lime-kiln owner, who paid one half of his workforce from parish funds under the old allowance system.

From the Poor Law Commission *Second Annual Report*, published in 1836. This is part of a report from W. J. Gilbert about the introduction of the new Poor Law in Devon.

SKILLS BUILDER

Read Sources C and D.

Nassau Senior's letter to George Villiers is very positive about what has been done by the commission and optimistic about the work that lies ahead for them.

How far does Source D challenge Source C?

Definition

Board of Guardians

Under the old Poor Law, unelected 'overseers of the poor' were responsible for the local administration of the Poor Law. They were severely criticised by the Poor Law Commission of 1832–4. Under the Poor Law Amendment Act, Poor Law guardians were similarly responsible for the local administration of the Poor Law, but they were elected by local ratepayers. The more property a ratepayer had, the more votes that ratepayer had to use in these elections. In practice, many of the old overseers were returned as guardians, thereby enabling not simply continuity between old and new ways, but also continuity of the old corrupt practices and attitudes to paupers. It was not until 1894 that the property qualification was abolished and women were thus able to become guardians.

The commission wasn't working randomly to implement the Poor Law Amendment Act. The commissioners had a definite and defined policy. Before we look further at the ways in which the act was implemented and received, we must consider first the policy that lay behind that implementation.

What was the Poor Law Commission's policy, 1834–47?

In 1847 the Poor Law Commission was abolished and replaced by the Poor Law Board, headed by a president who was a member of the government and had a seat in the Cabinet. From then onwards, there was increasing parliamentary scrutiny of the workings of the Poor Law. But what happened between 1834 and 1847? What were the priorities of the commission? And how were they implemented?

Poor Law policy, after 1834, had two priorities:

- the transfer of out-of-work and underemployed workers in rural areas to urban areas where employment was plentiful
- the protection of urban ratepayers from a sudden surge of demand from rural migrants prior to their obtaining regular employment.

It was possible to meet both priorities. A programme of workhouse construction met the first one: the setting up of a string of workhouses, offering relief to the able-bodied poor on the **less eligibility** principle, would, it was anticipated, drive potential paupers to find work in towns and cities. The Settlement Laws (see pages 4–7) met the second: the poor rates would be kept low, and would not fall disproportionately on the towns if the Settlement Laws were stringently applied, returning the seekers of relief to their home parishes.

Priority 1: a programme of workhouse construction

The programme of reducing able-bodied pauperism by building deterrent workhouses carried with it the assumption that outdoor relief for the able-bodied poor would stop, even though it was not expressly forbidden by the 1834 Poor Law Amendment Act. In this key area, the commissioners were only able to act fairly slowly. Amalgamating unions and building or adapting workhouses took time, even when there was no organised opposition (see pages 38–44) against the implementation of the act. The commission then acted to try to forbid outdoor relief for the able-bodied poor.

- **1830s:** the commission began issuing orders to specific unions in the rural south of England, prohibiting outdoor relief to the able-bodied poor; this was extended to the rural north of England in 1842.
- **1842:** General Prohibitory Order forbidding outdoor relief in all those unions previously covered separately.
- **1844:** General Outdoor Relief Prohibitory Order. This applied to all unions and forbade outdoor relief to the able-bodied poor.

Definition

Less eligibility

One of the definitions of 'eligibility' is 'the ability to choose'. When applied to the Poor Law, 'less eligibility' meant 'less worthy of choice'. In other words, the poor would not choose to become paupers if they could support themselves otherwise. It followed that conditions inside a workhouse had to be worse than those of the poorest individual who was existing on his or her own wages.

However, the issuing of orders and directives was one thing. Their implementation and effectiveness, as the commissioners were to find, was quite another. Outdoor relief did continue, and continued to be the most common form of relief given to paupers, particularly in industrial northern towns. The north of England was subject to enormous swings of cyclical unemployment beyond the control of mill- and factory-owners. There outdoor relief was not only the most humane of alternatives, it was also the cheaper alternative to building huge workhouses that would remain half empty for most of a working year. In 1855, for example, over 700,000 paupers out of a total of almost a million received relief outside the workhouse. This was, of course, before the full programme of workhouse-building was completed by about 1870. Even so, by 1871 only one union in six was operating under the 1844 order, and there is strong evidence to suggest that outdoor relief continued as the mainstay of those seeking temporary support in stressful periods of their working lives until well into the twentieth century.

Source E

A photograph of the workhouse in Oundle, Northamptonshire, taken in 1894. The workhouse was built in the years 1836–7, using £4,400 authorised by the Poor Law Commissioners for its construction, and was built to house up to 150 inmates.

Source F

The new measures were greeted with bitter opposition from working people. Inevitably, the Poor Laws affected the life of a labouring man at its most tender spots. In times of distress caused by unemployment, sickness, old age and death, he and his family were under strain and most in need of sympathetic help and consideration. Yet this was the last thing to be expected under the new regime. As they watched the building of the great, grim new workhouses, and heard the rumours of the prisonlike discipline enforced behind the high walls, the working classes were seized with a great and sudden fear. On the outskirts of every medium-sized town and at remote crossroads in country districts, the new, raw, redbrick buildings appeared. They looked like prisons and were called 'bastilles'.

From J. F. C. Harrison *The Early Victorians 1832–51*, published in 1971.

Priority 2: the Settlement Laws

Settlement legislation had been in operation since the sixteenth century (see page 4) and here, in the mid-nineteenth century, the Settlement Laws were seen as necessary if the cost of maintaining paupers was to be fairly spread between urban and rural parishes, and if workhouses were indeed to be true deterrents.

In 1840 around 40,000 paupers were removed from the parishes in which they were living and claiming relief, back to their parishes of settlement, theirs by virtue of birth or marriage. This was a costly process, both in practical and administrative terms, whilst the cost in terms of human suffering was incalculable.

The situation was complicated by the fact that before 1834 many parishes were paying relief to people for whom they were responsible, but who lived elsewhere. Removal was not seen as sensible or humane.

Opposition to the Poor Law Amendment Act: a serious threat or a futile protest?

Out in the parishes, it was mostly fear and anger that greeted the Poor Law Amendment Act and the ways in which it was implemented. But this fear and anger were not universal, and they found expression in different ways and at different times. In parts of Cumbria and north Yorkshire, for example, where there were few able-bodied male paupers, the act was considered irrelevant and protest against it unnecessary. Indeed, the Carlisle Union continued to divide its applicants into deserving and undeserving poor and treated them accordingly. But where communities were outraged by the changes in tradition and practice brought about by the act, there was an almost universal coming together of the powerful and influential with the poor and dispossessed to protest jointly.

Rumour and propaganda

Fear thrives on rumour, and propaganda makes good use of both rumour and the fear that feeds it. This is common in all stressful situations, and the period when the Poor Law Amendment Act was being implemented was no exception.

- Union workhouses were built some distance from the homes of most of those seeking relief. This fuelled the belief among the poor that they were extermination centres where paupers were helped effortlessly from life in an attempt to keep the poor rates low.
- The *Book of Murder*, widely circulated and erroneously believed to be the work of the Poor Law commissioners, contained suggestions that pauper children should be gassed.
- In Devon, many of the poor believed that bread distributed as part of outdoor relief was poisoned in order to reduce the numbers of those claiming this form of relief.

- Rumours circulated that all children over and above the first three in a pauper's family were to be killed.

- Many anti-Poor Law campaigners believed that the new Poor Law was introduced specifically to lower the national wage bill. Workhouses, it was argued, were supposed to force people onto the labour market, no matter how low the wages. A variant on this theme was the belief that mill-owners in the north wanted unemployed agricultural workers from the south to work for them, so limiting rising wages and bringing about a workforce that lived at subsistence level.

Genuine fears

People's fears were based on individual perceptions of the way in which society should be organised.

- Many attacked the centralisation implicit in the new Poor Law. The commissioners were seen as being London-based, with no real concern for, or understanding of, the ways of life outside the metropolis.

- Many feared that the replacement of the old Poor Law by the new would break the traditional, paternalistic bonds between rich and poor, which had resulted in a kind of social contract.

- Rural ratepayers realised that outdoor relief was cheaper than indoor relief and were worried that a programme of workhouse-building would lead to higher, not lower, poor rates.

- Ratepayers in northern industrial areas, prone to cyclical unemployment, realised that building a workhouse large enough to contain all those who might need relief in times of economic depression would be an enormously costly undertaking, if not an impossible one.

Protest in the rural south

In 1835 the commissioners began their work in the most heavily pauperised districts of southern England, which was the source of most of the evidence that had supported the report of the Poor Law Commission. Even though the implementation of the act began here in a period of economic recovery, when employment prospects were good for most labourers and fear of want was retreating, there were still sporadic outbursts of opposition. Local magistrates and clergy, angered at what they saw as unnecessary centralisation and the removal of the traditional master–servant relationship with its attendant responsibilities, joined with the poor, who were alarmed and fearful, to protest. The following two examples of different kinds of protest exemplify, first, protest against centralisation and removal, and, second, protest against the regime and institutionalism of the workhouse.

- In Buckinghamshire, people took to the streets when paupers from the old workhouse in Chalfont St Giles were being transported to the new union workhouse in Amersham. Only when the Riot Act was read, special constables sworn in and armed yeomanry put on the streets was it possible for the paupers to be transported the three miles to Amersham.

SKILLS BUILDER

Study Sources E and F and use your own knowledge.

How far do you think the author of Source F is exaggerating the fear of the workhouse felt by working-class people?

Definition

Tolpuddle Martyrs

In 1834 six agricultural labourers from Tolpuddle, Dorset, led by George Loveless, were sentenced to seven years' transportation for swearing illegal oaths. The oath-swearing was part of a loyalty ceremony that bound the men into a trade union. Although trade unions were not banned at this time, the government feared that unions of agricultural workers would heighten the general rural unrest and so used this device to nip such unions in the bud. After a series of mass campaigns, the men were pardoned and returned home in 1838.

- In East Anglia, newly built workhouses were attacked, the one at St Clements in Ipswich being particularly badly damaged, and relieving officers assaulted.

While the poor themselves took to the lanes and market squares of rural England, the more influential citizens used their positions to, for example, refuse strictly to apply the less eligibility rule, continue to provide outdoor relief to the able-bodied poor and generally to find all possible ways of circumventing what they saw as an inhumane and destructive law.

However, the recent fate of the Dorset labourers (the **Tolpuddle Martyrs**), sentenced to transportation for swearing illegal oaths, had tended to depress rural protest. By and large, most farmers and landowners, aided by good harvests and a more or less content workforce, enabled the Poor Law Amendment Act to be put into practice in the south of England.

Source G

The well-regulated system of employment, the boring detention, the discipline of our workhouses, and I trust a sincere desire to reform, has persuaded some who were unmarried to enlist as soldiers, and by entering the ranks in His Majesty's Services, they now form part of that body of men whose duty it is to support and maintain those laws and that peace which but a few months since they were amongst the foremost to outrage and disturb.

The great mass of those individuals who were so noisy against the new enactments, on the grounds of cruelty to the poor, are now silenced by the fact a saving of nearly £10,000 has been made.

From *Operations of the Poor Law Amendment Act in the County of Sussex*, published in 1836. Here, the auditor of the Uckfield Union in Sussex comments on reactions to the new Poor Law.

Source H

In the north of the county, where there were some disturbances, we found that the poor people were acting under the grossest deception.

There was not anything too horrible or absurd to be circulated and nothing too incredible for their belief. Few really understood the intended proceedings of the guardians, and the opposition was not against the execution of the law but the falsehoods in circulation. As soon as the intentions of the law were understood, the most riotous submitted and received the alterations gladly.

Amongst other ridiculous statements circulated, the peasantry fully believed that all the bread was poisoned, and that the only cause for giving it instead of money was the facility it offered for destroying the paupers; that all the children beyond three in a family were to be killed. I saw one poor person at North Molton look at a loaf with an expression of hunger, and when it was offered to her, put her hands behind her and shrink back in fear lest it should touch her. It was also believed that to touch the bread was like 'taking bounty' and the guardians would immediately seize them, kill their children and imprison the parents.

From the Poor Law Commission *Second Annual Report*, published in 1836. This is part of a report from W. J. Gilbert about the introduction of the new Poor Law in Devon.

Source I

There was determined resistance by the labourers to the New Poor Law in both rural and urban areas. Since the implementation of the Act began in the Midlands and South, the first outbreaks occurred there. Not surprisingly, many of the disturbances took place in areas marked by the Swing riots a few years earlier. Kent proved an especially difficult southern county to bring under the law. Throughout the autumn of 1834 and the winter of 1835, rural Wiltshire witnessed large demonstrations of workers, punctuated by incidents of incendiarism and threats against local officials deemed responsible for harsher policies. Labourers in Wales also showed a marked repugnance for the new system. When the Llanfyllin guardians voted to discontinue paying pauper rents, hundreds of workers surrounded the meeting, a red flag was waved and the guardians had to flee under a bombardment of eggs and other objects. There were also major anti-Poor Law riots in Suffolk, Devon and Cornwall. By 1837, however, the Poor Law Commissioners and local magistrates had restored order, using London police detachments as well as military units. But that same year, the north erupted in opposition.

From Anthony Brundage, *The English Poor Laws 1700–1930*, published in 2002.

SKILLS BUILDER

Read Sources G, H and I. How far does Source I challenge Sources G and H about:

a the nature and extent of protest against the Poor Law Amendment Act in the south

b the ways in which the protest ended?

Opposition in the north: industrial Lancashire and west Yorkshire

In the north of England, it was a different matter. Edwin Chadwick urged an early start on unionising the industrial regions of Britain, while times were relatively prosperous. The commissioners ignored him. It was not until 1837, during the onset of a trade depression, that they turned their attention to the north of England and in particular to industrial Lancashire and the West Riding of Yorkshire.

Many areas had already adapted their relief provision to meet the cyclical depressions with which industry was beset. Guardians, magistrates, mill- and factory-owners resented interference from Londoners who had little knowledge of industrial conditions and whose report and subsequent act were based upon an understanding of the rural south and bore little relevance to them. Workshop-, factory- and mill-workers, facing lay-offs and short hours, needed short-term relief to tide them over periods of temporary unemployment, not removal of whole families to workhouses.

Organised and fired up by the demands of the **Ten Hours Movement**, they turned to oppose what many saw as yet another assault on working people. Anti-Poor Law associations sprang up, uniting Tory paternalists like Richard Oastler and John Fielden with radical printers like R. J. Richardson and socialists like Laurence Pitkeithly. Huge public protest meetings were held, at which the 'Three Bashaws of Somerset House' and their 'Bastilles' were roundly denounced. Indeed, the South Lancashire Anti-Poor Law Association quickly set up some 38 local committees, determined to stop the onset of the new Poor Law.

Definition

Ten Hours Movement
A sustained campaign in the 1830s for the reduction of hours worked in textile mills to ten per day. The campaign was led inside Parliament by Lord Shaftesbury and John Fielden, and outside by Richard Oastler. In 1847 the Ten Hours Act limited the work of women and young persons (aged 13–18) in textile mills to ten hours a day for five days a week and eight hours on Saturday.

For a while, there was insurrection, as these examples show:

- Armed riots in Oldham, Rochdale, Todmorden, Huddersfield, Stockport, Dewsbury and Bradford were put down by the local militia.

- In Huddersfield the guardian, George Tinker, warned the commissioners in June 1837 that 'in the present alarming state of the district, it will be dangerous to put the law into operation'.

- In Bradford in 1838 the assistant commissioner Alfred Power was threatened by the mob and pelted with stones and tin cans (see Source A). Troops were sent out from London to quell the riots.

- London troops were sent to quell the 1838 riots in Dewsbury.

- John Fielden, radical MP and philanthropic factory owner, in 1838 closed his own factories in protest and refused to pay the new poor rate. His workers attacked the homes of local guardians; troops were required to restore order. The Poor Law Amendment Act was not implemented in Todmorden until 1877, long after John Fielden's death.

- In Stockport in 1842 the workhouse was attacked and bread distributed to the poor outside.

Richard Oastler

Source J

CHRISTIAN READER

Be not alarmed at the sound of the title. I cannot bless that which GOD and NATURE CURSE. The Bible being true, the Poor Law Amendment Act is false! The Bible containing the will of God, – this accursed Act of Parliament embodies the will of LUCIFER*. It is the Sceptre of BELIAL**, establishing its sway in the land of Bibles!! DAMNATION; ETERNAL DAMNATION to the accursed Fiend!!

I tell you deliberately, if I have the misfortune to be reduced to poverty, that the man who dares to tear from me the wife whom God has joined to me, shall, if I have it in my power, receive his death at my hand! If I am ever confined in one of those hellish Poor Law Bastilles, and my wife be torn from me because I am poor, I will if it be possible, burn the whole pile down to the ground.

RICHARD OASTLER

* Lucifer: the chief rebel angel, Satan, who became the Devil
** Belial: an alternative name for the Devil

From Richard Oastler, *Damnation! Eternal Damnation to the Fiend-Begotten Coarser Food New Poor Law*, published in 1837.

Source K

Fellow Rate-Payers

The time has come for you to give a practical demonstration of your hatred of the new Starvation Law.

The 25th March is the day for the election of the new Guardians for the ensuing year; therefore it will depend on your exertions, whether you will allow men to be elected who are the mere tools of the three Commissioners in carrying out their diabolical schemes for starving the poor, reducing the labourers' wages and robbing you, the ratepayers of that control you have hitherto exercised over your money and your township's affairs; or will you elect men of character and humanity, who will prefer death itself rather than sacrifice the rights of their neighbours and constituents at the bidding of three pensioned Lawyers residing in London, and living in princely splendour out of your hard-earned money.

Ratepayers, do your duty and select none who are in the remotest degree favourable to the hellish Act. Remember that the law is cruel, illegal and unconstitutional. The real object of it is to lower wages and punish poverty as a crime. Remember also that children and parents are dying frequently in the same Bastille without seeing one another, or knowing of one another's fate.

From the 10 March 1838 edition of the Chartist newspaper the *Northern Star*. It was a Leeds-based radical newspaper established by its owner, Feargus O'Connor, in November 1837 and was fiercely critical of the Poor Law Amendment Act.

SKILLS BUILDER

Sources J and K helped inflame the anti-Poor Law campaign in the north of England.

1 How does Richard Oastler (Source J) use religion as a weapon in the campaign?

2 How does the owner and editor of the *Northern Star*, Feargus O'Connor, try to persuade people to show their opposition to the new Poor Law?

3 Which method of persuasion do you find the most effective? Why?

How effective was the anti-Poor Law movement?

Despite the best efforts of the campaigners, the government was not going to back down and repeal the 1834 Poor Law Amendment Act. It was, however, prepared to make concessions. In 1838, the General Prohibitory Order was set aside for unions in Lancashire and the West Riding of Yorkshire. There, the guardians were allowed to administer relief according to the 1601 Elizabethan Poor Law, and a considerable amount of discretion was permitted to guardians in negotiating local settlements.

Question

Was flexibility in implementing the Poor Law Amendment Act indicative of strength or weakness on the part of the Poor Law Commission?

Very few workhouses, for example, were built until the 1850s and 1860s, and in Todmorden one was not built until 1877.

How did it all end?

The new Poor Law was established relatively easily in other urban areas. The Metropolitan Anti-Poor Law Association, founded in London by Earl Stanhope, had little effect; there were few problems in the industrial north-east of England; a strike in the Potteries and a major recession in the stocking industry in Nottingham failed to push working people into protest. But absence of violent protest did not necessarily mean acceptance. It was still possible for local Boards of Guardians, with an eye on local feelings, to ignore, adapt and amend directives from the commissioners. And many of them did.

Opposition was short-lived. In many places, it was a spontaneous reaction to unwelcome change and, because it was mostly unorganised, had no chance of success. Even where opposition was organised, as with the anti-Poor Law associations of Lancashire and Yorkshire, the unlikely combinations of paternalistic Tories and working-class radicals were bound to fall apart eventually. Those who remained to protest turned to Chartism, seeing in working-class representation in the Commons the only hope of improving their lot.

It ended, too, because ratepayers in the parishes saw an immediate change in the rates they paid.

Question

Does the fall in the cost of poor relief indicate that the government was right to pass the Poor Law Amendment Act?

Source L

The cost of poor relief (in £m) 1833–47.

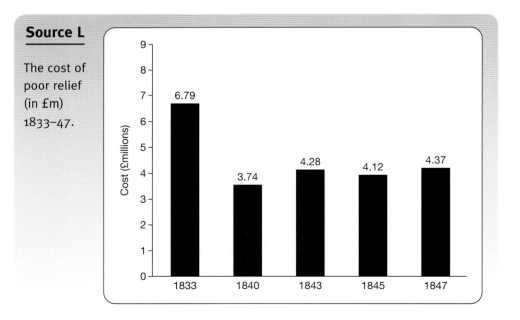

Were the commission's priorities successfully met?

The two important planks of Poor Law policy after 1834 were not implemented as the Poor Law commissioners wished. First, the Poor Law Amendment Act was implemented unevenly, and was implemented and interpreted in different ways by different Boards of Guardians in different parts of England and Wales. These differences were the consequence of many factors: the degree of local resistance to the act, long-established local customs, the vested interests of those in power and influence in the parishes (those who had been overseers of the poor before 1834 were frequently returned as Poor Law guardians afterwards) and the persuasive skills of assistant commissioners. Secondly, parishes were not insisting on the removal of paupers under the Settlement Laws, and they continued to prefer paying 'resident relief' after 1834 for those for whom they were responsible but who lived elsewhere. Despite the best efforts of assistant commissioners, over 80,000 paupers were still receiving relief in this way in 1847.

However, by the late 1860s the vast majority of parishes had been incorporated into Poor Law unions. And, even though most paupers received relief outside the workhouse, it was the workhouse and, perhaps overwhelmingly, the fear of the workhouse that stood as an awful symbol of deterrence for the most vulnerable members of Victorian society.

Unit summary

What have you learned in this unit?

You have learned that, although the Poor Law Amendment Act passed through Parliament with hardly any opposition, there was considerable opposition once the Poor Law Commission began implementing it in the parishes. The act itself left a considerable amount of discretion to the three commissioners and to its secretary, Edwin Chadwick, as to how the act was implemented and what orders they could issue to ensure its smooth implementation. The act itself did not forbid outdoor relief, although the building of workhouses implied that outdoor relief would end, and a lot of the opposition centred around the perceived ending of outdoor relief for the able-bodied poor. You have seen how, and understood why, there was opposition to the implementation of the act in the rural south and the industrialised north. Unlike the poor in the south, the poor in the industrial north were organised, used to radical protest and were backed by many mill-owners and industrialists who understood the vagaries of cyclical employment and the need of most workers for short-, not long-term relief. They were also suspicious of centralised control from London. You have seen how, for different reasons, protest ended or was ended by the superior forces of troops and police, good harvests in the south and the willingness of the commission to set aside orders forbidding outdoor relief in the north.

Source M

The Poor Law Commission began its work in the mid-1830s, steadily at first, establishing the union structures and issuing orders and regulations. But the administrative history of the New Poor Law in its first twenty years is one of conflict and compromise. In part, the compromise between central and local control represented in the New Poor Law is characteristic of the approach to government responsibility in the nineteenth century. But equally there was a mismatch between the intentions of central authority and the interests of many localities, especially in the industrial North.

From Alan Kidd, *State, Society and the Poor in Nineteenth-Century England*, published in 1999.

What skills have you used in this unit?

You have worked with a range of primary and secondary sources, using your skills of comprehension, inference and cross-referencing to evaluate for bias, challenge and support. You have begun to develop your skills of empathy in order to understand more fully the motives driving those opposed to the implementation of the Poor Law Amendment Act.

Exam style question

This is the sort of question you will find appearing on the examination paper as a (b) question.

Read Sources C, K and M and use your own knowledge.

Do you agree with the view, expressed in Source M, that there was a clash between the intentions of central authority and the interests of many localities, especially in the industrial north?

Exam tips

You tackled a (b) style question at the end of Unit 2. Look back at the Exam tips you were given there (see page 29). Now is the time to build on and develop those tips. What do you have to do to write a successful answer to a (b) question?

- What view is being expressed in Source M? Read Source M carefully and write the 'view' in the middle of a spider diagram.
- Read Sources C and K carefully. Establish points that support and challenge the view and set those as spider 'legs'.
- Think about appropriate knowledge and add a note of this to the different spider 'legs', using your own knowledge to both reinforce and challenge.
- Cross-reference between the different 'legs' for similarities and differences.

You are now ready to write up your answer.

- Combine the different points into arguments for and against the stated view.
- Evaluate the conflicting arguments by reference to the quality of the evidence used.
- Reach a supported judgment.

Remember, there is an Exam zone section at the end of this book (see pages 161–66) to help you further.

Now plan an answer to the question above and write a response.

RESEARCH TOPIC

Research the life and career of Richard Oastler, Feargus O'Connor or John Fielden. What did your chosen individual do to improve the lives of working people?

UNIT 4 Union workhouses: pauper palaces or bastilles?

What is this unit about?

A cornerstone of nineteenth-century Poor Law policy was the workhouse, with its attendant principle of less eligibility. The workhouse had to offer a way of life that was less attractive than survival outside. And herein lay a terrible dilemma. Conditions outside, for the poorest of the workforce, were pretty terrible. Urban workers in the midst of a depression and rural workers close to starvation lived and worked in conditions so poor that it would be hard for an institution to match them, let alone provide something worse. The state could not, in a civilised society, institutionalise dirt, disease and starvation.

This unit explores the ways in which the Poor Law Commission faced, and tried to resolve, that paradox.

Key questions

- How successfully was the principle of less eligibility applied?
- What was the reality of life in a workhouse?

Timeline

1834	**Parliament passes the Poor Law Amendment Act**
	Poor Law Commission established to implement and administer the act.
1835	**Sampson Kempthorne appointed architect to the Poor Law Commission**
	Produces basic workhouse plans to be adopted by guardians building new union workhouses.
1841	Rules, regulations and disciplines to be observed in workhouses set out by Poor Law Commission.
	Publication of the *Book of the Bastilles*, a compilation of workhouse horror stories by George R. Wythen Baxter.

SKILLS BUILDER

1 Look carefully at Source A. What point is the cartoonist trying to make?

2 Discuss in your group whether the cartoonist is for or against the new Poor Law.

Source A

A cartoon published in 1840, comparing life under the old and new Poor Laws.

Definition

Workhouse test
That all those seeking relief had to apply to their union workhouse.

The workhouse, as you have seen, was intended to be the last refuge for the destitute. It was intended that the principle of less eligibility, together with the deterrent conditions offered by the workhouse system, would be self-regulating. Few poor people would want to take the **workhouse test** and so only the genuinely destitute would apply. However, conditions inside could not, insofar as cleanliness, food and clothing were concerned, be made deliberately worse than the poorest labourer living outside. The state could not be seen to institutionalise dirt, disease and starvation. What was to be done? The Poor Law Commission attempted, in the face of this problem, to make the workhouses repellent by insisting on a monotonous routine and strict discipline, by building workhouses that looked like prisons and by trying in every way to dehumanise the paupers by removing from them their own individual identities. In these ways, the commission argued, the principle of less eligibility would be upheld.

Workhouse architecture: designed to deter?

The design and structure of workhouses were intended, in themselves, to act as a deterrent to would-be paupers. They were also supposed to instil discipline in the paupers they were designed to house. How were they to do this? Sampson Kempthorne, an architect with a London practice, was appointed architect to the Poor Law Commission in 1835.

He produced designs for the approval of the Poor Law commissioners that were then issued to Boards of Guardians as indicative of the standards to which they should work when commissioning new workhouses or altering existing ones.

Kempthorne produced two basic designs:

- The first was a Y-shaped building, two or three storeys high, inside a hexagonal boundary wall. The boundary wall held workrooms; one wing of the Y, kitchen, dining hall and chapel; the other two wings, dormitories and day rooms. The master's rooms were in the middle of the Y, where he and his staff could watch the three exercise yards that were divided from each other by the wings of the Y. This design was intended to accommodate around 300 paupers.

- The second design was a cruciform-shaped building, two storeys high, inside a square boundary wall. The wall held workrooms and the cross shape divided the space into four exercise yards. Each 'arm' of the cross held dormitories and dining rooms, a chapel and kitchens, schoolrooms and stores – sufficient accommodation for between 200 and 500 paupers.

Look at the ways in which Kempthorne's designs provided for the division and segregation of paupers. Before they could be segregated, paupers had to be classified. The report of the royal commission recommended seven categories of separation:

- aged and/or infirm men
- aged and/or infirm women
- able-bodied men over the age of 13
- able-bodied women over the age of 13
- girls aged 7–13
- boys aged 7–15
- children under 7 years old.

Why were they so classified? What was the point of it? Segregation enabled the workhouse officers to provide appropriately for each class of pauper; it added to the deterrence factor by splitting up families; and prevented the moral 'contagion' that would occur if the different categories mixed freely. Paupers, as soon as they entered the workhouse, would begin to lose their individuality and begin to be treated as impersonal units.

SKILLS BUILDER

Look carefully at Sources B and C.

1 How was each design intended to intimidate and dehumanise the paupers?

2 Which design would be likely to be the more popular with Boards of Guardians? Why? Discuss this in your group.

Source B

Sampson Kempthorne's design for a Y-shaped workhouse. One Poor Law union that adopted this design for its workhouses was the Winchester Union.

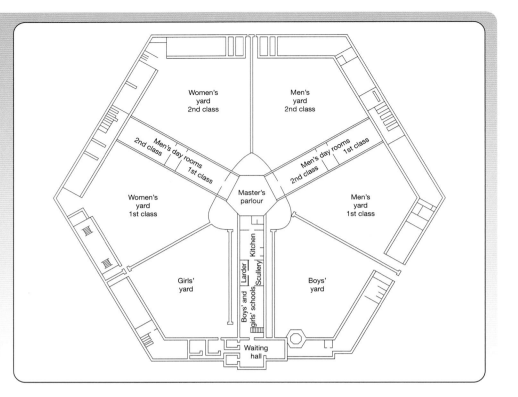

Source C

Sampson Kempthorne's design for a cruciform workhouse. One Poor Law union that adopted this design for its workhouses was the Watford (Hertfordshire) Union.

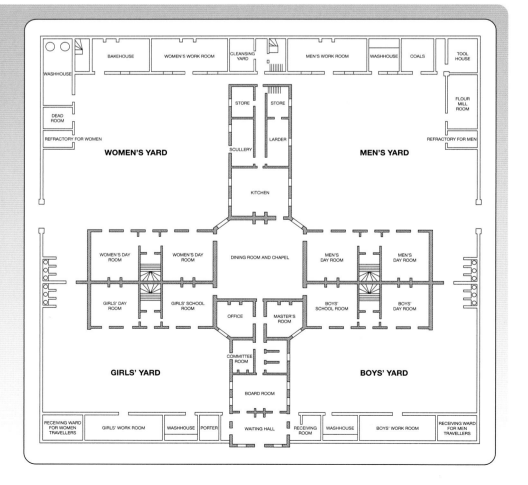

Not all Poor Law unions, however, welcomed this development. Many preferred to adapt their existing 'old' workhouses to accommodate this new classification and division of paupers.

Source D

In the first place, upon our system there is a great saving of expense; our Homes have cost us under £300. I dislike the appearance of all these new Houses all over the country. I fear the consequences. When we have eight workhouses there is hardly an inducement to pull down one only, and to pull them all down is next to impossible. Our system eludes the risk of insurrection. Besides this, how much more perfect is the classification. How secure are our separate schools from all contamination. How small are the masses of pauperism which we bring together compared with the congestion of one vast House. With us, our Houses are not like prisons, for we require no high wall to separate the classes; eight or ten miles distant is far more effectual than the highest walls.

From *An Address to the Board of Guardians of the Cranbrook Union on the Necessity of Building a Union Workhouse, by their late Chairman.* The 'late Chairman' was a Kent magistrate, and this address was written in 1839.

Source E

The very sight of a well-built efficient establishment would give confidence to the Board of Guardians; the sight and weekly assemblage of all those who were employed by the Guardians to run the workhouses would make them proud of their office, while the pauper would feel it was utterly impossible to fight against it. In visiting such a series of unions the Assistant Commissioner could with great facility perform his duty, whereas if he had eight establishments to search for in each union, it would be almost impracticable to attend to them.

From Sir Francis Head, *English Charity*, published in 1835. Francis Head was an assistant commissioner.

SKILLS BUILDER

1 Read Source D. The author clearly wants to keep the old workhouses; but is he opposed to the new Poor Law, too?

2 Now read Source E. How might Francis Head have replied to the author of Source D?

Who were the new paupers?

Outdoor relief continued to be the main form of support for paupers, despite the best efforts of the commissioners. This means that any analysis of the types of people opting for, or forced into, indoor relief cannot be taken as typical of the pauper population as a whole. But it is interesting to see just which people were given indoor relief and to bear this in mind when looking at workhouse provision, regimes and staff, and evaluating these for fitness for purpose.

Workhouses provided both short-term and long-term care, and at any one time around one-fifth of all inmates had been inside for five or more years. There were, of course, regional and local differences, but by and large, pauper populations within workhouses were surprisingly similar in structure:

- **Young people** were provided with a temporary shelter and a solution to a personal crisis. They moved in and out of workhouses, maybe several times a year, depending on variables such as the seasonality of employment, the harshness of the winter or the severity of a local epidemic.

Question

Given the context of the time, was there any other way in which these groups of vulnerable people could have been helped?

Definition

Apprenticeship
Originally a medieval system whereby young people (usually boys) were apprenticed to a master craft worker for a certain number of years to learn a specific trade. It continued, with variations, into the twenty-first century, where young people could obtain apprenticeships in shipbuilding and vehicle engineering, for example. In the nineteenth century, youngsters could be apprenticed to the many mills and factories in the industrial north and midlands, in order to learn skills that would make them self-supporting.

- **Vagrants** were considered less deserving than any 'settled' poor. They were given overnight accommodation in a 'casual ward', to which they were not admitted until the evening, when they were fed a meal of bread and water. In the better workhouses, they were stripped, deloused and had their clothes disinfected. These were considered to be the lowest of the low and believed to be beyond redemption; the only aim of workhouse staff was to get rid of them as soon as possible the following morning.

- **The elderly** received shelter and sustenance until death. In this group, men were more prominent than women. Women, when old, could more frequently be of domestic use to their families and so tended to be kept by their relatives rather than being sent 'on the parish'.

- **Children**, who made up between 25 and 40 per cent of all admissions, were both long- and short-stay inmates. The offspring of the transient able-bodied poor went in and out with their parents. However, most workhouse children were abandoned, orphans or ill. Many were the illegitimate sons and daughters of other inmates and were likely to spend all their childhood and early adolescence in the workhouse.

- **Single women**, who could not claim relief because they had nowhere to live except the workhouse, made up a significant proportion of any workhouse community and included widows, abandoned wives, single mothers and prostitutes.

- **The mentally ill** accounted for a growing number of inmates, increasing from 1 per 100 to 1 per 8 inmates as the century progressed.

Workhouse regime: designed to demoralise?

Workhouses had to provide for the most vulnerable and needy members of society, both as transient and as long-term inmates. They had, too, to impose the workhouse test to ensure that the principle of less eligibility was being maintained. Inevitably, these demands and expectations conflicted as Boards of Guardians struggled to match their own prejudices and preconceptions with the demands of their localities and the requirements of the Poor Law commissioners.

Routine, rules and regulations

Every aspect of workhouse life was governed by a stream of rules and regulations laid down by the commissioners in London. The routine was designed to be unpleasant and was intended to deter people from seeking relief.

- Upon entry to a workhouse, the pauper family was given a medical inspection and then split up. Husbands were separated from wives and parents from their children, although children usually stayed with their mothers until they were about seven years old. The assumption was that the pauper had given up all responsibility for his family and so was separated from them.

- Children were sent to the workhouse school and, when they were nine or ten years old, **apprenticed** (often to the cotton mills of Lancashire) without their parents' consent and sometimes without their knowledge.

- Paupers had to wear workhouse uniform that sometimes fitted them and sometimes did not. Guardians were allowed to add variety to the uniform clothing, but few of them did.

- Men were given razors to shave once a week and all paupers had a weekly bath. Workhouse staff watched while this happened. This was to prevent any attempt at self-mutilation or drowning and to add to the sense of loss of personal privacy.

- No personal possessions were allowed and there were no lockers or cupboards in which paupers could put clothes or shoes. This was to prevent any expression of individuality.

- The daily routine was designed to be boring and monotonous:

07.00–08.00	Breakfast
08.00–12.00	Work
12.00–13.00	Dinner
13.00–18.00	Work
18.00–19.00	Supper
20.00	Bedtime

- Each day began and ended with prayers, starting and ending an hour earlier in the summer.

Work

It was essential, within the whole scheme of things, that workhouse inmates worked. The primary aim of this work was to rehabilitate the paupers and restore them to the workforce outside. As an aim, this was praiseworthy, but when translated into practice, huge problems arose, both of an ideological and practical nature. What work could the paupers do that would equip them for a useful working life outside?

- The work had to be available in the locality of the workhouse, and it had to be able to be done inside the confines of the workhouse.

- It could not diminish available employment outside the workhouse to the extent that the able-bodied working poor became paupers.

- The attitudes of the commissioners made the situation even more difficult. They held that work done inside the workhouse could not pay more than it cost the workhouse to maintain the pauper. If it did, they argued, there would be no incentive for the pauper to return to the labour market.

Read Source F.

1 These regulations were published seven years after the Poor Law Amendment Act was passed by Parliament. Does this mean that, in that time, workhouses had become rowdy places?

2 How did the Poor Law commissioners believe that these regulations would maintain the principle of less eligibility?

Source F

Workhouse (Rules of Conduct)

Any pauper who shall neglect to such of the regulations herein contained as are applicable to him and binding on him:

Or who shall make any noise when silence is ordered to be kept;

Or shall use obscene or profane language;

Or shall by word or deed insult or revile any person;

Or shall threaten to strike or to assault any person;

Or shall not duly cleanse his person;

Or shall refuse or neglect to work after having been required to do so;

Or shall pretend sickness;

Or shall play at cards or other games of chance;

Or shall enter or attempt to enter, without permission, the ward or yard appointed to any class of paupers other than that to which he belongs;

Or shall misbehave in going to, at, or returning from public worship out of the workhouse, or at prayers in the workhouse;

Or shall return after the appointed time of absence, when allowed to quit the workhouse temporarily;

Or shall wilfully disobey any lawful order of any officer of the workhouse;

Shall be deemed DISORDERLY.

Any pauper who shall, within seven days, repeat any one or commit more than one of the offences specified above,

Or who shall by word or deed insult or revile the master or matron, or any other officer of the workhouse, or any of the Guardians;

Or shall wilfully disobey any lawful order of the master or matron after such order shall have been repeated;

Or shall unlawfully strike or otherwise unlawfully assault any person;

Or shall wilfully or mischievously damage or soil any property whatsoever belonging to the Guardians;

Or shall be drunk;

Or shall wilfully disturb the other inmates during prayers or divine worship;

Shall be deemed REFRACTORY.

It shall be lawful for the master of the workhouse to punish any DISORDERLY pauper by substituting, during a time not greater than forty-eight hours, for his or her dinner, as prescribed by the dietary, a meal consisting of eight ounces of bread, or one pound of cooked potatoes, and also by withholding from him during the same period, all butter, cheese, tea, sugar or broth.

And it shall be lawful for the Board of Guardians to order any REFRACTORY pauper to be punished by confinement to a separate room, with or without an alteration to the diet, for a period no longer than twenty-four hours.

From the Poor Law Commission *Seventh Annual Report*, published in 1841.

It looked as though the commission was expecting trouble in the union workhouses!

Source G

REFUGE FOR THE DESTITUTE—WARD FOR FEMALES.

REFUGE FOR THE DESTITUTE—THE MALE WARD.—(See next page.)

Refuge for the Destitute was produced in 1843 and shows the rough type of accommodation that was common in both male and female wards.

SKILLS BUILDER

Look at Sources G and H. How far are the aims of the Poor Law Commission being put into action here?

Source H

The women's yard in a union workhouse, some time after 1837.

So, what work was done?

- Some paupers, mainly women and children, worked to help maintain the workhouse. They worked in the laundries, kitchens and sick rooms. They worked as cleaners, attendants, child-minders and sloppers-out.

- If work that was economical and easy to perform within a workhouse could not be found, dispiriting and monotonous work was given to the paupers. They made sacks and unravelled ropes so that the fibres could be reused; they chopped wood and smashed limestone that was used to make roads; and they ground animal bones into dust to be used by farmers as fertiliser. Paupers were, by and large, doing the same work as convicts and with the same loss of dignity.

Dietaries

The supply of food to paupers, while it just about kept them alive, served also to degrade and to discipline. The Poor Law commissioners issued six model diets from which Boards of Guardians could choose the one, or ones, that best suited their pockets and inclinations. Here, again, the principle of less eligibility had to hold sway, as far as possible. However, many urban and rural able-bodied poor were only just about existing on what amounted to a subsistence-level diet outside the workhouse. Not even the most badly disposed guardians would want to take their paupers right to the edge of starvation. So, the aim of the published dietaries was to sustain and maintain life but to make meals as boring and tedious as possible. Paupers were to get no pleasure from the food they ate.

Questions

1 How nutritious is this dietary?

2 How far does the information regarding the elderly, sick and children mean that the paupers are being well looked after?

Source I

Dietary for able-bodied Men and Women.

		BREAKFAST		DINNER				SUPPER			
		Bread.	Gruel.	Cooked Meat with Vegetables	Lobscouse .	Soup with Vegetables	Suet Pudding	Bread.	Cheese.	Broth Thickened.	OLD PEOPLE of 60 Years of Age and upwards, may be allowed 1oz. of Tea, 7oz. of Sugar, and 5oz. of Butter per Week, in lieu of Gruel for Breakfast, if deemed expedient to make this change.
		oz.	Pints.	oz.	Pints.	Pints.	oz.	oz.	oz.	Pints.	
Sunday…	Men	7	1½	6	—	—	—	5	—	1½	
	Women	6	1½	5	—	—	—	4	—	1½	
Monday…	Men	7	1½	—	—	1½	—	6	2	—	CHILDREN under Nine Years of Age to be allowed Bread and Milk for their Breakfast and Supper, or Gruel when Milk cannot be obtained, also such proportions of the Dinner Diet as may be requisite for their respective ages.
	Women	6	1½	—	—	1½	—	5	2	—	
Tuesday…	Men	7	1½	—	—	—	14	6	2	—	
	Women	6	1½	—	—	—	12	5	2	—	
Wednesday.	Men	7	1½	6	—	—	—	5	—	1½	
	Women	6	1½	5	—	—	—	4	—	1½	
Thursday…	Men	7	1½	—	—	1½	—	6	2	—	CHILDREN above Nine Years of Age to be allowed the same quantities as Women.
	Women	6	1½	—	—	1½	—	5	2	—	
Friday…	Men	7	1½	—	2	—	—	6	2	—	
	Women	6	1½	—	2	—	—	5	2	—	
Saturday…	Men	7	1½	—	—	—	14	6	2	—	SICK to be Dieted as directed by the Medical Officer.
	Women	6	1½	—	—	—	12	5	2	—	

"SOUP" made in the proportion of One Pound of Beef or Mutton to One Gallon of Water, with Vegetables.
"PEAS SOUP" made in the proportion of One Pound of Beef or Mutton and One Pint of Peas to One Gallon of Water.
*The VEGETABLES are EXTRA, and not included in the above specified.

This dietary was used in the Stafford Union workhouse.

The way in which meals were taken was designed to instil repressive uniformity. Until 1842, all meals were to be taken in silence. Paupers had the right to have their food weighed in front of them; many workhouses used this regulation to delay the serving of food until it was stone cold, thus further adding to paupers' humiliation.

Definition

Adulterate

Spoiling food or drink by adding something to it, for example, adding chalk to bread to make it look white (to mislead as to its quality).

Source J

The following articles were found on her person: three-quarters of a pint of rum, two pounds of pork, half a pound of sausages, six eggs, some apples, some bread, half a pound of cheese, three packets of sweetmeats, two bunches of keys, £1 9s 0d in silver, 7d and 3 farthings in copper, and in her box, £5 10s 0d in gold and many articles of clothing.

> These items were found on Elizabeth Stannard, an inmate of the Shipmeadow workhouse in the Wangford Union of Suffolk, when she returned, drunk, from her usual Sunday outing. She had been living in the workhouse for 15 years.

There were, too, other ways to degrade. The meat, oatmeal, cheese and bread that formed the mainstay of pauper meals were of poor quality and often **adulterated**. The meals themselves were poorly and carelessly prepared and cooked. In the 1830s some workhouses did not allow paupers to use cutlery, and they were forced to scoop up their food with their hands and drink from bowls.

Discipline

The ways in which workhouses implemented the multitude of rules and regulations did of themselves bring about a discipline that was intended by those who drew up these rules.

Workhouses were often rowdy places. Staff and paupers frequently hurled verbal and physical abuse at each other. Disturbances ranged from full-scale riots to the swift exchange of foul language. Among the paupers themselves there were frequent outbreaks of bullying and blackmail, and there are recorded instances of sexual abuse between staff and paupers and between pauper and pauper.

Workhouse staff used a complicated system of rewards and punishments in order to maintain order. Paupers could be punished for being in the wrong part of the building, making too much noise, working too slowly or cheeking a member of staff. On the other hand, paupers could be rewarded with food, 'clean' jobs or pocket money. Paupers were usually very clear as to which of them were favoured by the authorities and which were not. Often, systems of rewards and punishments had no legal backing and had grown up through custom. There were, however, specific punishments laid down by the Poor Law commissioners, and a standard punishment book was kept, in which all punishments were formally recorded.

In some ways, many punishments were enlightened. Under the old Poor Law, paupers were very much at the mercy of the overseer, who could, and did, abuse paupers with impunity. Operating within the new system, the guardians and staff did at least know that there were limits to their powers and that these limits were determined and universally applied by the Poor Law commissioners. Girls and women, for example, could not be beaten; although the reduction of rations was a common punishment, there was a minimum below which they could not be reduced. Most workhouses had punishment cells, and paupers were shut up there for minor misdemeanours. Some workhouse masters developed their own refinements, such as forcing stubborn paupers to spend the night in the workhouse mortuary. For more serious crimes, the usual processes of the law came into play.

Part of the problem in trying to manage an orderly workhouse was that a proportion of the population was mobile. These transient, itinerant paupers – drifting in and out of relief – brought with them the tensions, stresses and petty crime of the outside world. Indeed, all paupers were free to come and go as they pleased: only three hours' notice was required if paupers wanted their own clothes returned so that they could leave.

Source K

Case	Name	Date	Offence	Punishment
17	Bernard Quinn	Jan 5	Visiting the women's day room after having been cautioned	Three meals bread and water
18	William Ryecroft	Feb 2	Not returning for three days after being allowed the usual days' leave of absence	Leave of absence and tobacco stopped
19	William Edwards	March 7	Fighting by striking a boy and making his nose bleed	Stopped from attending the Christmas tree
20	Catherine Briggs	April 5	Absconding with Union clothing	Committed to gaol for 14 days
21	William Johnson (vagrant)	June 9	Refusing to perform his task	Committed to gaol for 7 days
22	George Grey (vagrant)	June 15	Refusing to perform his task	Committed to gaol for 21 days
23	Bates May	Aug 13	Refusing to obey the laundress and insolent to the Matron	One meal low diet
24	Kelly Peter Kelly William Kelly John Durkin, John Thomas	Sept 12	Bad conduct and insolent to the Trainer	Caned
25	Quinn Bernard	Sept 14	Visiting the women's yards and dayrooms	Two meals low diet
26	Riddiough Florrie	Sept 22	Playing truant	Two meals low diet
27	Williams, James	Sept 25	Brought in by police for climbing boundary wall of Horton Hall, breaking glass and throwing stones at fruit trees.	Caned
28	Kelly William	Nov 1	Insolent to the boys' trainer and refusing to obey him	Caned
29	Larkin Thomas Raper Thomas	Oct 30	Refusing to complete their task of corn grinding	Taken before the magistrates. Larkin committed to 14 days and Raper to 5 days hard labour
30	Towley Elizabeth	Apr	Absconding with workhouse clothing	Sentenced to 5 weeks hard labour
31	Marston Mary		Using abusive language and striking the matron in the face with a scrubbing brush	Confined in the cell for half an hour. Afterwards examined by the doctor and transferred to the imbecile ward.

Extracts from the Bradford Union workhouse punishment book, late nineteenth century

SKILLS BUILDER

1 Think about Source J. Use your knowledge to explain why you think Elizabeth Stannard was allowed to make these outings every Sunday.

2 Use Source K. List the punishments in order of severity and link them to the 'crimes'. Can you see a pattern?

3 What does this tell you about priorities in keeping order in this particular workhouse?

Workhouse staff could not prevent paupers from leaving, neither could they refuse to readmit them. Many paupers exploited this to the full. It was not until 1871 that an act of Parliament gave guardians the power to limit the number of times in a week a pauper could leave a workhouse.

What about the children?

The very act of entering a workhouse meant that a pauper child's parents had relinquished responsibility for them. Children, unlike their able-bodied parents, could not be held responsible for their own poverty. On the other hand, they were paupers and their situation, under the less eligibility rule, could not be made better than that of poor children outside the workhouse – but it was.

Pauper children received a basic education in the workhouse, better medical attention than they could have hoped for outside and, when they were about nine years old, they were apprenticed to a trade.

However, the education was often rudimentary in the extreme, and they could be apprenticed to any passing tradespeople and taken far away. Children, unlike pauper adults, could not leave a workhouse of their own free will; if they ran away and were caught, they would be returned. They quickly became institutionalised and unable to cope with life beyond the walls of the workhouse. It was the **Elementary Education Act (Forster's Act) of 1870** that placed the education of pauper children firmly within the elementary school system and so helped their integration into society.

Workhouse staff: appointed to intimidate?

The 1846 report from the Poor Law commissioners stated: 'The workhouse is a large household. It resembles a private family on an enlarged scale.' Pious and praiseworthy though these sentiments were, one is left wondering just what kind of family the commissioners had in mind. Even the most repressive Victorian patriarch did not aim to make life as unpleasant as possible for members of his family so that their main purpose in life would be to leave.

Definition

Elementary Education Act (Forster's Act), 1870
This act provided for local elementary schools to be set up where there were gaps in the Church provision of schools. These 'Board' schools were to be financed from the locally levied rates. Many workhouses sent their children to Board schools rather than try to provide education within the workhouse walls.

A workhouse, like any large institution, required staff in order to function at all efficiently. There had to be, for example, cleaners, porters, washerwomen, cooks, scullery maids and chimney sweeps. Some of this work was carried out by the paupers themselves; some by casual labour brought in from outside; most by the poor themselves who lived outside the workhouse and did menial work for long hours and low pay in order to keep themselves and their families out of the institution they helped to make function.

There were some key posts that were unique to the workhouse. Those who held these posts had enormous influence on the way the workhouse was run and on how it was perceived by the paupers inside and society outside. These people had it in their power to make a workhouse a place of grim terror and dread, or a place where the most vulnerable in society were given help when they most needed it.

Master and matron

The key individuals in a pauper's day-to-day life were the master and matron of the workhouse. They were underpaid, overworked and frequently operated without close supervision from their Board of Guardians. The master was responsible for the discipline and economy of the workhouse; the matron for the female paupers and the domestic side of life. Cruel or kind, they both enjoyed tremendous power over staff and paupers. No member of staff could leave the workhouse without the master's permission and no one, not even the guardians, had an automatic right of entry except the paupers. Many were simply not up to the job. The very nature of the work meant that it attracted married couples with no roots: demobbed army non-commissioned officers and their wives, for example, who had no experience of managing large institutions. Many masters wielded power by interpreting rules and regulations with unnecessary and ignorant tyranny; many matrons saw in the paupers a ready supply of 'free' servants and aspired to a lifestyle beyond their means.

However, not all were like this. The 1,238 masters and matrons in the 600 Poor Law unions that had been set up by 1846 were a mixed bag:

- At Ashford (Kent) the union workhouse was run by a retired, and much decorated, naval officer and his wife. It was renowned for its efficiency and for its compassion, and held up by the commissioners as a model to which others should aspire. When the master retired, paupers wept.

- Colin M'Dougal, an ex-sergeant major, ran the Andover workhouse in Hampshire. In 1846 it was the subject of questions in the House of Commons and a formal enquiry when it was reported that starving paupers were sucking the bones they were pounding into fertiliser in a vain attempt to find sustenance. Conditions in this particular workhouse pointed up some of the weaknesses in the Poor Law Amendment Act and were instrumental in bringing about the fall of the Poor Law Commission (see page 70).

- George Catch, an ex-policeman, moved from workhouse to workhouse in London, inflicting terror and cruelty wherever he went. Boards of Guardians gave him excellent testimonials simply to get rid of him, and it was not until the 1860s that, after a career of depravity, corruption and murder, he finally threw himself under a Great Western train.

- The master of Cerne Abbas workhouse (Wiltshire) lasted as master for just two weeks. He had little education and simply could not cope with the paperwork demanded by the commissioners. The guardians appointed the workhouse porter in his place.

Clerk

Some Boards of Guardians tried to save money by combining the posts of master and clerk. This simply did not work: both posts, done properly, were full-time jobs. It was the clerk who ordered, and budgeted for, the food, clothing, equipment, furniture and supplies coming into the workhouse; he supervised building work, either new or repairs. Under the master, he was responsible for just about everything, from boilers to brushes. The opportunities for corruption were enormous.

Medical officer

Medical officers were appointed on short-term contracts on the lowest possible pay and had to supply all their own drugs and bandages. Unlike other workhouse posts, the Poor Law commissioners did not recommend specific salaries for medical officers. Local doctors in each Poor Law union were invited to tender for the job. In some unions, they refused to tender, not wanting to undercut each other; in other unions, they first agreed a minimum salary among themselves.

The job was not a popular one and the status was low. At the beck and call of the workhouse master, the medical officer was part of the disciplinary structure of the workhouse. Masters could, and did, ignore medical officers' advice regarding special diets and restrictions on work. Medical officers, as well as dealing with routine sickness, had to cope with the chronic, venereal and infectious diseases that the voluntary hospitals refused to treat.

Conditions in workhouse infirmaries, until the 1860s, were pretty grim. Poor pay and workhouse accommodation were hardly incentives to recruitment. The sick were forced to depend on the ministrations of pauper 'nurses' who were supervised by the workhouse matron.

Teacher

Poor Law teachers were kept firmly under the master's control. As well as teaching the pauper children, they were expected to be responsible for their cleanliness and general appearance. But here again the principle of less eligibility stumbled. Teachers were supposed to teach – but what? Thousands of poor children never set foot in a school. Many Boards of

Questions

1 Where did power lie in the hierarchy of workhouse staff?
2 Which workhouse staff had the best opportunities for:
   a doing harm
   b doing good?
3 Why do you think workhouse staff were so poorly paid?

Guardians were wary of teaching paupers to read: what would they do, it was believed, but read **Chartist** pamphlets or write Swing letters? But they did realise that teaching pauper children to read and write would make them less likely to become a charge on the parish when they grew up. In 1836 the Bedford Board of Guardians 'solved' the problem. The guardians would have their pauper children taught to read, but not to write. This 'solution' was disallowed by the commissioners on the grounds that this would stigmatise pauper children because, when other children learned to read, they also learned to write.

In many unions the problem solved itself. At Salisbury in 1840, the schoolmaster was an alcoholic and the schoolmistress could not read; at Coventry the teacher was a pauper who did not attempt to teach reading and writing because she was herself illiterate; in Deptford the 'teachers' were illiterate seamen who specialised in swearing, bullying and drunkenness.

Chaplain

Workhouse chaplains were usually poor curates, anxious to supplement their livings. Chaplains had to hold one service in the workhouse chapel every Sunday, visit the sick and minister to the dying. Here again, they were subject to the vagaries of the 'rule' of the workhouse master and matron as to when they could visit those of their flock who needed spiritual help and guidance. Many a poor young curate would have struggled indeed against the tyranny of a workhouse master and the unruly and probably blaspheming nature of his workhouse flock.

Definition

Chartism
Chartism was a radical movement that began in the 1830s, after the 1832 Reform Act had failed to give the vote to working people. Chartists supported the six points of the People's Charter: annual elections, equal electoral districts, payment of MPs, universal manhood suffrage, the secret ballot and the abolition of a property qualification for MPs. Chartism as a movement died out in the 1850s, but by 1920 all its demands (except for annual parliaments) had been realised.

Source L

The *Book of the Bastilles* began with a stage direction for a mock dialogue: 'Scene: The outside of a new-built "union": Groans, weeping and gnashing of teeth and the agonising cries of innocents writhing under the lash heard from within' and the incidents and anecdotes which followed lived up to this promising introduction.

No novelist, surely, could have bettered the tale of poor Widow Deacon of Woburn, who, having honourably raised four children with the help of out-relief, after being told 'some time before Michaelmas 1836 that she was not to have relief except in a workhouse', drowned herself.

Equally impressive were the cases of an 18-year-old girl discovered living in a haystack near Chester and eating 'the grass of an adjacent field as she feared being sent to the union', and a 12-year-old boy found 'cuddled up like a hedgehog under the wall' near Stockport, who had fled from Stowmarket workhouse, after he had discovered his sister 'fastened in a kind of stocks. They were cutting her hair off, and they were flogging her because she cried.'

'So much', commented Baxter, 'for the means by which savings are achieved under the administration of the New Poor Law Amendment Act. I blush for its supporters and am proud to be numbered among its most active opponents.'
From Norman Longmate, *The Workhouse*, published in 1974.

Source M

Harriet Decoster Rushworth, twenty years old, with her daughter, an infant nine months old, were placed in the workhouse of St George's-in-the-East. Her baby was taken from her and two other babies were put to her to suckle. This was done the very day she went in. A little boy, having been separated from his mother in Nottingham Union, raged in all the agony of despair, and actually tore off his own hair by handsful.

From a letter written by Richard Oastler and sent to Lord John Russell on 3 March 1838.

Source N

Upwards of half a dozen girls in the Hoo workhouse, some of them verging on womanhood, have at times had their persons exposed in the most brutal and indecent manner, by the Master, for the purpose of inflicting on them cruel floggings; and the same girls, at other times, have, in a scarcely less indecent manner, been compelled by him to strip the upper parts of their persons naked, to allow him to scourge them with birch rods on their bare shoulders and waists, and which, from more than one of the statements from the lips of the sufferers, appears to have been inflicted without mercy.

From The Times, 26 December 1840.

Pay and conditions

Overall, the Poor Law did not attract well-qualified, dedicated people to work in its service. This was mainly because of the ludicrously low rates of pay the commissioners offered. A prison governor, responsible for, say, 900 long-term convicts, was paid around £600 a year. Yet a workhouse master and matron, responsible for a shifting population of around 600 paupers, received a salary of around £80 a year between them; the highest salary on record was £150. A prison chaplain received on average £250; a workhouse chaplain, £100; a surgeon, £220; a workhouse medical officer, £78. Apart from the pay, workhouse staff complained about long hours, few holidays and of being tied to the workhouse and the whim of the workhouse master.

Source O

The Poor Law Commissioners regret to learn that their Assistant Commissioner, Mr Hall, on visiting the Chelsea workhouse, found it in a very unsatisfactory state. There was throughout a lack of order, cleanliness, and ventilation, the heat in the female wards being excessive, in consequence of there being a number of unnecessarily large fires kept up.

Some of the paupers were in their own clothes, Article 7 of the workhouse rules having been, in this case, neglected.

Smoking was going on in several of the rooms, both bedrooms and day rooms. The Commissioners think the allowance of such a practice, particularly in the bedrooms, highly objectionable.

The Commissioners also learn that extra articles of food are freely admitted to be brought into the workhouse. The Commissioners think it desirable that a dietary should be prescribed for the inmates of the workhouse, the practice of allowing provisions to be brought into the workhouse as presents, cannot, in the opinion of the Commissioners, fail to produce many irregularities.

From a letter written by Edwin Chadwick on 27 May 1843, to the Clerk of the Poor Law Guardians, St Luke Chelsea, London.

Source P

The Guardians caused, on receipt of your letter, a minute inspection of the house to be made. We have to state, that with the exception of the need for a little whitewashing, and that only here and there, there is no lack of order, cleanliness and ventilation in the Chelsea workhouse, as erroneously stated in your letter.

As to the charge of 'the heat in the female yards being excessive', the Guardians found that there has been for some time past but one fire, and that only a moderate one, in the infirm wards.

As to some of the paupers wearing their own clothing, there are some who do; but they are of the elder class, and who have been allowed to wear their own clothes on account of their former respectability.

The Guardians find smoking is confined to five old infirm women, who smoke medicinally. Some old men also smoke, but this is allowed by the Guardians.

As to 'extra articles of food', these, the presents of friends, have been permitted but it is only to a trifling extent.

Part of a letter from T. M. Loveland, Clerk to the Board of Guardians,
St Luke Chelsea, to the Poor Law Commissioners on 15 June 1843.

SKILLS BUILDER

1 Read Sources O and P. How far, according to Source P, are Edwin Chadwick's complaints (Source O) justified?

2 To what extent would you agree that, in this particular workhouse, the principle of less eligibility had not been applied?

Concern, protest and outrage

As soon as the first union workhouse admitted the first paupers, letters of concern were sent to prominent individuals and the newspapers, and stories of atrocities began to circulate. George R. Wythen Baxter published some of the stories in his *Book of the Bastilles* in 1841.

There was a different sort of protest from Edwin Chadwick! But, as you will see from Source P, the Chelsea Poor Law guardians fought back.

Unit summary

What have you learned in this unit?

You have learned that the Poor Law commissioners faced a dilemma in trying to apply the principle of less eligibility to the union workhouses. They could not make life within a workhouse worse than the living conditions of the poorest labourer outside, because this would have meant institutionalising dirt, disease and near starvation. They solved this problem by creating a regime so grim that only the destitute would want to take the workhouse test and enter a workhouse. You have found that not all workhouses were run on the lines recommended by the Poor Law commissioners, and not all Poor Law guardians wanted them to be so. You have seen that reports and accounts of abuse and cruelty perpetrated within the union workhouses were circulating and that they had become places of fear and dread.

What skills have you used in this unit?

You have evaluated a range of source material in order to discover what the lives lived by paupers in the union workhouses were like, and you have discovered a range of different experiences. You have worked with workhouse plans, regulations, a dietary and a punishment book to help you understand how the Poor Law Commission interpreted and applied the principle of eligibility. You have seen how the commission struggled to persuade the guardians of some workhouses to conform and how the principle of less eligibility was being turned into a regime of cruelty that was gradually being made known to the general public.

Exam style question

This is the sort of question you will find on the exam paper as an (a) question.

Study Sources G, N and P.

How far do Sources G and N challenge the view given of workhouses in Source P?

Exam tips

You tackled an (a) type question at the end of Unit 1. Look back at the exam tips you were given there (page 15) before developing and building on them here. Follow these tips to write a successful answer to an (a) question.

- Get 'underneath' the sources and make inferences from them.
- Compare the sources by analysing their similarities and differences.
- Contextualise the sources, giving weight to the significance of their origin, nature and purpose.
- Reach a judgment on 'how far' by using the sources as a set.

Remember, there is an Exam zone section at the end of this book (see pages 161–66) to help you further.

Now plan an answer to the question above and write a response.

RESEARCH TOPIC

Many novels, ballads and broadsides were written at the time about life in a workhouse. Use your research skills (and the internet) to locate one of these, access it and read it or relevant sections from it.

Use your knowledge of the period to decide whether you are reading propaganda or something that mirrors reality. Here are three suggestions to start you off:

- Charles Dickens, *The Adventures of Oliver Twist*, first published in 1838.
- Mrs Frances Trollope, *Jessie Phillips, a Tale of the Present Day*, published in 1844.
- Bradford broadsheet, *The New Starvation Law Examined*.

Alternatively, find a modern novel about life in a workhouse and decide whether you are reading romantic fiction or a story that closely mirrors reality.

5 How did the Poor Law develop between 1847 and 1875?

What is this unit about?

1847 was a watershed in the development of the Poor Law. The initial teething troubles, caused by the painstaking implementation of the main principles of the Poor Law Amendment Act, had been dealt with by commissioners and assistant commissioners with some measure of success. Opposition had, broadly, died down. Those seeking relief knew what to expect, and those paying for the relief knew what they were paying for.

However, 1847 was a watershed in another, more concrete, way. The Andover workhouse scandal, although undoubtedly exaggerated, had brought some of the worst abuses of the new Poor Law system to the attention of Parliament and the public. The scandal had provided the trigger for the abolition of the Poor Law Commission. It was replaced by the Poor Law Board, whose president was a cabinet minister and accountable to Parliament. In 1847 the stage was set for development, and this unit explores the changes that happened after 1847 and examines the continuity with the 1834–46 regime. But first it begins with the trigger that pushed the government into action.

Key questions

- Why was the Poor Law Commission replaced by the Poor Law Board?
- To what extent did the treatment of paupers change between 1847 and 1875?

Timeline

1845–6	**Andover workhouse scandal and enquiry**
1847	**Poor Law Commission replaced by Poor Law Board** This makes the administration of the Poor Law directly accountable to Parliament.
1848	**District Schools Act** This act enables unions to combine to provide schools for pauper children off the workhouse site.
1852	**Outdoor Labour Test Order** Able-bodied men required to undertake monotonous work in return for outdoor relief.
1865	**The Union Chargeability Act** This act puts the financial burden of caring for the poor on the Poor Law union as a whole and not on individual parishes, thus spreading the cost.
1867	**The Metropolitan Poor Act organised London into 'asylum' districts** Each district provided general, specialist, isolation and mental hospitals.

1867 **Parliamentary Reform Act**
      The act almost doubled the electorate from 1 million voters to just under
      2 million. In several industrial boroughs (Oldham, for example) the majority of
      the electorate were working class.

1869 **Poor Law Loans Act**
      Guardians could now take out loans for capital projects and extend the
      repayments over a period of 30 years.

1870 **Elementary Education Act (Forster's Act)**
      Board schools set up for all children and Poor Law guardians encouraged to
      send pauper children to them.

1871 **Poor Law Board replaced by the Local Government Board**

The Andover scandal

Source A

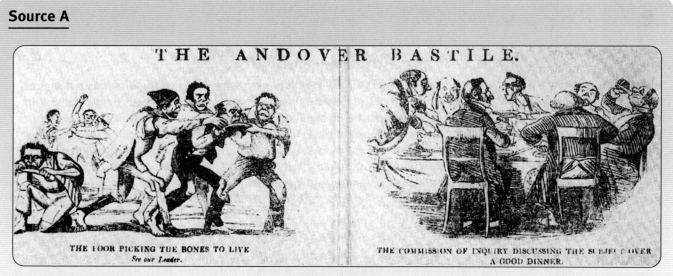

WORKHOUSE ATROCITIES—Just before the Prorogation of Parliament, Mr. Wakley asked Sir James Graham if he had heard "that the paupers of a union in Hampshire were employed in crushing bones, and that while so employed they were engaged in quarrelling with each other for the bones, in extracting marrow from them, and in gnawing off the meat from the extremities."

With regard to the immediate case before us, it appears, from the investigation (observes the *Times*) which has taken place into this truly shocking affair, that the paupers are employed in crushing bones collected from various sources, including frequently the bones of horses as well as of other animals, and "occasionally" some from churchyards.

"They must have been ground down by hunger to a condition as low as that of the very dogs, for we have it in the words of the paupers themselves that they are 'ready to fight over the bones', and, 'as soon as one sees a good bone which is unobserved by the rest, he contrives to steal it away, and hides it until he gets an opportunity of gnawing it.'"—DISPATCH

A cartoon in the *Penny Satirist*, published 6 September 1846.

SKILLS BUILDER

1 Look at the cartoon, Source A. What point is the cartoonist making by using the two very different images?

2 Read Source B. Bone-crushing was work commonly given to paupers in workhouses. Crushed animal bones were in demand as an agricultural fertiliser and were sold to local farmers. Why, then, would contemporaries find Charles Lewis' evidence particularly disturbing?

   Is Charles Lewis being asked leading questions, or is he giving his evidence freely? Does it matter?

3 Now look at Source A and Source B together. How do you think these two sources could be used by opponents of the new Poor Law to criticise the Poor Law Commission and the principle of less eligibility?

Source B

Evidence of Charles Lewis, Labourer

Q What work were you employed about when you were in the workhouse?
A I was employed breaking bones.

Q Were other men engaged in the same work?
A Yes.

Q During the time you were so employed, did you ever see any of the men gnaw anything or eat anything from those bones?
A I have seen them eat marrow out of the bones.

Q Have you often seen them eat the marrow?
A I have.

Q Did they state why they did it?
A I really believe they were very hungry.

Q Did you yourself feel extremely hungry at that time?
A I did, but my stomach would not take it.

Q You could not swallow the marrow?
A No.

Q Did you see any of the men gnaw the meat from the bones?
A Yes.

Q Did they use to steal the bones and hide them away?
A Yes.

Q And when a fresh set of bones came in, did they keep a sharp look out for the best?
A Yes.

Q Was that a regular thing?
A Yes.

The evidence of an inmate of the Andover workhouse, from the *Report from the Select Committee on the Andover Union*, published in 1846.

Thomas Wakley, MP

Why did the Andover scandal lead to the end of the Poor Law Commission?

The Andover Union in Hampshire had for a long time been held up as being the model of post-1834 Poor Law administration. Outdoor relief had been abolished, and the strictest dietary used in the union workhouses. Indeed, the union administration was praised in the annual reports of the Poor Law commissioners. In 1837, the guardians appointed Colin M'Dougal and his wife as the Andover workhouse master and matron. So confident were they that they had the right people for the job that they made only cursory inspections afterwards. Reports began filtering out that all was not well. Thomas Wakley, who was MP for Finsbury and a strong opponent of the new Poor Law, asked a question in the House of Commons about the situation in the Andover workhouse and the Poor Law Commission ordered Henry Parker, assistant commissioner with responsibility for the area, to investigate.

Henry Parker discovered that the rumours were all true and that a range of dreadful abuses were being perpetrated in the Andover workhouse, ranging from sexual abuse of the female paupers by M'Dougal and his son to serving even less food than laid down by the worst dietary. The Poor Law Commission tried to extricate themselves from the situation by sacking M'Dougal, by blaming Parker for not uncovering the abuses sooner (conveniently forgetting that they had reduced the number of assistant commissioners from 21 to 9, thus making his job impossible) and sacking him, and by issuing an order forbidding bone-crushing. But it was too little, too late. Parker struck back by writing a well-argued pamphlet, gaining the support of Edwin Chadwick, who never lost an opportunity of undermining his superiors, and precipitating an enquiry by a select committee of the House of Commons. You read part of the report from that enquiry in Source B. The full report was highly critical of the Poor Law Commission, and it was clear that a major shake-up in the administration of the Poor Laws was highly likely.

The Andover scandal was not the only problem that central government had with the commission, and the select committee's enquiry revealed more than the straightforward maladministration of one workhouse.

Problems with the Poor Law Commission

The apparent autonomy given by Parliament to the three commissioners was largely driven by the need to implement the Poor Law Amendment Act quickly and efficiently. It was always envisaged that the power given to the commissioners would be temporary, and the 1834 act limited the life of the commission to five years. After 1839 the commission's powers were renewed on an annual basis. However, by 1842 opposition to the implementation of the Poor Law Amendment Act was waning. It looked as though Parliament would not have to intervene and so it extended the commission's contract for a further five years to 1847. So why wasn't it extended beyond 1847?

- The Andover scandal (1845–6) revealed the worst abuses of the workhouse system and the apparent lack of willingness of the commission to detect and correct such matters.

- The way the commission itself pilloried the assistant commissioner responsible for the Andover workhouse alarmed those who knew how administrators should be treated in problematic situations.

- The select committee revealed that there were considerable tensions within Somerset House, where the commission worked. Edwin Chadwick, for example, had never reconciled himself to the 'lowly' position of secretary and had always wanted to be a commissioner. He used the Andover scandal to criticise his employers.

Administering the Poor Law 1847–75

From Poor Law Commission to Poor Law Board

Gradually, Parliament became convinced that the commission had served its purpose and had to go. In 1847 the government replaced the Poor Law Commission with the Poor Law Board. It was intended, not only to rid the administration of the Poor Law of arrogance, rigidity and hypocrisy, but also to link it more firmly to government.

Who was running the Poor Law Board?

- The president of the board, Charles Buller, and the parliamentary secretary, Lord Ebrington, were both in the House of Commons.

- George Nicholls (one of the three former Poor Law commissioners) was appointed permanent secretary and was responsible for the day-to-day operations of the commission. Nicholls had been an avid supporter of bone-crushing and, furthermore, had blamed the dreadful occurrences at Andover on the depravity of the paupers themselves. In many ways it seems odd that he, alone of the three commissioners, should have been kept on in his post. However, his salary was reduced from £2,000 to £1,500 and this could be seen as a criticism of his earlier role.

- The assistant commissioners were kept on, their numbers increased from 9 to 13 and they were renamed 'poor law inspectors'. Here, the importance of their personalities became obvious. The skilled negotiator, John Walsham, for example, was able to achieve more in the north-east of England than the irascible John Mott in Lancashire and Yorkshire. But, with large districts to supervise, inspectors were able to visit individual unions no more than a couple of times a year.

Two of the three men who were Poor Law commissioners in 1846 were promoted to prestigious posts. Sir Edmund Head was appointed governor-general of New Brunswick and George Cornewall Lewis became secretary to the Board of Control for India. What happened to Edwin Chadwick? He had no place at all on the Poor Law Board. He was appointed a member of the General Board of Health, where, as you will read later, he had considerable impact.

Questions

1 The Poor Law inspectors were responsible for large districts. Would this be likely to mean that unions could afford to be flexible in meeting local needs, or that they were more able to abuse paupers in their care?

2 Are you surprised at the appointment of George Nicholls to the post of permanent secretary to the Poor Law Board?

Source C

In 1834 it was thought that the persons who were to be invested with the discretionary powers to be exercised by a central authority [the Poor Law Commissioners] ought not to form any part of the Executive Government; that they should be free from popular pressure. It was at that time thought better, also, that no political changes should be allowed to affect those who were to be entrusted with these powers. Upon these grounds, the Poor Law Commission was separated from the Executive Government.

Looking at the results of that arrangement and experience, I think I may assert that it has not been as successful as was anticipated. The responsibility of the Poor Law Commissioners to Parliament was indirect and imperfect. The power they exercised was free from that check which is imposed upon those public officials who are obliged to listen in this House to charges made against them, and they [the Commissioners] were not able to answer their accusers. They have laboured under a major disadvantage in this respect.

Under the existing Poor Law Commission, what really happens? Complaints are made, and questions asked of the Home Secretary who is expected to give an answer; but his first answer has to be that he is entirely ignorant of the matter, but that he will enquire into the case and give a reply on a future day. Consequently, he obtains an explanation from the Commissioners, but still without a knowledge of all the circumstances, he is expected to give full information to the House on the subject. This, unquestionably, leads to a great inconvenience; and the administration of the Poor Law Amendment Act has been, to a certain degree, prejudiced by it.

The principle, therefore, of the bill which I have to propose, is that there should be a general superintending authority immediately responsible to Parliament and the existing powers of the Commission shall be transferred to a new Board.

From *Hansard* (an official publication recording parliamentary debates), May 1847. Sir George Grey, the Home Secretary, explains why he wants to replace the Poor Law Commission with a Poor Law Board.

Definition

Parliamentary Reform Act, 1867

This increased the number of voters to over two million men, and included the 'respectable' working classes by allowing occupiers of dwelling houses who had lived there for 12 months to have the vote.

From Poor Law Board to Local Government Board

In the latter half of the nineteenth century, and particularly after the **Parliamentary Reform Act of 1867**, the government became increasingly aware of, and concerned with, the welfare of the people. The new legislation that affected, for example, housing and public health was dependent upon the local authorities for enforcement. It did not make any administrative sense to keep the Poor Law separate from this and so, in 1871, the Poor Law Board was replaced by the Local Government Board. However, the government still retained its control, as the president of the Local Government Board was invariably a cabinet minister.

These administrative shifts reflected, too, a shift in the attitude to poverty among legislators and the public. Poverty, and therefore pauperism, came to be seen less as a disgrace associated with deliberate idleness and more of a misfortune associated with events beyond the control of an individual or with personal inadequacy and accident. This change in attitude was itself a part of a growing belief that society had a duty to protect its more vulnerable members.

Did the financial situation improve?

One of the driving forces for change in 1834 had been the rising cost of the poor rate. The 1834 Poor Law Amendment Act grouped parishes into unions, but each parish within the union had to pay for the maintenance of its own paupers. The result of this was that struggling parishes with the most paupers levied the highest poor rates, yet were the least able to afford them. Conversely, prosperous parishes with few paupers levied a low poor rate and their prosperity was further enhanced. In some areas, the burden of the poor rate was so heavy that parishes could not meet their commitments.

Source D

	Average expenditure (in £ooos)	% increase or decrease on previous period	Per head of population
1844–8	5290	+11	6s 2d
1849–53	5198	−2	5s 10d
1854–8	5791	+11	6s 0d
1859–63	5880	+2	5s 10d
1864–8	6717	+14	6s 2d

The poor rate, 1844–68.

SKILLS BUILDER

1 Read Source C. What reasons does George Grey give for wanting to replace the Poor Law Commission with a Poor Law Board?

2 From what you know of the situation, do you believe that these are the only reasons?

3 Does he blame anyone for needing to make the change?

SKILLS BUILDER

Use Source D to answer these questions.

1 Did looking after the poor get cheaper or more expensive in the period 1844–68?

2 How could supporters of the new Poor Law use this data to claim the law was meeting its main objective?

3 How could opponents of the new Poor Law use this data to claim the law wasn't working?

The situation was resolved in 1865 by the Union Chargeability Act, which placed the financial burden of relief on the union as a whole. Each parish contributed to a common fund and its contribution was based upon the rateable value of properties in the parish, not the number of paupers for whom the parish was responsible. Thus, richer parishes subsidised the poorer ones, and those owning larger properties paid higher poor rates than those living in more modest dwellings.

Even so, there was no uniform rating system so that, pound for pound, the owner of a property in, say, Hertfordshire would pay the same poor rate as the owner of a similar property in, say, Lancashire. Most Boards of Guardians, too, were middle class and committed to keeping the rates as low as possible. These factors combined to lead some Poor Law unions to claim they could not afford to build, for example, the separate accommodation required by the 1834 act for different classes of paupers. The 1869 Poor Law Loans Act attempted to ease the situation by allowing guardians to extend the repayments on loans from the Public Works Commissioners to up to 30 years. Guardians could thus contemplate applying for the level of loan that would enable them to upgrade their facilities without adding too much to the poor rate they levied.

What balance was achieved between indoor and outdoor relief?

All legislation attempting to deal with the problems thrown up by the poor and destitute stumbled when it came to the problems of coping with the able-bodied poor. All legislators saw the need to distinguish between those who could not work and those who would not work. They differed in how they categorised able-bodied paupers and in how they treated them, once categorised. The prime movers behind the 1834 legislation had no inhibitions. The 1834 Report of the Royal Commission on the Poor Laws was adamant in recommending that all outdoor relief should end. Outdoor relief did, it was believed, encourage laziness as it removed from the poor the need to work. If all relief were obtainable solely in workhouses, only the truly desperate would apply and the much-vaunted principle of less eligibility would be seen to operate. With fewer able-bodied poor applying for relief, the labour market, and hence the economy, would remain buoyant, the poor rates would be kept low and the poor would retain their self-respect. This, at least, was the theory. Reality was, of course, different.

By 1847 it had become clear that it was going to be impossible to abolish outdoor relief in rural as well as urban areas. In 1844 the commissioners had issued the Outdoor Relief Prohibitory Order, prohibiting outdoor relief for the able-bodied poor (see page 30). At this time, the assistant commissioners were experiencing tremendous problems in implementing the new Poor Law in the industrial north, and so the order did not extend there. Instead, the Outdoor Labour Test Order was supposed to apply. This insisted that the workhouse test had to be paralleled by the 'labour test' whereby monotonous and unpleasant work had to be undertaken by the pauper in return for outdoor relief. This was intended to be temporary, to tide over the industrial areas while the problems of introducing the Poor Law Amendment Act were ironed out by the relevant assistant commissioners. But it was not to be. Their irregular and infrequent visits meant that local variations were not just possible but became the norm. In 1846 – the commission's last full year – there were approximately 1,300,000 paupers in England and Wales. Of these, only 199,000 received relief inside union workhouses.

The Poor Law Board made an attempt, in 1852, to incarcerate all the able-bodied paupers in workhouses by issuing a general order forbidding outdoor relief to the able-bodied. It failed. Many Boards of Guardians used all the loopholes possible (the most common one being sickness in the family) to continue giving outdoor relief. Indeed, aware that poor rates were again rising, cost-conscious guardians preferred the cheaper alternative of outdoor relief.

- In East Anglia in 1860 it cost 3s 5½ d a week to keep a pauper in a workhouse and 1s 9d if that same pauper were on outdoor relief.
- In London in 1862 it cost 4s 8d a week to keep a pauper in a workhouse and 2s 3d if that same pauper were on outdoor relief.

The superiority of outdoor relief over indoor was endorsed in 1863. In the early 1860s, the American cotton crop failed, causing a crisis in the Lancashire cotton mills. Thousands of operatives needed short-term outdoor relief. In order to ease the situation, the Public Works Act of 1863 allowed local authorities to borrow money to set up work schemes to employ paupers. It did not really work because the crisis passed before it could come into play. But the point was that a basic principle of the 1834 Poor Law Amendment Act – the ending of outdoor relief for able-bodied paupers – had been breached, and breached by Parliament.

The Local Government Board and relief

When the Local Government Board took over responsibility for the administration of the Poor Law in 1871, it tried desperately to reduce the number of paupers receiving relief:

- It issued a circular condemning outdoor relief on the basis that it took away from the poor all desire to save for bad times by offering relief to them in their own homes whenever they needed it.
- It supported local authorities when they took a harsh line with the able-bodied poor asking for relief. Poplar, in east London, for example, set up a deterrent workhouse that set the undeserving poor to harsh work. Others followed suit. They were able to do this because a growing number of charities were beginning to provide charity payments for the deserving poor.
- It authorised Boards of Guardians to take part in emigration schemes, whereby groups of paupers (either whole families or specific categories of poor and paupers) were sponsored to emigrate.

However, one factor remained constant. Although the ratio of paupers relieved inside the workhouse to those receiving outdoor relief changed over time, the greater number of paupers were always relieved *outside* the workhouse.

Source E

Year	Total number of paupers relieved	Number receiving indoor relief	Number receiving outdoor relief
1840	1,199,592	169,232	1,030,297
1850	1,008,700	123,004	885,696
1860	844,633	113,507	731,126
1870	1,032,800	156,800	876,000
1880	792,499	215,377	577,122

From the Local Government Board's 31st Annual Report, showing the number of paupers receiving indoor and outdoor relief 1840–80.

SKILLS BUILDER

Look at the data shown in Source E and use your own knowledge to answer the following:

1 Why were the authorities unable to stop outdoor relief?

2 Does the fact that outdoor relief continued to be the most popular way of giving help to the poor mean that the principle of less eligibility had failed?

Did the treatment of paupers change, 1847–75?

The rigour and deterrent principles embodied in the 1834 Poor Law Amendment Act were directed at able-bodied men. It was never intended that Boards of Guardians apply them to the more vulnerable members of society: the elderly, the sick, the mentally ill and children. Indeed, the royal commission of 1834 (see page 27) recommended the separation of different categories of paupers within a workhouse and that the paupers within each category should be treated differently. However, this ideal stumbled over the enormous cost implications. Initially, therefore, the 'general mixed workhouse' became the norm, something to which Chadwick, for one, was never reconciled.

It was not until later in the century that Poor Law administrators returned to Chadwick's thinking. In the 1870s, the Local Government Board advised Boards of Guardians to divide up paupers in their workhouses according to what it was that caused their poverty and to create a scale of 'comforts' for each category, with the most deserving receiving the most. This was all very well in theory, but in practice it was a difficult thing to do without government funding, which was not forthcoming. There were, as always, vast local differences in provision.

Pauper children

The special needs of pauper children were almost universally recognised. It was generally considered undesirable, even before 1834, that children should mix freely with adult paupers and there was a growing belief that education was the way to ensure that pauper children did not return to the workhouse as pauper adults. After 1834, children under the age of 16 made up, fairly consistently, around one-third of all paupers in workhouses. So what was done and how did provision for children change?

- **1834:** workhouse schools were established and became one of the first forms of state education. These breached the principle of less eligibility because they provided an education for pauper children that was better, although their curriculum was narrower, than that provided by voluntary schools outside the workhouse. Indeed, the poorest children outside the workhouse rarely had any education at all.

- **1846:** a government grant was made available to Boards of Guardians to enable them to pay the salaries of workhouse schoolteachers.
- **1848:** the District Schools Act allowed Poor Law unions to combine to provide district schools, where pauper children were educated in buildings often far distant from the workhouse in which they lived. Some progressive Boards of Guardians, like those in Leeds and Manchester, set up industrial schools, where pauper children lived and took 'honest and useful industrial courses', enabling them to become 'good servants or workmen'.
- **1850s:** some Boards of Guardians abandoned district schools in favour of smaller, on-site schools where boys were taught a trade and girls learned domestic skills.
- **1860s:** some Boards of Guardians began to experiment with boarding pauper children with working-class families.
- **1870:** Forster's Education Act set up Board schools and guardians were encouraged to send their pauper children to these, enabling them to mix with children outside the workhouse.

SKILLS BUILDER

Read Sources F and G. How far do the sources, taken together, explain the problems involved in educating workhouse children?

Source F

There was a promising flurry of district school creation during the first year. Six new districts, in and around London, where it seemed easiest to procure the consent of boards of guardians, were created. By 1849, however, the movement's force had been spent, and only three more districts were created throughout the remainder of the century. The problem, especially in the rural areas, was the parsimony and scepticism of guardians. Many a farmer and village tradesman-guardian, usually wretchedly educated themselves, were worried that decent schools might cause their pauper charges to set their sights higher than farm labour and domestic service. If pauper children could be better educated than the sons and daughters of independent labourers, it might even be an inducement for parents to throw themselves on the ratepayer – a perverse inversion of the 'less eligibility' principle.

From M. A. Crowther, *The Workhouse System 1834–1921*, published in 1981.

Source G

An advertisement for a schoolmistress to teach in a workhouse.

> # BROMSGROVE UNION.
>
> ## APPOINTMENT OF SCHOOLMISTRESS.
>
> THE BOARD of GUARDIANS OF this UNION, at their Meeting on TUESDAY, the 9th day of May next, intend to elect a SCHOOLMISTRESS for the WORKHOUSE. The person appointed will be required to instruct both boys and girls, and to perform such duties as are set forth in the General Consolidated Orders of the Poor Law Board. The salary will be £20 per annum, subject to such increase as may be awarded by the Committee of Council on Education, with Rations, Lodging, and Washing in the Workhouse.
>
> Applications in the handwriting of the candidates, with testimonials as to character and ability, to be sent to me on or before Monday, the 8th of May next, and the applicants will be expected to attend at the Board Room on the following day (Tuesday), at Eleven o'clock in the Forenoon. No travelling expenses will be allowed.
>
> By order of the Board,
>
> THOMAS DAY, Clerk.
>
> Board Room, Bromsgrove, 25th April, 1865.

Sick and mentally ill paupers

Illness of the main breadwinner in a family was a major cause of poverty and eventually pauperism, yet the early Poor Law administrators paid little attention to the problem. It is true that the Poor Law Amendment Act allowed for the employment and payment of medical officers, but these were invariably poorly paid and were seen as part of the disciplinary structure of the workhouse (see page 61). Boards of Guardians frequently left their sick, injured and pregnant paupers to be treated in their own homes by Poor Law medical officers. Indeed, this was one of the major forms of outdoor relief after 1834. In this way, costs were kept to a minimum; in 1840 only £150,000 from a Poor Law expenditure of £34.5 million went on medical services.

The change and development in Poor Law medical services happened, not in response to any plan or ideology, but in response to need and public opinion, as the following points show:

- **1841:** a poor person receiving a smallpox vaccination from a Poor Law medical officer did not, because of this, become a pauper.
- **1850s:** Poor Law unions set up public dispensaries, which dispensed medicines to the general public as well as to paupers.
- **1852:** a poor person who could not pay for medical treatment or prescribed medicines automatically qualified for outdoor relief.

However, matters came to a head when Poor Law medical officers began complaining through the Poor Law Medical Officers' Association and through the Workhouse Visiting Society about the conditions in workhouse hospitals. Letters of complaint were published in *The Lancet*, which itself initiated an enquiry into conditions in London workhouse hospitals. Gradually, the public became aware that something had to be done. 'Sickness and poverty are different things', thundered *The Times* in 1866. Gathorne Hardy, president of the Poor Law Board, agreed. In doing so, he signalled a major change of policy. Sick paupers were to be treated in hospitals that were separate from the workhouses. Thus began the separation of pauperism from illness.

These 'pauper' hospitals were often the only places where ordinary working people could get medical help. This was particularly the case in London, where the 1867 Metropolitan Poor Act had organised London into 'asylum' districts, which provided general, specialist, isolation and mental hospitals.

The Poor Law was thus beginning to provide a national, state-funded system of medical care for paupers and poor people. The connections between medicine and less eligibility were well and truly broken. Gradually, the move had been made from stigmatised, pauperised medicine to a basic medical service for the poor for which they did not have to pay.

Source H

At St Martin-in-the-Fields, the ground floor rooms look like basement cellars, and this is due to the fact that the site is part of an ancient and well-stocked churchyard; and these rooms, with this offensive amount of churchyard earth blocking up the windows on one side, have been converted into surgical wards.

At Greenwich the site is below water-mark, and the foundations are liable to be flooded. Several wards (e.g. the maternity ward) have no water service at all.

Part of the report from a commission sent by *The Lancet* to investigate conditions in workhouse hospitals. The report was published in 1865. *The Lancet* was (and still is) an important medical journal.

Source I

An advertisement, dated 7 December 1861, for a workhouse ward keeper.

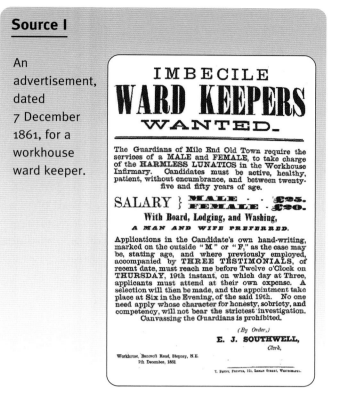

IMBECILE
WARD KEEPERS
WANTED.

The Guardians of Mile End Old Town require the services of a MALE and FEMALE, to take charge of the HARMLESS LUNATICS in the Workhouse Infirmary. Candidates must be active, healthy, patient, without encumbrance, and between twenty-five and fifty years of age.

SALARY } MALE - - £25.
FEMALE - £20.

With Board, Lodging, and Washing,

A MAN AND WIFE PREFERRED.

Applications in the Candidate's own hand-writing, marked on the outside "M" or "F," as the case may be, stating age, and where previously employed, accompanied by THREE TESTIMONIALS, of recent date, must reach me before Twelve o'Clock on THURSDAY, 19th instant, on which day at Three, applicants must attend at their own expense. A selection will then be made, and the appointment take place at Six in the Evening, of the said 19th. No one need apply whose character for honesty, sobriety, and competency, will not bear the strictest investigation. Canvassing the Guardians is prohibited.

(By Order,)

E. J. SOUTHWELL,
Clerk,

Workhouse, Bancroft Road, Stepney, N.E.
7th December, 1861.

T. PROUT, PRINTER, 123, LEMAN STREET, WHITECHAPEL.

Source J

My father was a ratepayer for 32 years and never troubled the parish for a farthing. When the poor old man was taken ill, of course my wife had to attend to him. She was pleased enough to do it. But she had her little family to see to, and she had been accustomed to bring in about two shillings a week by going out charring.

[Joseph then asked the Guardians for outdoor relief.]

Well, they refused me that, and said that my father could go into the workhouse, and I could pay one-and-sixpence a week towards his expenses.

My blood boiled up at that. What! My honest, respectable old father turned into the workhouse to end his days – never! I up and said to these gentlemen 'I'd sooner rot under a hedge than he should go there!'

And he did not go. He died under his own roof and he breathed his last breath in my arms.

From *The Autobiography of Joseph Arch*, published in 1898. Here he is recounting an event in the early 1870s.

SKILLS BUILDER

1 Read Source H. How reliable do you think this is as evidence of poor conditions in workhouse hospitals?

2 Read Source I. How useful is this source as indicative of conditions in the Mile End Old Town workhouse?

3 Now take Sources H and I together. How far does Source I challenge Source H about conditions in workhouse hospitals?

Elderly paupers

The separation of elderly married paupers was perhaps the one provision of the 1834 administrative arrangements that caused most anguish among the paupers and most disquiet among the general public. Attempts were made to ease this compulsory separation. In 1847, the Poor Law Board ruled that separate bedrooms should be provided for couples aged over 60 if they asked for them, but in reality few were made available.

Source K

When the Local Government Board began its crackdown on outdoor relief in the 1870s, it faced a problem. For, although the logic of the Poor Law supported a toughening of conditions for the able-bodied poor, it was hard to justify any imposition of such conditions on those who were poor through illness or age.

Deterrent workhouse conditions were to an extent consistent with general thinking behind the New Poor Law. Without some incentive to do otherwise, it was feared that the elderly would automatically throw themselves on the rates. Labouring people, according to this way of thinking, should put something aside for their old age or ensure that they had families to support them.

From Peter Murray, *Poverty and Welfare 1830–1914*, published in 1999.

SKILLS BUILDER

1 How might the guardians have explained why they would not give outdoor relief for the care of Joseph Arch's father?

2 To what extent do Sources J and K explain why the elderly poor were terrified of the workhouse?

These arrangements might seem humanitarian for the time; nevertheless many poor working people viewed their old age with fear and trepidation. The workhouse cast a long shadow.

Letting the poor speak

So far, we have not had much indication of what the poor themselves felt about the ways in which they were treated. All the arguments, philosophising, categorising and ordering were made by those who were totally unlikely ever to become the recipients of the dubious benefits of the Poor Law Amendment Act. The records of the Poor Law Commission and, later, the Poor Law Board are full of letters written by, or on behalf of, paupers and the poor. They reveal the depths of poverty experienced in nineteenth-century England and Wales, the vagaries of Boards of Guardians in applying the law, and the relative powerlessness of the central administration to intervene on their behalf.

Source L

I beg permission to lay a case before you of one name of Wm Martin hawker by occupation; which has a wife and five children . . . who is reduced by five months sickness of his wife. The surgeon stated that she was in danger of losing her eyesight if she be not cautious. She asked him if moving to the seashore would help and he replied that he thought it would. So I appeared at the Board of Guardians the Tuesday following and I asked them if they would be so kind as to grant me a trifle of money to take her to the seashore. They asked me if I had got a certificate from the surgeon, I answered no sir, they answered if I had brought one they could have done better with me. So I prolonged the time one more week and I got a certificate from Mr Patchett the surgeon. So I appeared again at the Board, on the Tuesday following and they would not grant me one penny. So I resolved before she should lose her eyesight I would sell all my chattels. So on Sunday following I contrived for her to go down to Blackpool, and she remained there a few days, and returned home again much the better. And in a few days afterwards she was struck with the cholera.

On 13th December 1849 she went to the Relieving Officer and he gave her an order for the workhouse and she asked him for a horse and cart for it is twelve miles from my cottage and I am sure my children cannot walk such a distance, but he answered he would not.

Part of a letter from William Martin to the Poor Law Board in 1850 about his treatment by the Clitheroe Union. Across the letter is written 'State that the Board have no power to order relief, but will make enquiry of guardians as to his case.'

Source M

We your humble servants the Inmates of the above workhouse humbly ask your protection from the cruelties practised upon us by the Master. We are kept locked in the cell yard to break stones and kept on bread and water every other 24 hours because we cannot break 5 bushels of stone per day, being mechanics who never broke everything before. The stones being so that men that have been used to get their living by breaking them cannot do the task. We have been these last three weeks kept on bread and water, not having any meat but on Sundays, have become very weak. Most of us have large families and are not allowed a days liberty to look for work. So we have no chance of taking our families out of this place. The cruelty going on in this place is beyond description. It is a disgrace to a Christian land boasting of humanity.

> This is part of a petition from paupers in the Bethnal Green workhouse in London. It was written in 1850. The master, when contacted by the Poor Law Board, said the men were troublemakers and they were being punished for general cheek and rudeness.

Source N

Gentlemen

It is right you do cum and see oure children bad for months with hich and gets wors the Master nor gardens wont see to it and if we give oure names we shall get loked up Haste to see all and sum name Sarle and Sisel – soon as you can.

A Mother

> This letter was written to the Poor Law Board from a pauper mother in the Bethnal Green workhouse in 1857. A Poor Law inspector scribbled on the letter that he would visit the workhouse as soon as possible.

SKILLS BUILDER

Read Sources L, M and N, and use your own knowledge. How far do these letters show:

a change from

b continuity with

the attitudes of the Poor Law commissioners who administered the Poor Law until 1847?

Source O

Increasing specialisation within the workhouse system, at least in the larger urban areas, was a return to Chadwick's vision from the 1830s of a range of designated buildings for the sick, the aged, children, the insane and for the able-bodied. Hence, from the 1860s, the central authority officials urged guardians to classify inmates more clearly, and to distinguish in treatment and diet between them on grounds of the causes of their poverty and assessments of their character.

> From Alan Kidd, *State, Society and the Poor in Nineteenth Century England*, published in 1999.

Source P

The Poor Law Commissioners had been active policy makers, prejudiced in their approach to the problem of poverty, but not inert. The Poor Law Board, in contrast, was characterised by inactivity, and the Local Government Board did little better.

> From M. A. Crowther, *The Workhouse System 1834–1921*, published in 1981.

Unit summary

What have you learned in this unit?

You have learned about the change from Poor Law Commission to Poor Law Board and, later, the change from Poor Law Board to Local Government Board, and the reasons for these changes. You have seen how the Poor Law Board, answerable to Parliament for the administration of the

Poor Law, was run and you have looked at the continuity and change between the work the board did and the earlier work of the Poor Law Commission. You have looked at the changing financial situation with regard to the cost of caring for paupers, and you have considered the balance between the provision of indoor and outdoor relief. You have understood that, despite the best efforts of the authorities, outdoor relief remained the most usual way of giving relief to the poor. Finally, you have considered the ways in which the treatment of paupers by the Poor Law Board and the Local Government Board changed over time.

What skills have you used in this unit?

You have used your skills of source analysis in order to deepen your understanding as to why the Poor Law Commission was replaced by the Poor Law Board. You have analysed different sorts of data to enhance your understanding of the complexity of the changing financial situation with regard to the support of paupers and the persistence of outdoor relief. You have evaluated source material relating to the different categories of pauper and you have tried to resolve apparent differences by cross-referencing to your own knowledge. Finally, you have looked at the voices of the poor themselves in order to deepen your understanding of the complexity of the development of the Poor Laws after 1847.

Exam style question

This is the sort of question you will find appearing on the exam paper as a (b) question.

Study Sources I, O and P, and use your own knowledge.

Do you agree with the view, expressed in Source P, that the 'Poor Law Board was characterised by inactivity'?

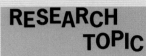

RESEARCH TOPIC

The place where you live will have been part of a Poor Law union in the nineteenth century.

Find out what that union was, where your local workhouse was situated and how the paupers were treated with regard to both indoor and outdoor relief.

Exam tips

You tackled (b) style questions at the end of Units 2 and 3. Look back to the exam tips you were given there because you will need them to answer this question. At the end of Unit 3 you created a spider diagram as a plan. This time, use whichever sort of plan works for you. But whatever you do, be sure to plan!

- Be very sure you know what view is being expressed in Source P.
- Analyse and interpret Sources I and O so as to establish points that support and points that challenge the view given in Source P.
- Cross-reference between the sources by focusing on challenge and support.
- Use your wider knowledge both to reinforce and to challenge the points derived from the sources.
- Combine the points into arguments for and against the view given in Source P.
- Evaluate the conflicting arguments by considering the quality of the evidence used, involving a consideration of provenance (where appropriate) and the weight of evidence and range of knowledge you can find in support.
- Present a supported judgment as to the validity of the stated view and/or any alternatives.

6 Dirt, disease and public health: the nature of the problem

What is this unit about?

Poverty and pauperism affected the most vulnerable members of society: those who had few saleable skills and less education, who were at the mercy of market forces and the vagaries of employers. Disease, on the other hand, was no respecter of persons, and effective public health was essential if the prevalence and spread of disease were to be controlled.

The improvement in the health of the community has always posed problems for those intent on developing public health provision. There has to be appropriate technical skill and knowledge of sanitary engineering; there has to be appropriate medical knowledge about the cause and prevention of disease; and there has to be the willingness of the public, local authorities and Parliament to legislate, carry through and uphold that legislation. This was to be no easy task in a Britain wedded, in the early years of this period, to the doctrine of *laissez-faire*, and where the **germ theory of disease** was not known until the 1860s.

Pressure for change – for improvement in public health – came not necessarily from those most affected or likely to be most affected. It came, in some measure, from local authorities and, in a greater measure, from scientists, doctors, administrators and philanthropists who, sometimes working together and sometimes alone, were concerned about various aspects of health problems in society.

This unit explores the nature of the problem. It considers the impact of population growth and movement on the public health of urban communities, on the connection made at the time between dirt, disease and death and the influence this had on the health of the general public, and on the adequacy of public health provision before about 1848.

Key questions

- What impact did population growth have on the health of urban communities?
- How significant a difference did understanding of the causes of disease make to the provision of public health?

Definition

Germ theory of disease
By the beginning of the nineteenth century, most scientists and doctors knew of the existence of micro-organisms. Many believed that they were caused by disease, not that they were the cause of disease. Some people believed that disease was caused by miasma, or gases in the air. In the 1860s Louis Pasteur (1822–95) made the link between micro-organisms (commonly called germs) and disease. It was Robert Koch (1843–1910) who took the next step of linking specific diseases with certain microbes.

Timeline

1801–51	**Population of Britain doubles**
1821	**Mortality in Leeds reaches 1 in 55**
1837	**Civil registration of births, deaths and marriages introduced**
1844	**Friedrich Engels writes *The Condition of the Working Class in England***

1845	Bradford Woolcombers form their own Protective Society
1851	50 per cent of British population living in towns
1861	Louis Pasteur publishes his germ theory of disease

Source A

	REGISTRATION DISTRICT					West London			
	1849. DEATH in the Sub-district of _West London_ in the _City of London_.								
Columns :— 1	2	3	4	5	6	7	8	9	
No.	When and where died	Name and surname	Sex	Age	Occupation	Cause of death	Signature, description, and residence of informant	When registered	Signature of registrar
100	Eighteenth June 1849 106 Shoe Lane St. Brides	Maria Woolf	Female	32 years.	Wife of George Woolf Accountant.	Diarrhoea 8 days Cholera 4 days Premature Labour 32 hours Exhaustion. Certified.	G. Woolf Present at the Death 106 Shoe Lane London.	Nineteenth June 1849	William Nason Registrar

Death certificate of Maria Woolf, dated 18 June 1849.

SKILLS BUILDER

Look carefully at Source A.

What questions would you need to ask of this source that would lead you to an understanding of the state of public health in the City of London at that time?

Question

Why do you think that life-threatening diseases hit rich and poor alike?

Maria Woolf, wife of a struggling law clerk, died, as you can see in Source A, from cholera in 1849 when she was 32 years old and pregnant. The baby was stillborn. Her husband George survived the cholera only to die from tuberculosis two years later. Prince Albert, husband to Queen Victoria, died from typhoid on 14 December 1861, aged 42. Their daughter Alice died from diphtheria in 1878, when she was 35 years old.

People on the move: a crisis in the making?

Before the Industrial Revolution

In pre-industrial Britain, there were few pressing public health problems. True, there were no drains or sewerage systems, no clean piped water and no effective measures to prevent the spread of disease. From time to time, edicts and directives were issued by government and town councils regarding, for example, the removal of waste from the streets and the emptying of privies. There were periodic outbreaks, too, of **bubonic plague**. But while there was some concentration of people in fairly crowded conditions in London and some provincial towns, the vast majority of people lived, thinly spread, in rural areas. Apart from a couple of particularly virulent outbreaks of plague, there were really no opportunities for disease to get a hold. There was certainly no perceived need for anything like a national public health system.

However, change was to come: enormous, cataclysmic change. Between 1801 and 1851 the population of Britain doubled, and it doubled again by the beginning of the twentieth century.

Source B

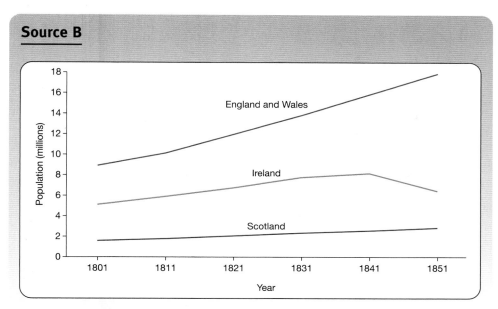

Population of the UK in millions.

Definition

Bubonic plague
A highly infectious epidemic disease. It was carried by fleas that lived on rats, and transmitted to people via flea bites. Bubonic plague first appeared in Europe as the Black Death in around 1348–9 and returned at regular intervals, disappearing from England in the 1660s. Mortality rates were very high.

Why did the population increase?

The overall population increase in Great Britain was rapid in the years between 1815 and 1851. This was due almost entirely to the consequences of industrialisation.

The death rate fell due to:

• the medical industry producing the vaccine that prevented smallpox, which had killed so many people
• the agricultural industry producing food that was better in quantity and quality
• the chemical industry producing soap that was cheap and readily available, enabling people to keep themselves and their clothes cleaner than before
• the textile industry producing cotton cloth that was cheap to buy and easy to wash and so keep clean.

The birth rate rose because:

• fewer people dying when young meant that more people survived into their twenties and thirties to have babies
• more babies living to adulthood meant that their generation, too, would have more children, and so on through following generations.

The marriage rate rose because:

• in rural areas, farmers employed fewer live-in servants. It was therefore easier for male and female agricultural labourers to begin life together on their own, and so they married earlier
• in industrial areas, unskilled workers were replacing skilled craftsmen who had had to work a seven-year apprenticeship. Therefore industrial workers could marry as soon as they had a job or even if they didn't have one
• earlier marriages, in the days before contraception, meant more babies.

Definition

Civil registration

In 1538 Thomas Cromwell instructed every parish to keep books in which the vicar should enter every baptism, marriage and burial at which he officiated. This entry should be made after the service on Sunday with a churchwarden as a witness. This practice continued, with more or less efficiency and accuracy, until the nineteenth century. The rise of non-conformity, the fall in church attendance and the increasing mobility of the population made parish registers increasingly unreliable. In 1837 the system of civil registration was introduced, which meant that national, civil certificates of births, marriages and deaths were issued as legal documents and records kept, initially, at Somerset House.

It was not just the size of the population that changed; the distribution changed, too. In 1801 around 33 per cent of the population lived in towns. This had increased to 50 per cent in 1851 and 72 per cent in 1891. The steady and relentless growth conceals the even more dramatic growth of individual towns. In the 1820s Bristol grew by 70 per cent, Bradford by 66 per cent, Leeds, Liverpool and Manchester by 46 per cent, Sheffield and Birmingham by 41 per cent. Censuses were held every ten years, and it was not uncommon for industrial centres to add one-third to their population at each count. Individual parishes, particularly in London where one-third of a million migrants settled in the 1840s, were overwhelmed.

Civil registration of births, deaths and marriages – introduced in 1837 – revealed a young, fertile and actively reproducing population in most urban centres. Urban birth rates were continually above death rates and so natural increase, from the 1840s, added to the increase from internal migration. But these global rates, too, conceal as much as they inform. In Manchester in the 1840s, for example, 57 per cent of babies died before their fifth birthday.

It was not so much the *fact* of urban growth that created public health problems, but the *rate* of urban growth. It was the pace of this growth that created almost insuperable problems and daunting challenges insofar as public health was concerned.

Source C

	Pre-1801	1831	1841	1851	1861	1871
London	775	1,685	1,948	2,362	2,804	3,254
Birmingham	42	144	183	233	296	344
Bradford	4	44	67	104	106	146
Brighton	3	41	47	66	78	90
Bristol	55	104	124	137	154	183
Cardiff	–	6	10	18	33	40
Edinburgh	85	162	166	194	203	242
Glasgow	62	202	275	345	420	522
Leicester	13	41	53	61	68	95
Leeds	24	123	152	172	207	259
Liverpool	35	202	286	376	444	493
Manchester	30	182	235	303	339	351
Newcastle	33	54	70	88	109	128
Norwich	39	61	62	68	75	80
Sheffield	27	92	111	135	185	240
Swansea	4	15	20	25	33	43
York	13	26	29	36	40	44

Population of some towns and cities in thousands, from E. J. Evans, *The Forging of the Modern State 1783–1870*, published in 1983.

SKILLS BUILDER

1 Look back at the section headed 'Why did the population increase?' Use the information there to construct a spider diagram or flow chart to show how changes in the death rate, marriage rate and birth rate are linked. What do you think is the most important factor that brought about change?

2 Look at Source C.

   a Which towns would you expect to experience the greatest challenges with regard to public health? Why?

   b How would you explain the differences in the growth rates shown here?

Questions

1 What public health problems would arise because of the rapid growth of towns?

2 What solutions could you suggest?

What impact did the Industrial Revolution have on people's living conditions?

Public health is closely connected to people's living conditions. The influx of many thousands of people into small market towns and cathedral cities that had had the fortune, or misfortune, to have one or more industries located there had a catastrophic effect on the existing housing and sanitation provision. This, in turn, led to the explosion of what the Victorians called 'filth diseases' such as typhoid, diphtheria, tuberculosis, scarlet fever and, most dreaded of all, cholera. Other nineteenth-century killers, like measles and whooping cough, became endemic.

Housing

Bad housing was nothing new and it certainly was not a product unique to the industrial revolution. There had been slums in medieval London and, throughout the centuries, agricultural labourers had lived in conditions that were frequently no better than those of the animals they tended. What was unique about the industrial revolution was that it resulted in widespread, dense overcrowding.

Urban communities responded, first, by using up and adapting existing 'vacant' living space and, second, by building new dwellings. Cellars and attics were filled with working people and their families, and were used as workplaces as well. In the 1840s in Bradford (West Yorkshire), for example, there were more than 10,000 woolcombers (see page xii) living and working in their own homes. Conditions were appalling; the average age of death of a woolcomber was 14 years 2 months. In 1845 the Bradford woolcombers formed a Protective Society and appointed their own 'Sanatory Committee' to report on their living conditions, part of which you can read in Source D.

Question

Does the fact that the woolcombers themselves commissioned their own report in an attempt to draw attention to their plight mean that it cannot be accepted as reliable?

Source D

NELSON COURT

A great many woolcombers reside in this court. It is a perfect nuisance. There are a number of cellars in it utterly unfit for human dwellings. No drainage whatever. The Visitors [those compiling the Report] cannot find word to express their horror of the filth, stench and misery which abounds in this locality, and were unable to bear the overpowering effluvia [smell] which emanates from a common sewer which runs beneath the houses. Were this to be fully described, the Committee might subject themselves to the charge of exaggeration. We trust that some of those in affluent circumstances will visit these abodes of misery and disease.

HOLGATE SQUARE

A miserable hole, surrounded by buildings on all sides. This place resembles a deep pit – no chance of ventilation; a number of men and women work in the cellars near charcoal fires, seven feet below the surface.

From the *Report of the Bradford Woolcombers Sanatory Committee*, published in 1845.

Source E

First, there is the old town of Manchester. Here the streets, even the better ones, are narrow and winding, as Todd Street, Long Millgate, Withy Grove and Shude Hill, the houses dirty, old and tumble-down, and the construction of the side streets utterly horrible. Going from the Old Church to Long Millgate, there is a row of old-fashioned houses at the right, of which not one has kept its original level; these are remnants of the old pre-manufacturing Manchester, whose former inhabitants have moved with their descendents into better-built districts. Here, [back in the old town] one is in a working-men's quarter for even the shops and beer houses hardly take the trouble to exhibit a trifling degree of cleanliness. But all this is as nothing compared to the courts and lanes that lie behind, to which access can be gained only through covered passages, in which no two human beings can pass at the same time. Every scrap of space left by the old way of building has been filled up and patched over until not a foot of land is left further to be occupied.

From Friedrich Engels, *The Condition of the Working Class in England*, published in 1844.

Source E not only creates a vivid impression of housing in industrial Manchester, but it also reveals a new development. Prior to the industrial revolution, rich, poor and 'people of the middling sort' lived in close proximity in Britain's towns and cities. In industrialising Britain, the absence of affordable public transport meant that industrial workers had to be housed close to the mills and factories in which they worked. The middle classes moved out, beyond the pollution and smut-laden pall that covered the industrialising cities.

Source F

Let us compare the mortality in Leeds with that of an agricultural district. In 1821, the population of the town and borough of Leeds was 83,796 and the burials were 1,516, or one death for every 55 people. Pickering Lythe returned in 1821 a population of 15,232 and the number of burials 205, or one death for every 74 people. Taking, then, the mortality in Pickering Lythe as the natural one, there was an excess of deaths in Leeds during 1821. Allowing for the increase in population since that year, we may fairly say that at least 450 persons dies annually in Leeds from the injurious effects of manufactures, the crowded state of the population and the consequent bad habits of life. We may say that every day of the year is carried to the grave the corpse of an individual whom nature would have long preserved in health and vigour; every day we see sacrificed to the artificial state of society, one, and sometimes two, victims, whom the destinies of nature would have spared.

From C. Turner Thackrah, *The effects of the principal arts, trades and professions on health and longevity, with a particular reference to Leeds*, published in 1831.

Most of the housing for those moving to live and work in the fast-growing cities had to be newly built. These new homes varied wildly in style: rows of industrial cottages were common in the north, back-to-back houses in parts of industrial Lancashire and Yorkshire, enclosed courtyards in Birmingham and vast tenements in Glasgow. They also varied in standard. Many were poorly built, with floors being nothing more than bare boards over beaten earth. Others were planned carefully, but the most careful planner could not legislate for the number of families that would occupy a house designed for one.

Source G

A plan of eight houses to be built in Holme Top Street, Little Horton, Bradford, dated 1852.

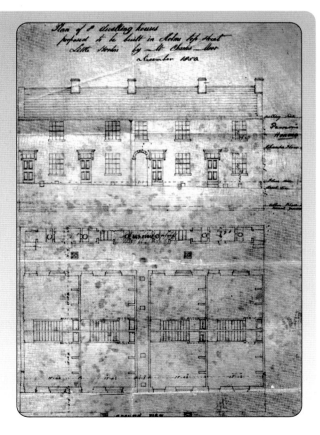

Question

Source F was published in 1831. Sources D and E were published in 1845.

Are you surprised that nothing seems to have been done to improve public health in the 14 years between the publication of Source F and Sources D and E?

SKILLS BUILDER

1 Read Sources D and E. How far do they agree with each other about housing conditions?

   What public health problems can you detect in these two accounts?

2 Read Source F. What does the author blame for the mortality in Leeds being higher than that in Pickering Lythe?

   Is his argument correct? Could there be other reasons?

3 Study Source G. With a partner, work out how living in one of these houses proposed for Holme Top Street, Bradford, could be healthier than living in the places described by the Bradford woolcombers (Source D) and Friedrich Engels (Source E).

Urban sanitation: dirt, disease and death

Source H

The houses were wholly unprovided with any form of drainage or arrangements for cleansing, one mass of damp filth. The ashes, garbage and filth of all kinds are thrown from the doors and windows of the houses upon the surface of the streets. The privies are few in proportion to the number of inhabitants. They are open to view both in front and rear and are invariably in a filthy condition and often remain without the removal of any portion of the filth for six months.

From *Parliamentary Papers Vol, 3*, describing housing in the City of Leeds, 1845.

Sanitation

It was the lack of services to a house rather than the house itself that caused problems, no matter how overcrowded it was with occupants. Most housing in the first half of the nineteenth century lacked drainage, sewerage and a regular water supply.

Lavatories (or privies) were usually outside, in the courtyards and alleys, and emptied into cesspits. Human waste collected in these cesspits that were, from time to time, cleaned out by 'night-soil' men. They piled what they had collected in huge dunghills and then sold it on to local farmers at a price per ton. Some houses (as in the back-to-back houses in the architect's plan for Holme Top Street) had their own privies. These were ash privies where, instead of flushing, the users covered the contents with ash. Some middle-class houses had flushing lavatories, but these flushed either into a cesspit in the cellar or into a closed sewer. These, as with the ash privies, had to be physically emptied.

Water was needed for washing, cooking and drinking; not only was it in short supply, but it was also expensive. Its supply, too, was controlled by vested interests in the form of private water companies. Water companies sometimes took their water from deep, natural underground reservoirs and springs, but more usually from local rivers. The middle classes had water piped to their houses and, because the supply was frequently irregular and uncertain, stored it in huge cisterns so that they could, quite literally, have water on tap. The poorer areas of towns and cities had to make do with standpipes, and the inhabitants queued with buckets and saucepans to buy what they could afford when the water company turned on the supply. People too poor to buy water, or to buy enough water for their needs, either didn't bother or took what they could from local wells and streams.

Source I

This contemporary picture of Jacob's Island, Bermondsey (London) illustrates the nub of the problem. The wooden shacks are privies emptying into the stream. The stream provides water for those living in the houses.

Source J

A cartoon by the caricaturist George Cruikshank, published in 1832.

SKILLS BUILDER

1 Study Sources H and I. How far does Source I support Source H with regard to public health issues?

2 Look at Source J. What point is George Cruikshank making?

3 Now, working with a partner, compare Sources I and J.

a Explain which source:

i gives the most information about public health problems

ii has the most impact.

b What can be learned from these sources about attitudes towards public health?

Questions

1 Do you find it odd that children should be using their own death as the focus of a game? (Source K)

2 Children today play skipping games that involve counting. Why would you not, now, find them singing about death?

Disease

The connection between dirt and disease had been appreciated for hundreds of years, but what was not known was just what that connection was. That had to wait until 1861, when Louis Pasteur published his germ theory of disease. In the first half of the nineteenth century, overcrowding and a lack of sanitation and clean water meant that disease was rampant and life expectancy of the working classes was low, for the following reasons:

- People living in overcrowded, unsanitary conditions and without easy access to a supply of clean water housed body lice, which spread typhus fever, from which many people died. There were typhus epidemics in 1837 and 1839; an outbreak in 1847 killed 10,000 people in north-west England alone.

- Influenza, scarlet fever, tuberculosis (often called the white plague) and measles were endemic and were often killers.

- Typhoid and diarrhoea were common.

- Smallpox raged between 1837 and 1840, killing over 12,000 people in 1840 alone, and scarring many more for life.

- Cholera hit Britain in four massive epidemics: 1831–2, 1848–9, 1853–4 and 1866. The first epidemic killed 31,000 and the second, 62,000. Maria Woolf (Source A) was caught by the second huge epidemic and was one of the (approximately) 62,000 to die.

Death

Victorians were familiar with death. Most parents could expect to lose some of their children. In some urban areas, one baby in four died before their first birthday. Brothers and sisters could expect at least one of their siblings to die, sometimes along with their mother in childbirth. The table of urban and rural death rates on page 119 indicates that many children, before they became adults, buried at least one parent.

Victorians usually buried their dead. It wasn't until 1885 that the first official cremation took place in Woking, Berkshire, and cremation didn't become a popular way of disposing of the dead until well into the twentieth century. The nineteenth-century Anglican clergy had a vested interest in keeping all burials within their churchyards, but, as the death rate soared, the acreage of parish graveyards remained constant. London, for example, had 200 acres of cemeteries. Every year around 50,000 dead were added, and the sheer quantity of burials made overcrowding a public health hazard.

Source K

Witness	In the year 1831 I was first employed by Mr Watkins the head grave-digger at St Clement's churchyard.
Question	How long did you work before you were taken ill?
Witness	I worked there between five and six years before I was taken ill. I got up one Sunday morning and went into the ground in Portugal Street. We had a grave to open. I believe it was ten feet. I went in and I completed the work, and I cut four or five coffins through in that piece of ground, and the bodies of some. I placed the flesh behind and I went home for my breakfast. It was our church time. We did not dare do any more till the people were in church, for the sound of cutting away the wood was so terrible that mobs used to be around the railings and looking.
Question	How many coffins have you dug through, and bodies cut through, to get to a depth of ten feet?
Witness	To get ten feet of ground you must cut through at least five or six. In the almshouses I could uncover and expose a dozen coffins within the hour.
Question	How near is the wood of the coffins to the surface?
Witness	There are coffins now within a foot of the surface.

From evidence given to the Select Committee on the Improvement of the Health of Towns in 1842.

Source L

Grandmother,
Grandmother
Tell me the truth.
How many years am I
going to live?
One, two, three, four . . . ?

A nineteenth-century children's skipping game.

Question

To have cemeteries in the state described in Source K was clearly distasteful and distressing. But why did they constitute a public health hazard?

Theories of disease

Public health is about the prevention of disease and about the spread of disease in the community. It is not about curing disease, which is the function of medicine. Nevertheless, the two are connected. The causes of disease have to be understood before effective cures can be developed. If the causes of specific diseases (especially those diseases the Victorians regarded as 'dirty') are understood, then the spread of those diseases within a community can be reduced to a minimum or eliminated altogether.

In the nineteenth century, there were two main theories about what caused disease. The first was the miasma theory; this was replaced, though not all at once and not by everyone, by the germ theory of disease. These two theories had a profound effect on public health in the years 1830–75.

The miasma theory of disease

People had understood for hundreds of years that there was a link between dirt and disease. However, they were unsure just what that link was. In the nineteenth century, the most popular explanation was 'miasma', or bad air.

Definitions

Miasma

People who believed in the miasma theory of disease said that a miasma was a poisonous vapour characterised by a bad smell created by decaying matter. The existence of a miasma in the air, they said, caused disease.

Micro-organism

Tiny organisms, such as a virus or a bacterium, which can only be seen under a microscope.

Question

Explain how the miasma theory both helped and hindered the development of effective public health.

This was an old theory, developed first in the Middle Ages. Diseases, it was believed, were caused by the presence, in the air, of a **miasma**, a kind of poisonous gas in which, so it was said, were suspended minute particles of decaying matter that couldn't be seen by the naked eye. It was characterised by a foul smell. So, the theory went, if you were breathing in a miasma, you were going to be ill because the miasma carried disease. As Edwin Chadwick said, 'Smell is disease'. Diseases were spread because the poisonous gases were carried from person to person and place to place on the air.

It was a neat theory, and it made a lot of sense to people who were trying to improve public health in the nineteenth century. Industrialisation and the rapid growth of towns had created many filthy, foul-smelling areas in most cities. It was these areas in which disease was rampant, epidemics common and death rates high. So the answer was clear: clean them up, improve housing and sanitation, and public health would automatically improve.

The germ theory of disease

Scientists became very interested in decaying matter and in the maggots and flies that lived on and in it. The development of microscopes (principally by Joseph Lister, who in 1830 built a microscope that could magnify 1,000 times without distortion) enabled them to observe **micro-organisms** in rotting material that were much, much smaller than flies and maggots. Where did these micro-organisms come from? There were two ideas:

- the decaying material created the micro-organisms
- micro-organisms in the air were attracted to the decaying material.

Which was correct?

During the 1860s, a French scientist, Louis Pasteur, conducted a series of experiments that proved that micro-organisms existed in the air and were not created by the decaying material. It was a small step from this to his germ theory. He discovered that a disease in silkworms was caused by a particular micro-organism. If micro-organisms could cause a disease in silkworms, surely different micro-organisms (germs) could cause diseases in people? And he was right. Germs could, and did, cause disease in humans. Not everyone believed him and many influential people were slow to let go of the miasma theory, as you will see in Unit 7.

It was left to a German doctor, Robert Koch, to prove this once and for all, and in the 1880s and 1890s he and his team identified the germs that caused most of the killer diseases of the nineteenth century.

How adequate was public health provision before 1848?

There were three main stumbling blocks in the way of adequate public health provision:

- lack of compulsory national legislation
- opposition of vested interests
- ignorance of the ways in which disease was spread.

This did not, however, mean that local authorities simply ignored the issue. Pioneering work was done in certain towns and cities by individual medical people and administrators. Thomas Percival and John Ferriar of Manchester were behind the formation of the Manchester Board of Health in 1795, and in Scotland Robert Graham, Robert Cowan and James Cleland published reports on public health in the early nineteenth century that prompted authorities to action. But the point is that this was piecemeal and initiatives were only applied locally. Given a different local administration with different personnel and different priorities, public health schemes would collapse.

Equally piecemeal were the many private acts of Parliament obtained by local authorities that related to public health. London, for example, was administered by 300 different bodies with an interest in public health, and these operated some 250 acts. Just one London parish, St Pancras, had 16 street paving boards acting under 29 acts of Parliament. It was an administrative nightmare. The nightmare was not confined to London. In 1831–2, for example, the county of Lancashire had an act passed for 'Lighting with Gas the Town of St Helens'; and the City of Exeter asked for an 'Act For Better Paving, Lighting, Watching, Cleansing And Otherwise Improving The City Of Exeter'. These, and many other private acts of Parliament, allowed improvement commissioners to be elected by the ratepayers to deal with the specific problems detailed by the acts. Many towns ended up with different sets of improvement commissioners dealing with, say, lighting, paving, street-cleaning and other town improvements.

By the 1830s, many people were beginning to criticise the corrupt nature of town-improvement committees and, sometimes, the town corporations themselves. In some towns, elections were rarely held and the various groupings of officials became self-perpetuating **oligarchies**. Many operated to serve the interests of selected groups of citizens. **Vested interests** – from night-soil men to clergy and owners of water companies – were either paid off or, more likely, represented on the improvement committees themselves.

It was becoming clear that the different ways of addressing public health issues were grossly inadequate.

Unit summary

What have you learned in this unit?

You have learned that industrialisation enabled the rapid growth of population, and that this, coupled with the movement of people into the industrial towns, created tremendous public health problems. This was largely due to overcrowding, poor housing and lack of sanitation.

Definitions

Oligarchy
Strictly speaking, this means 'government by a small group of people'. A self-perpetuating oligarchy would be a group of people who kept themselves in office, year after year.

Vested interest
This phrase is used to suggest that people are more likely to support a measure if they, their families or social group will benefit from the measure. People with power – whether that power rests in land, money, trade or industry – will look very carefully at measures that might damage that power.

The lack of drainage, sewerage and a regular water supply enabled diseases like tuberculosis, cholera, smallpox, measles, scarlet fever, typhus and typhoid to become killers. While many people knew there was a connection between dirt and disease, it was not until 1861 that Louis Pasteur published the germ theory of disease. Until then, people who thought about it believed that disease was caused and spread by 'miasma', or bad air. Many town councils had acts passed that enabled such things as paving, lighting and street-cleaning to be carried out, but these were not co-ordinated and, most importantly, were not universal. They were hampered, too, by corruption and vested interests. It was becoming clear that something needed to be done if the health of the people was not going to deteriorate.

RESEARCH TOPIC

Select a town that grew rapidly in the years to 1848. Research the improvement acts that related to that town (see page 130). How did they (a) help and (b) hinder improvements in public health?

What skills have you used in this unit?

You have worked with different kinds of data in order to explore the rate of growth of the UK population, and the differential distribution of population in the UK, especially concerning the rate of growth of different towns. You have analysed different sources and cross-referenced between written and pictorial material concerned with living conditions in Britain before about 1848 and related these to public-health issues. You have looked, too, at the contemporary reasons given for the high death rates and raging epidemics in urban areas insofar as they related to public health.

Exam style question

This is the sort of question you will find appearing on the examination paper as an (a) type question.

How far does Source G challenge the descriptions of urban sanitation given in Sources D and E?

Exam tips

You tackled (a) style questions at the end of Units 1 and 4. Now let's develop what you learned there about approaches to the (a) question.

- What is the question asking you to do? It is asking how far Source G challenges Sources D and E.
- Consider the sources carefully, and make inferences and deductions from them rather than using them as sources of information.
- Remember that Source G is a *plan* and, while it may represent attitudes to living conditions, does not give us evidence that these houses were ever built.
- Evaluate the evidence, assessing its reliability and quality in terms of how much weight it will bear and how secure the conclusions are that can be drawn from it.
- Reach a judgment about how far Source G can be said to challenge Sources D and E.

UNIT

7 Cholera: the impetus for reform?

What is this unit about?

There were two strong stimuli for reform in the 1830s: the reports, investigations and enquiries of sanitary reformers, organisations and commissions, and disease itself. Together they provided the impetus for local reforms and, finally, reform on a national scale. This unit focuses on the importance of cholera as a stimulus to action on the part of the authorities, on the investigative and experimental work of Dr John Snow in discovering that cholera was a water-borne disease, and on the contribution made to public health, partly as a consequence of this discovery, by John Simon and Joseph Bazalgette.

Key questions

- How effective was the response of the authorities to the cholera epidemics?
- How critical was the work of Dr John Snow?
- How far did John Simon and Joseph Bazalgette carry John Snow's work further?

Timeline

1831 **Board of Health established**
Set up by the government in response to fears that cholera was approaching Britain.

Local Boards of Health established
Issued advice, set up fever hospitals and quarantine regimes.
Folded once cholera epidemic over.

1831–2 **First cholera epidemic**
32,000 people die.

1832 **Cholera riots**
Liverpool and Exeter badly affected.

1848–9 **Second cholera epidemic**
62,000 people die.

1853–4 **Third cholera epidemic**
20,000 people die.

John Snow creates theory that cholera is water-borne
Empirical research in Soho culminating in the removal of the handle from the Broad Street pump. Cholera deaths plummet.

1855 **Publication of *On the Mode and Communication of Cholera* by John Snow**

Metropolitan Board of Works established

1856	**Joseph Bazalgette appointed Chief Engineer to the Metropolitan Board of Works**
	Draws up plans for a comprehensive sewerage system.
1858	**The 'Great Stink'**
	A hot summer turns the River Thames into a stinking sewer.
	The Metropolis Local Management Amendment Act
	The Metropolitan Board of Works given a free hand to establish a sewerage system for London.
	Joseph Bazalgette's project gets under way
	A system of interconnecting sewers and pumping stations under construction.
1865	**The Prince of Wales opens Bazalgette's sewerage system**
1866–7	**Fourth cholera epidemic**
	14,000 people die.
1870	**Final acceptance that cholera is a water-borne disease**
	John Simon, Chief Medical Officer of Health, in his annual report to the Privy Council, accepts Snow's theory that cholera is a water-borne disease.

SKILLS BUILDER

Look carefully at Source A.

What can you learn from this cartoon about the state of public health at the time?

Source A

A cartoon published in the satirical magazine *Punch* in 1852.

A COURT FOR KING CHOLERA.

Why did cholera epidemics lead to public health reform?

Cholera was unknown in Britain before 1831. Endemic in India, it was believed to have spread to China, and then along the trade routes to Europe. It hit Britain in four massive epidemics:

- 1831–2, resulting in 32,000 deaths
- 1848–9, resulting in 62,000 deaths
- 1853–4, resulting in 20,000 deaths
- 1866–7, resulting in 14,000 deaths.

The cholera epidemics, more than endemic diseases like typhoid and tuberculosis, had a profound effect upon the public and the legislators that was out of all proportion to their statistical importance. This was for two main reasons:

1 the high percentage of fatalities (40–60 per cent) among those contracting the disease

2 the speed with which cholera could strike.

Cholera

Causes

Cholera is caught by swallowing water or food that has been infected by the cholera *vibro*, a minute bacillus (germ). This bacillus can live for up to a fortnight in water, and a week in meat, milk or cheese. It is most often spread by water contaminated by the excrement of cholera victims, or by flies that have fed upon the excrement.

Symptoms

The first stage of cholera consists of violent, explosive diarrhoea and vomiting. Often the body loses several pints of fluid in a few minutes. Dehydration causes the patient to become shrunken and shrivelled. The second stage of cholera begins with acute pain in the fingers and toes. This spreads to the limbs and chest and is often accompanied by stomach cramps. The patient's features collapse and the skin turns black and blue. By now the patient is breathing with difficulty. If this stage is survived, collapse follows. This can last for a couple of hours to a week or more. The patient lies unmoving, with eyes turned up. Although conscious, the patient doesn't appear to hear or understand what is said and only occasionally replies in a feeble whisper. Coma and death soon follow.

In the same year that the *Methodist Magazine* was reporting on the fear that cholera engendered, there were 30 recorded 'cholera-phobia' riots in towns and cities throughout Britain. Principally affected were Birmingham, Bristol, Edinburgh, Exeter, Glasgow, Leeds, Liverpool, London, Manchester and Sheffield.

The Liverpool riots, 1832

The Liverpool riots were worse than those that happened anywhere else in Britain, and some of those were pretty bad. Between 29 May and 8 June 1832, eight major street riots occurred, with minor disturbances as well. The rioters were not protesting against the disease (which would not have been very sensible!) but against the local medical men. It was a generally held belief that cholera victims were being taken to the local hospital where they died, doubtless murdered by the doctors in order to provide bodies for dissection. There was some basis for this belief. In 1826, 33 bodies had been found on the Liverpool docks, ready to be shipped to Scotland for dissection. Two years later, a local surgeon, William Gill, was tried and found guilty of running a grave-robbing system in order to

Source B

To see a number of our fellow creatures, in a good state of health, in the full possession of their wonted strength, and in the midst of their years, suddenly seized with the most violent spasms, and in a few hours cast into the tomb, is calculated to shake the firmest nerves, and to inspire dread in the stoutest heart.

From the *Methodist Magazine*, 1832.

provide bodies for dissection. The riots ended abruptly, largely because of pleas from the local Catholic clergy and a well-respected local doctor, James Collins.

The Exeter riots, 1832

In Exeter, the authorities had instituted regulations for the disposal of choler-infected corpses and their clothing and bedding. People rioted, and even attacked gravediggers, because they objected to the burial of cholera victims in local graveyards.

It seems clear that cholera riots were not directed at the authorities for failing to contain the epidemic, but arose because of specific fears that:

- doctors were murdering cholera victims
- medical students were stealing bodies for their anatomy classes
- victims were being buried in unconsecrated ground
- victims were being buried hastily, possibly before they were dead, and without proper religious ceremonies
- victims were being buried in local graveyards where infection could contaminate the ground.

The Times newspaper wrote of 'great panic' and 'complete panic', but this is probably exaggerated. After all, the first two cholera epidemics occurred at a time of a great deal of political and social unrest: pressure for the reform of Parliament in 1831–2 and intense Chartist activity in 1848 (see page 62). But governments were not overturned and the fabric of society held firm.

A cure for cholera?

The problem with cholera was that it was silent, deadly and had no known cause or cure. Thousands of people tried avoidance rather than attempt prevention or a cure, although plenty of 'cures' were on offer.

Question

Are you surprised that the people were not rioting against the failure of the authorities to contain the cholera epidemic?

Source C

The victim could be dead within a few hours of the first apparent symptoms. But more generally he died after several days of suffering from violent stomach pains, vomiting, diarrhoea, and total prostration, during which the body turned cold, the pulse became imperceptible and the skin wizened. During the final stages the afflicted might well be taken for dead, and gruesome stories circulated of premature burial and the poor victim's anguished attempts to claw free of the coffin. The sudden death of apparently healthy people added still further to the fear. Cholera was thus a 'shock disease'.

From Anthony Wohl, *Endangered Lives*, published in 1983.

Source D

In all quarters there were the sick, the dying, the dead. The general silence of the city, save when broken by the tolling of the funeral bell, was most remarkable; the streets were deserted, the hurried steps of the medical men and their assistants, or of those running to seek their aid, alone were heard, while the one-horse hearse, occasionally passing on its duty, was almost the only carriage to be seen in the usually busy streets.

A description of the city of Wolverhampton in 1832, written by a doctor who worked there.

Source E

An advertisement printed in London in 1832.

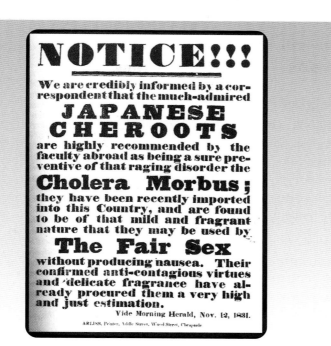

NOTICE!!!

We are credibly informed by a correspondent that the much-admired **JAPANESE CHEROOTS** are highly recommended by the faculty abroad as being a sure preventive of that raging disorder the **Cholera Morbus;** they have been recently imported into this Country, and are found to be of that mild and fragrant nature that they may be used by **The Fair Sex** without producing nausea. Their confirmed anti-contagious virtues and delicate fragrance have already procured them a very high and just estimation.

Vide Morning Herald, Nov. 12, 1831.

ARLISS, Printer, Addle Street, Wood Street, Cheapside.

For those unwilling – or unable – to flee, there was a host of remedies and preventatives from which to choose.

- The **contagionist theory** suggested that cholera was spread by contact with cholera victims. Eminently sensible, it met with considerable opposition. If true, it meant that houses, streets or even whole cities had to be put into quarantine. Opponents pointed to the potential loss of trade and consequent increase in poverty and unemployment. They argued that not everyone in the same household fell ill with cholera and so the theory could not be true.

- The **miasma theory** (see page 93) suggested that cholera was spread by a 'miasma of filth' that was breathed in from infected air. At least the results of this theory – the removal of heaps of excrement, for example – were steps in the right direction. The connecting of sewers to rivers and other water courses, however, was not.

- In 1831 *The Lancet*, a journal written by doctors for doctors, reported that a community of Jews in Wiesniz had kept themselves free from cholera by rubbing themselves with an ointment made from wine, vinegar, camphor, mustard, pepper, garlic and the crushed bodies of beetles.

- **Patent medicines** grew and multiplied, as did their claims. The most well known were Moxon's Effervescent Universal Mixture, Daffey's Elixir and Morrison the Hygienist's Genuine Vegetable Universal Mixture. All claimed to cure cholera, and, because many who took them undoubtedly did survive, they had a great following who believed in their curative properties.

- **Prayer** was recommended by all the main Christian Churches. Cholera, many believed, was God's punishment for lax and immoral behaviour.

SKILLS BUILDER

1 Read Sources B, C and D, and use your own knowledge. How far do you agree with the view that cholera was a 'shock disease'?

2 Study Source E. What can you learn from the source about the 1832 cholera epidemic?

Repent and all would be well. As with patent medicines, many of those who prayed for themselves survived, as did those for whom they prayed: prayer, the arguments went, was proven to be efficacious.

How did the government react?

Central government had done nothing about the endemic fevers and 'dirty' diseases that were common among all classes in all large towns and which claimed the lives of thousands more people than cholera. Cholera, however, was different. It was deadly, it was swift – and it was capable of engendering fear in a way that typhoid and tuberculosis could not. The government had to take action.

In 1831, realising that cholera was fast approaching the shores of Britain, the government sent two medical commissioners to St Petersburg, in Russia, to assess the situation. Their report, coupled with general alarm among government officials, resulted in a temporary Board of Health being quickly set up. It consisted of the president and four fellows of the Royal College of Physicians, the superintendent-general of quarantine, the director-general of the Army Medical Department, the medical commissioner of the Victualling Office and two civil servants.

Source F

Take for dinner a moderate quantity of roast beef in preference to boiled, with stale bread and good potatoes, two glasses of wine with water, or an equivalent of good spirits and water, or of sound porter or ale. Eat garden-stuff and fruit sparingly, and avoid fat, luscious meats. In short, while under apprehension of cholera, use a dry nutritive diet, sparing rather than abundant. Observe great caution as to eating suppers, for cholera most frequently attacks about midnight, or very early in the morning.

Dietary advice given by the Board of Health, 1832.

What did the Board of Health do?

- It advised local government areas to set up their own boards of health, which would be in a position to deal with problems at grass-roots level.
- It suggested that these local boards of health should include one or more magistrates, a clergyman, some 'substantial householders' and one or more medical men.
- It recommended that the local boards of health appoint district inspectors to report on 'the food, clothing and bedding of the poor, the ventilation of their dwellings, space, means of cleanliness, their habits of temperance'.
- It issued advice.

What advice did the Board of Health give?

- Houses were to be whitewashed and limed and all infected furniture and clothing were to be fumigated.
- People with cholera were to be put into strict quarantine.
- Food and flannel clothing were to be distributed to the poor.
- Temporary fever hospitals were to be set up.

In the absence of any knowledge about the causes of cholera, the Board of Health was understandably a trifle hazy about what people should do once they had caught the disease. It suggested a variety of remedies:

- bleeding by leeches
- warm baths followed by rubs of castor oil and laudanum
- plasters of mustard, peppermint and hot turpentine.

This sort of advice could do no harm and perhaps would do some good. What is important is that here central government is, for the first time, officially recognising that cleanliness, adequate clothing and food were necessary factors in public health. Later, Edwin Chadwick was to change the emphasis to water supply and sewerage.

What did the local boards do?

A number of cities were sufficiently frightened by the advance of cholera and did set up their own boards of health, as suggested by the central board. There were inspectors who did submit reports to their local board, and local boards sent returns to the central board, noting the cases of cholera in their area and deaths from the disease. But this tended to be information gathering, not disease prevention or cure.

Some areas set up cholera hospitals and other areas tried to institute a quarantine regime. However, in the absence of firm knowledge and understanding as to what caused cholera, any measures tended to be rather hit-or-miss affairs.

Question

How effective was the advice given by the Board of Health likely to have been?

Source G

That, with a view to check, and as far as possible, prevent the further extension and spreading of the Disease called Cholera into these Towns and Neighbourhoods, all Parish-Officers, Constables, Peace-Officers and others, are enjoined and required to prevent all Beggars, Vagrants, Trampers and Persons of suspect characters, and especially those coming from Newcastle, Gateshead and other infected Places, from having any communication with the inhabitants of the said towns: and that they do arrest and detain all persons who shall be found committing acts of Vagrancy, by begging or otherwise; and do bring them, as soon as maybe, before one or more Magistrates, in order that they may be examined and dealt with according to the Law.

From a notice posted in Sunderland, 4 January 1832.

Source H

On 26th [May 1832] the first case of CHOLERA occurred in the Blue Bell Fold, a small, dirty cul-de-sac containing about 20 houses inhabited by poor families on the North side of the river in an angle between it and an offensive beck or streamlet which conveys the refuse water from numerous mills and dye-houses. The income of one family of eight persons, of whom four died in succession at the very start of the disease, had not averaged more than twelve shillings per week for the four preceding months.

The disease ran through Blue Bell Fold, spread with considerable rapidity, became general in the beginning of July, was at its height in August and the Board of Health ceased to have reports from its district surgeons on 12 November.

Amid a population of 76,000 persons, not more than 14 streets have sewers. Most [of the streets] are unsewered, undrained, unpaved, built on clayey soil and broken up by vehicles of every description. The only wonder is that diseases of this pestilential nature do not oftener and more fatally prevail. The disease has prevailed in those parts of the town where there is a deficiency, and often an entire lack, of sewerage, draining and paving. In three parallel streets, for a population of 386 persons, there are but two single privies.

From the privies in the Boot and Shoe yard, which do not appear to have been thoroughly cleansed for the last thirty years, 70 carts of manure were removed by order of the Leeds Board of Health.

From the *Report of the Leeds Board of Health*, published in 1833.

Source I

A contemporary illustration showing anti-cholera precautions taken in Exeter by burning barrels of tar to purify the air.

Source J

Everywhere cholera was much less fatal than pre-conceived notions had anticipated. The alarm was infinitely greater than the danger. When the disease gradually disappeared almost everyone was surprised that so much apprehension had been entertained.

Report from the Annual Register, 1832.

Almost immediately, legality became a problem. What legal right did the boards have to insist that people co-operate with them? Could individuals be compelled to have their houses limed? Could children be separated from their parents and sent to fever hospitals? In 1832 temporary 'Cholera Acts' were passed to allow local authorities to enforce some measures and to finance them from the poor rates. Even so, and despite people's fear of cholera, local action was haphazard. Local boards were only temporary, and, once the first cholera epidemic had died down, they were disbanded.

SKILLS BUILDER

1 Read Sources G and H. What can you learn from these sources about local boards of health?

2 Study Sources G, H and I. How far does Source I challenge Sources G and H about what was believed to be the cause of cholera?

3 Use your own knowledge to explain whether or not you find the sentiments expressed in Source J surprising.

The complacency displayed in Source J was shaken some 15 years later (1848–9) when cholera again swept the country. But even then, few local boards were set up to combat the epidemic. Where they were set up, they were quickly wound down once the epidemic had passed.

Indeed, the Bridgend (Glamorgan) board reported: 'The Cholera having ceased for some days in this District, the board consider they may dispense with the services of Dr Camps.' Most towns and cities preferred to rely on their long-established, inefficient, ignorant and often corrupt improvement commissions.

The significance of the work of John Snow

It was the third visitation of cholera (1853–4) that provided the answer to the question 'How is it spread?' that had dogged rich and poor, educated and untaught since the early 1830s. In 1831 John Snow had fought single-handed a cholera outbreak at Killingworth colliery (Newcastle). In the years that followed, he became increasingly convinced that cholera was a water-borne disease, but few people were inclined to agree with him. This was partly because his own retiring nature didn't allow him to push himself forward, and partly because of the hold the miasma theory had on the minds of doctors, surgeons, administrators and the general public. The third cholera epidemic was to change this. The 1853 outbreak found him working as a general practitioner in Frith Street in Soho, London, and again struggling to contain and control the terrifying disease. His suspicions fell upon a pump in Broad Street, whose water enjoyed a high reputation locally for taste and purity. However, once John Snow had persuaded the authorities to remove the pump handle and its users were forced to go elsewhere, the number of deaths fell dramatically.

Source K

If the Broad Street pump did actually become a source of disease to persons dwelling at a distance, we believe that this may have depended simply in the fact of its impure waters having participated in the atmospheric infection of the district. On the evidence, it seems impossible to doubt that the geographical distribution of cholera in London belongs less to the water than to the air.

From the *Report of the Committee for Scientific Enquiry into the Recent Cholera Epidemic*, published in 1855.

Source L

A copy of John Snow's map of 1854, plotting cholera deaths in the Broad Street area of Soho, London.

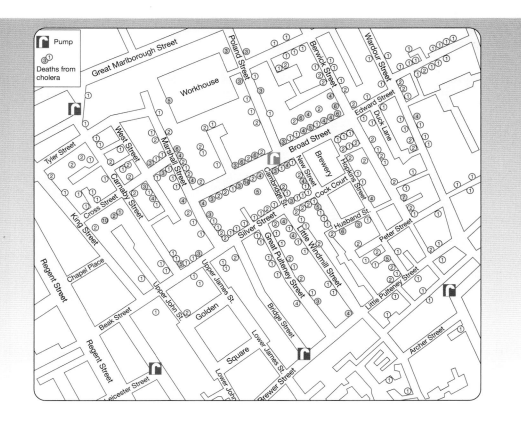

Biography

John Snow (1813–58)

The eldest son of a Yorkshire farmer, at the age of 14 he was apprenticed to William Hardcastle, a surgeon in Newcastle-upon-Tyne. During this time he became a vegetarian and gave up alcohol. He worked as a colliery assistant and, while still unqualified, fought almost single-handed a cholera outbreak at Killingworth colliery in Newcastle (1831–2). Moving to London, he became a medical student. Working at Westminster Hospital, he became a member of the Royal College of Surgeons in May 1838, a licentiate in the Society of Apothecaries in October 1838 and in 1844 graduated as an MD from London University. After doing some lecturing in forensic medicine, he worked as a general practitioner in Soho (London). Here he investigated the ways in which cholera spread and became convinced that cholera was a water-borne disease. He became interested in the values and importance of anaesthetics and administered chloroform to Queen Victoria at the birth of Prince Leopold (1853) and at the birth of Princess Beatrice (1857). He died in June 1858 as the result of a stroke.

Source M

The most terrible outbreak of cholera which ever occurred in this kingdom is probably that which took place in Broad Street and the adjoining streets a few weeks ago. Within two hundred and fifty yards of the spot where Cambridge Street joins Broad Street, there were upwards of five hundred fatal attacks of cholera in ten days.

As soon as I became acquainted with the situation, I suspected some contamination of the water of the much frequented street pump in Broad Street, near the end of Cambridge Street.

On proceeding to the spot, I found that nearly all the deaths had taken place within a short distance of the pump. There were only ten deaths in the houses situated decidedly nearer to another street pump. In five of these cases, the families of the deceased persons informed that they always sent to the pump in Broad Street, as they preferred the water to that of the pump that was nearer. In three other cases the deceased were children who went to school near the pump in Broad Street. Two of them were known to drink the water, and the parents of the third think it probable that it did so, too.

With regard to the deaths occurring in the locality belonging to the pump, there were sixty-one instances in which I was informed that the deceased persons used to drink the pump water from Broad Street. This water was used for mixing with spirits in all the public houses around. It was used in the same way at dining rooms and coffee-shops. The keeper of a coffee shop in the neighbourhood, which was frequented by mechanics, and where the pump water was supplied at dinnertime, informed me she was already aware that nine of her customers were dead.

There is a brewery in Broad Street, near to the pump, and on perceiving that no brewer's men were registered as having died of cholera, I called on Mr Huggins, the proprietor. He informed me that there were about seventy workmen employed in the brewery and none of them had suffered from cholera – at least not in a severe form – only two having been indisposed, and that not seriously, at the time the disease raged. The men are allowed a certain quantity of malt liquor, and Mr Huggins believes they do not drink water at all; and he is quite certain that workmen never obtained water from the pump in the street.

I had an interview with the Board of Guardians of St James' parish on the evening of Thursday 7th September and represented the above circumstances to them. In consequence of what I said, the handle of the pump was removed on the following day.

From John Snow, *On the Mode of Communication of Cholera*, published in 1855.

How did this come about? Dr John Snow made a study of one small area of central London during the 1853–4 cholera epidemic. Using careful observation, house-to-house interviews and meticulous research, he constructed a detailed picture of the progress of the cholera epidemic there.

Snow supported his theory with a vast amount of anecdotal evidence:

- Seven workmen, who lived outside the area but who were working in Broad Street and drinking from the pump, all died.
- 535 people lived in the local workhouse close to the Broad Street pump, but they got their water from another source. Only five inmates died from cholera.
- A widow, who used to live in the area and had a large bottle of Broad Street pump water delivered to her Hampstead home every week, died of cholera and none of her neighbours caught the disease.
- 200 people worked in a factory on Broad Street and got their water from the Broad Street pump. Eighteen factory workers died.

Even so, the medical establishment was not impressed, and for some years the idea that cholera was water-borne was referred to as 'Dr Snow's theory'.

SKILLS BUILDER

1 Study Sources L and M. What methods of investigation did Dr John Snow use to try to discover the reason why the cholera epidemic was so much worse in the area of the Broad Street pump?

2 Now read Source K. The authors of the report clearly believed in the miasma theory of disease, and there was some logic in their conclusion.

 Set up a debate between a supporter of John Snow's theory and a supporter of the miasma theory. Call the debate 'Air or water?' and argue the matter out as to what made the cholera worse in the area around the Broad Street pump. Remember that Pasteur had not yet discovered that disease was spread by germs in the air. All that was known was that there was a connection between dirt and disease.

3 Read Source N. Who, or what, does the anonymous author of this letter blame for public health problems in Soho?

4 Study Source O. Are you surprised that this source was produced in 1866? Use your knowledge, as well as the source, in your answer.

5 Now take Sources N and O together. Did those who produced these sources know more about the causes of cholera than the authorities?

Source N

Sir

May we beg for your protection and power? We are, Sir, living in a wilderness so far as the rest of London knows anything of us. The rich and great people do not care about us. We live in muck and filth. We ain't got no privies, no dust bins, no drains, no water supplies, and no drain or sewer in the whole place. The Sewer Company, in Greek Street, Soho Square, all great, rich, powerful men take no notice whatsoever of our complaints. The stench of a gulley-hole is disgusting. We all of us suffer, and numbers are ill, and if the cholera comes, Lord help us.

From a letter published in *The Times* newspaper in 1849, referring to the Broad Street area of Soho, London.

Source O

A cartoon published in the magazine *Fun* in August 1866.

Source P

Not only is it now certain that the faulty water supply of a town may be the essential cause of the most terrible epidemic outbreaks of cholera, typhoid fever, dysentery and other allied disorders; but even doubts are widely entertained whether these diseases, or some of them, can possibly obtain general prevalence in a town except where the faulty water supply develop them. Dr Snow was not able to furnish proofs of his theory, but afterwards (and happily before his death in 1858) distinct experiments, as well as much new collateral information, established as almost certain that his bold conjecture had been substantially right.

From the annual report by John Simon, chief medical officer of health to the Privy Council in 1870.

A much larger study than that of John Snow was made by John Simon, the medical officer of health for the City of London. John Simon's study covered some 500,000 south Londoners and was published in 1856. He showed that customers of the Lambeth Water Company had a death rate in the 1854 cholera epidemic of 37 per 1000, compared with 130 per 1000 among those who took their water from the Southwark Water Company. What was the difference? Lambeth took its water from Ditton, up-river from London, while Southwark took its water close to an out-flowing sewer in Battersea.

Even so, it was another 14 years before the medical establishment accepted that cholera was a water-borne disease. It was not until 1870 that John Snow's breakthrough in showing that cholera was water-borne received universal acclaim. John Simon, by then chief medical officer of health to the Privy Council, finally abandoned his attachment to the miasma theory of disease.

Joseph Bazalgette: combining ideas and technology

It is one thing to have ideas and theories, even proven theories, and quite another to be able to act upon them. So there would be little point in believing, or even knowing, that cholera was a water-borne disease, if there was not the technology, the civil engineering skills and the will to put theories into action.

London gets organised?

London's local government was chaotic, with different specialist authorities and improvement commissions having authority over different streets or even parts of streets. All of these bodies had to agree in order to provide services (such as drains, water and sewerage) that crossed their boundaries. This clearly made any public-health initiatives virtually impossible to implement. In 1837 an attempt was made to set up a London-wide elected authority to provide and administer services, but this was defeated by the vested interests of the wealthy districts of Marylebone and Westminster. In 1854 there was another attempt to rationalise the administration of London. The Royal Commission on the City of London proposed dividing London into seven boroughs, with each borough represented on a Metropolitan Board of Works. The proposal relating to the boroughs was defeated, but the Metropolitan Board of Works was set up in 1855.

The Metropolitan Board of Works took over the responsibilities of the Metropolitan Buildings Office and the Metropolitan Commission of Sewers. Both these bodies were short-lived. Indeed, the only marked 'success' of the Metropolitan Commission of Sewers had been to order all cesspits to be closed and that house drains should connect to sewers and empty into the River Thames, thus markedly adding to the death rate in the 1848–9 cholera epidemic. The new Metropolitan Board of Works was not an elected body, but consisted of 45 nominees from the principal local authorities in London. One of their earliest, and possibly best, actions was to appoint Joseph Bazalgette as its chief engineer.

Bazalgette's plans

By the time Bazalgette was appointed chief engineer in 1856, the Thames as it flowed through London was little more than an open sewer. No fish swam in its water and there was no wildlife along its banks. The problem was that the rapid growth of London had not been accompanied by the development of an infrastructure that could deal with the huge amount of sewage produced every day. Instead, the sewage contributed to the severity of the cholera epidemics and to other 'dirty' diseases such as diphtheria and typhoid.

Bazalgette drew up a comprehensive plan whereby London's sewage was channelled through miles of street sewers into a series of larger intercepting sewers. These large sewers took the waste far to the east of London where it could be pumped into the tidal part of the Thames; from here it would be swept far out to sea.

The plans were good, but the members of the Metropolitan Board of Works and its political boss became locked in fruitless argument, mostly about money, until the summer of 1858.

Source Q

The Metropolitan Board of Works shall cause to be commenced, as soon as may be after the passing of the Act, and to be carried on and completed with all convenient speed according to such plan as to them may seem proper, the necessary Sewers and Works for the Improvement of the Main Drainage of the Metropolis, and for preventing as far as may be practicable, the sewage of the Metropolis from passing into the River Thames within the Metropolis.

The first clause of the *Metropolis Local Management Amendment Act*, introduced into the House of Commons in 1858 by Benjamin Disraeli, the Tory leader of the House.

Question

Read the section 'London gets organised?' (above). What does this reveal about the difficulties involved in implementing public health reforms in London?

Biography

Joseph Bazalgette (1819–91)

Born in Enfield (Middlesex), Joseph was the son of a naval commander and the grandson of a French merchant who was so wealthy that he had been able to lend money to the Prince Regent, later George IV. At the age of 17, Joseph was apprenticed to John MacNeill, who had worked with Thomas Telford as a principal road- and bridge-builder. In 1838 he became a graduate member of the Institute of Civil Engineers; by 1842 he had set up his own engineering business. 13 years later, Joseph was appointed chief engineer to the Metropolitan Board of Works. Within ten years, Joseph had designed and had ordered the building of around 1,000 kilometres of sewers, which discharged more than 400 million gallons of sewage a day into the Thames further downriver, where the sewage could be swept out to sea. In 1862 the board was ordered to build an embankment along the Thames from Blackfriars to Chelsea, which Joseph designed. He also modernised most of the bridges that spanned the Thames, built new ones for Putney and Battersea, and designed the Blackwall Tunnel under the Thames.

What was the 'Great Stink'?

The summer of 1858 was unusually hot. The Thames was overflowing with raw sewage, and the warm weather encouraged bacteria to thrive. The resulting smell was so powerful that business in the House of Commons was suspended while members decided whether or not to move up-river to Hampton Court, and plans were made to evacuate the law courts either to Oxford or to St Albans. On 7 June *Hansard* (an official publication recording parliamentary debates) reported a claim by one MP that *'It was a notorious fact that the Hon Gentlemen sitting in the Committee Rooms and in the Library were utterly unable to remain there in consequence of the stench which arose from the river.'* Eleven days later the House of Commons debated the state of the river, and the debate continued until well into July.

Source R

The truth is, that this is a case where the fool's argument 'Something must be done' is applicable. The sewage of a mighty city lies in a broad stream under our very noses. The actions of the Metropolitan Board were crippled in two most important respects. It had no money and it had no power; it had no authority to raise the means required, and its engineers were liable to be confronted with engineers appointed by government and armed with a veto. If we wait for agreement on this subject, we shall never stick a spade in the ground or construct either a drain or a tunnel, or get, in fact, a single inch beyond the recent expedient of correcting Thames water with tons of lime. The stench of June was only the last ounce of our burden. That hot fortnight did for the sanitary administration of the Metropolis what the Bengal mutinies did for the administration of India.

From *The Times*, 21st July 1858.

Source S

In a late contribution to the debates on the Amendment Act, Viscount Ebrington was close to the truth when he remarked that 'this Bill had been forced upon the government by a panic rather than with dignity.' A later commentator observed, more succinctly, that 'the "Great Stink" concentrated minds wonderfully.' Whatever the reasons, the 'centralisers' had won. Parliament had given the Board more authority than any of its predecessors had enjoyed to construct a new system of drainage for London according to their own judgement, with little danger of interference. Bazalgette could at last begin to build.

From Stephen Halliday, *The Great Stink of London: Sir Joseph Bazalgette and the Cleansing of the Victorian Metropolis*, published in 1999.

Solving London's sewerage problems

Bazalgette, indeed, could begin to build. The project was a massive one, involving hundreds of kilometres of brick-lined sewers linked to four massive pumping stations, two on each side of the River Thames. As well as being responsible for building underground sewers, Bazalgette also managed to change the face of London by designing the Thames Embankment that housed the large sewers running parallel to each side of the Thames, carrying the contents to the pumping stations that delivered the untreated sewage downstream into the Thames. The need for treatment works wasn't recognised until much later.

Bazalgette designed large, brick-lined egg-shaped sewer tunnels rather than the narrower pipes favoured by Chadwick, and this was a sensible decision because they rarely got blocked. When planning the size of the sewers, Bazalgette started with the densest areas of population, calculated the amount of sewage each person would generate, and then doubled it.

The whole sewerage system was opened by Edward, Prince of Wales, in 1865, thus giving it the royal seal of approval.

Unit summary

What have you learned in this unit?

You have learned about the fear and panic that accompanied the four major cholera epidemics to hit Britain between 1831 and 1867 and that this was because of the swiftness with which the disease struck and the likelihood of death. You learned that the government reacted to the arrival of cholera in Britain by setting up a Board of Health and encouraging the establishment of local boards of health. Although these did some good by, for example, encouraging street-cleaning, as soon as the cholera epidemic passed, the boards folded. The prevailing theory was that the disease was spread by miasma, or 'bad air'. Many of the precautions dictated by the miasma theory, such as the removal of smelly excrement, worked – but for the wrong reason.

John Snow suspected that cholera was water-borne, and his meticulous observations in the Soho area of London led him to persuade the authorities to remove the handle of the water pump in Broad Street. Once people were no longer able to use this particular pump, the number of cholera deaths fell. Even so, the miasma theory continued to find favour with the medical profession until the 1870s, when further experiments had disproved it conclusively. You learned about the ways in which London tried to organise the administration of the city so as to bring about public health reforms, and of the work done by Joseph Bazalgette in creating a sound and effective sewerage system for the capital. The cholera epidemics led to the discovery that cholera was a water-borne disease and this had long-term implications for public health. Nonetheless, whether cholera was spread by germs or miasma, it had a profound effect upon public health: the government began to get involved and the need for effective sewerage systems was understood.

SKILLS BUILDER

Use Sources Q, R and S and your own knowledge. How far would you agree with the view that improvements in London's sewerage system happened only because of the 'Great Stink'?

Question

How would Bazalgette's sewerage system have satisfied those who believed in the miasma theory of disease and those who thought John Snow was right?

Exam tips

You tackled an (a) type question at the end of Units 1, 4 and 6. Look back at the exam tips you were given there before developing and building on them here. Follow these tips to write a successful answer to an (a) question.

- Get 'underneath' the surface of the sources and make inferences from them.
- Two of the sources are cartoons. Do they convey the same message?
- Compare the sources by analysing their similarities and differences.
- Contextualise the sources, giving weight to the significance of their nature, origin and purpose.
- Reach a judgment on 'how far' by using the sources as a set.

Remember, there is an Exam zone section on pages 161–66 to help you further.

Now plan an answer to the question above and write a response.

What skills have you used in this unit?

You have worked with a range of sources and used your skills of comprehension, inference-making, cross-referencing and analysis to understand how it was that people came to fear cholera and the avoidance measures they took. The sources concerned with John Snow and the Broad Street pump have merited particularly detailed work, and this has led to an understanding of the way in which the meticulous work of one man challenged the miasma theory of disease. Your work with the source material has led you to understand that government (national and local) was beginning to get involved in developing and encouraging public health measures, although this involvement was spasmodic. You have seen how the work of Joseph Bazalgette combined engineering skill, an understanding of technology and government backing to bring about a huge public health reform in London.

Exam style question

This is the sort of question you will find appearing on the exam paper as an (a) question.

Study Sources A, N and O.

How far does Source O challenge Sources A and N about the causes and transmission of cholera?

RESEARCH TOPIC

There were many sewage-related occupations before adequate public health systems were introduced:

toshers   grubbers   mudlarks   night-soil men   flushermen   rat-catchers

Find out:

a how these people made a living and how what they did helped or hindered public health

b how their work was regarded by contemporaries. The work of investigative journalist Henry Mayhew will be a good starting point. His book *London Labour and the London Poor* contains descriptions of the lives and occupations of many people regarded by the Victorians as an 'under-class'.

8 Reports, investigations and enquiries: what was their impact on public health reform?

What is this unit about?

The nineteenth century was a time of investigating and reporting, of collecting and collating information. Many reports were local and went no further than the local town hall; others found their way to central organisations, like the Board of Health. Some reports were the result of the enquiries of select commissions, set up for specific enquiries by Parliament; others were generated by bodies such as the Poor Law Commission. These reports and enquiries sometimes resulted in the establishment of various associations, formed for a specific purpose, like the improvement of public health in towns. Together they were to form public opinion and move the government to action. This unit explores the more influential reports, their findings, conclusions and impact.

Key questions

- Why were reports on people's living conditions considered necessary in nineteenth-century Britain?
- What was the impact of the reports?

Timeline

1831–2 **First cholera epidemic**
32,000 people die.

1832 **Dr James Kay appointed secretary to the Manchester Board of Health**
Publication of *The Moral and Physical Condition of the Working Classes Employed in the Cotton Manufacture of Manchester*, compiled by Dr James Kay.

1837–8 **London hit by typhus epidemic**
Poor Law commissioners authorise Edwin Chadwick to undertake a pilot study on the connection between dirt and disease in the worst affected areas of London.

1839 **Chadwick asked by Parliament to undertake a similar survey covering the whole country**

1842 **Chadwick publishes his *Report on the Sanitary Condition of the Labouring Population of Great Britain***
The report is published privately at Chadwick's expense, as the Poor Law commissioners refused to allow Chadwick's report to be published in its original form because of the criticisms it made.

- **1843   Royal commission set up to enquire into the public health of towns**
  First *Report of the Royal Commission for Inquiry into the State of Large Towns and Populous Districts* published.

- **1844   Health of Towns Association founded**
  A pressure group agitating for reform of public health.

- **1845   Second *Report of the Royal Commission for Inquiry into the State of Large Towns and Populous Districts* published**
  Contains proposals for future legislation.

Source A

The Rookery, St Giles, London, published in *The Illustrated London News* in 1850.

THE "ROOKERY," ST. GILES'S, 1850.

SKILLS BUILDER

1 What public health hazards can you spot in Source A?

2 Why had nothing been done about these problems?

The moral and physical condition of the working classes of Manchester in 1832

It was the 1832 cholera epidemic (see page 98) that brought Manchester's Dr James Kay to the attention of those in authority. Cholera hit the city on 17 May 1832 and a board of health was set up, with Kay as its secretary, to co-ordinate the work of the city's 14 district boards. Kay personally visited each area to investigate conditions there, and what he found formed the basis of his report.

Biography

James Kay-Shuttleworth (1804–77)

James Kay qualified in medicine in 1827 and rapidly developed a reputation as a well-respected doctor in Manchester. He became aware of the suffering of the poor and as a consequence became involved in sanitary and educational reform. As a result of treating people in the slum areas of the city during a cholera outbreak in 1832, he wrote *The Moral and Physical Condition of the Working Classes Employed in the Cotton Manufacture in Manchester*. In 1835 he was appointed Poor Law commissioner for the eastern counties and London. Four years later he was appointed secretary to the Privy Council's Committee on Education, where he worked hard to establish a public system of elementary education, supervised by a national body of inspectors. In 1840 he founded England's first teacher-training college in Battersea. His wife was Janet Shuttleworth, daughter and heiress of the wealthy Robert Shuttleworth of Gawthorpe Hall, near Burnley (Lancashire), and because of this he added 'Shuttleworth' to his name. He died in 1877, having been a leading member of the Lancashire Liberal Party, but failing in his attempt to become a Liberal MP.

What was the importance of Dr James Kay's report?

Source B

The state of the streets powerfully affects the health of their inhabitants. Sporadic cases of typhus chiefly appear in those which are narrow, ill ventilated, unpaved, or which contain heaps of refuse. The confined air and noxious exhalations, which abound in such places, depress the health of the people, and on this account contagious diseases are also most rapidly propagated there. The houses are unclean and ill provided with furniture. An air of discomfort, if not of squalid and loathsome wretchedness pervades them. They are often dilapidated, badly drained, damp; and the habits of their tenants are gross – they are ill fed, ill-clothed, and uneconomical – at once both spendthrifts and destitute – denying themselves the comforts of life in order that they may wallow in the unrestrained licence of animal appetites. Lack of cleanliness, of forethought, and economy, are found in almost invariable alliance with dissipation, reckless habits and disease.

The object of the author is simply to offer to the public an example of what he conceives to be too generally the state of the working classes, throughout the kingdom, and to illustrate by specific instances, evils everywhere requiring the immediate interference of legislative authority.

Part of the report *The Moral and Physical Condition of the Working Classes of Manchester*, compiled by Dr James Kay in 1832.

SKILLS BUILDER

Read Source B.

1 How does James Kay make the connection between dirt and disease?

2 How far are the findings of Source B supported by Source A?

Kay's report was one of the first detailed reports on the condition of a specific group of working people. He was one of the first people to demonstrate the connection between dirt and disease, and as well as demonstrating that dirt and diet affected the health of working people, James Kay threw into the equation (as did most nineteenth-century writers) the moral condition of the poor.

The implication here, of course, was that 'dirty' living led to 'dirty' habits, and this proved to be a powerful motivational force for would-be reformers. This report was important, not simply for the information it contained, but because it set the scene for later investigations.

What was the connection between public health and the Poor Law?

Edwin Chadwick

In 1837–8, London was hit by a typhus epidemic and the numbers applying for poor relief increased dramatically as a result. East London Poor Law guardians spent money from the poor rates on removing filth from the streets and on prosecuting negligent landlords. They were clearly acting upon the demonstrated connection between epidemics and living conditions. However, when the time came to have the East London Union account books audited, the government auditors disallowed this expenditure. The Whig home secretary, Lord John Russell, referred the matter to the Poor Law commissioners. Edwin Chadwick, the commissioners' secretary (see page 28) argued forcefully that, because disease caused pauperism, the prevention of disease and so the prevention of pauperism did fall within the competence of Poor Law guardians. The commissioners agreed with him. They went further: they authorised a pilot study on the connection between environment and disease in the worst areas of London, and detailed Edwin Chadwick to set it up.

It was important to Chadwick that the people he selected to work on this investigation were likely to come up with the solutions he wanted. This was, you will remember, exactly the procedure he adopted with respect to the investigation carried out by the royal commission into the operation of the old Poor Law (see page 25). Any reforms they recommended had to be based on the need for sanitary engineering, the disposal of refuse and the provision of clean water.

The three doctors Chadwick chose were all well known to him and all had previous experience in sanitary investigations:

- **Neil Arnott**, who had worked as a ship's surgeon for the East India Company, where he had a particular interest in improving seamen's health and had made considerable progress in identifying connections between 'exotic' diseases like cholera and sanitation

- **James Kay**, who had worked among, and reported on, the poor in Manchester (see page 114) and who later became a Poor Law commissioner in the eastern counties

- **Southwood Smith**, who had worked for over ten years at the London Fever Hospital and as a physician to the Eastern Dispensary and the Jews' Hospital in Whitechapel.

Arnott and Kay investigated Wapping, Ratcliff and Stepney. They reported *'On the prevalence of certain physical causes of fever in the Metropolis which might be prevented by proper sanitary measures'*. Southwood Smith turned his attention to Bethnal Green and Whitechapel. His report was entitled *'On some of the physical causes of sickness and mortality to which the poor are particularly exposed and which are capable of removal by sanitary regulations, exemplified in the present condition of the Bethnal Green and Whitechapel districts, as ascertained by personal inspection'*. Not exactly the most concise of titles, either of them! But their reports backed up what James Kay had found in Manchester and, as the titles of their reports imply, they suggested how the situation could be improved. Underlying the reports was the argument that, no matter how expensive sanitary improvements would be, the cost of pauperism that would result from inaction would be even higher. What was important about the reports, too, was that they received official sanction because they were published as appendices to the annual report of the Poor Law Commission. In this, they brought their conclusions to the attention of Parliament:

Dr Neil Arnott

- In areas inhabited by thousands of people, healthy conditions could not be achieved under existing circumstances.
- The personal habits of people were of less significance in producing disease than overcrowding, poor ventilation, an inadequate water supply and a lack of proper refuse control.

Chadwick's *Report on the Sanitary Condition of the Labouring Population of Great Britain*, 1842

Edwin Chadwick now had the ammunition he wanted to make the case for a full-scale Poor Law enquiry. In 1839, prompted by Chadwick, the bishop of London, Dr Blomfield, proposed in the House of Lords that a similar survey should be made of the prevalence of disease among the labouring classes throughout the whole country, and not just London.

Sir James Graham, the new Conservative home secretary, asked that the survey be completed and a report submitted by the beginning of the 1842 session of Parliament. Chadwick's report was in three volumes: two volumes of local reports from all over Britain, based on questionnaires sent to all local Boards of Guardians, and a third volume containing his own conclusions and proposals for the way forward. Almost immediately he hit a problem: the Poor Law commissioners refused to allow it to be published in its original form because it criticised the water companies, the medical profession and local administration. It named names, too. Eventually, in July 1842, Chadwick had the whole report published under his own name and at his own expense.

Source C

The annual loss of life from filth and bad ventilation are greater than the loss from death or wounds in any wars in which the country has been engaged in modern times.

The various forms of epidemic, endemic and other disease are caused, or aggravated, or propagated chiefly among the labouring classes by atmospheric impurities produced by decomposing animal and vegetable substances, by damp and filth, and close and overcrowded dwellings.

That such disease, wherever its attacks are frequent, is always found in connection with the physical circumstances above specified, and that where these circumstances are removed by drainage, proper cleansing, better ventilation, the frequency and intensity of such disease is abated; and where the removal of the noxious agencies appears to be complete, such disease almost entirely disappears.

Of the 43,000 cases of widowhood, and the 112,000 cases of destitute orphans relieved by the poor rates in England and Wales alone, it appears that the greatest proportion of deaths of the heads of families occurred as a result of the above specified and other removable causes.

The primary and most important measures, and at the same time, the most practicable, and within the recognised province of public administration, are drainage, the removal of all refuse from habitations, streets and roads.

The chief obstacles to the immediate removal of decomposing refuse in towns and habitations have been the expense and annoyance of the labour and cartage required.

This expense may be reduced to one-twentieth or to one-thirtieth, by the use of water and removal by improved and cheaper sewers and drains.

For all these purposes, as well as for domestic use, better supplies of water are absolutely necessary.

From *Report on the Sanitary Condition of the Labouring Population of Great Britain*, 1842, by Edwin Chadwick.

SKILLS BUILDER

Read Source C.

1 What connections did Chadwick make between dirt and disease?

2 How does Chadwick link public health with the Poor Law?

3 What solutions did he propose?

4 Why was this report so controversial?

Questions

1 Anthony Wohl describes Chadwick's report as 'protest literature'. Do you agree?

2 We now know that the miasma theory of disease, in which Chadwick believed, was wrong. Does this, then, mean that his *Report on the Sanitary Condition of the Labouring Population of Great Britain* was unimportant?

Source D

Comparative chances of life expectancy in different classes of the community.

Average age of the deceased

Place	Professional	Trade	Labourers
Truro	40	33	28
Derby	49	38	21
Manchester	38	20	17
Rutland	52	41	38
Bolton	34	23	18
Bethnal Green (London)	45	26	16
Leeds	44	27	19
Liverpool	35	22	15
Whitechapel (London)	45	27	22
Strand (London)	43	33	24
Kensington (London)	44	29	26
Kendal	45	39	34

From the *Report on the Sanitary Condition of the Labouring Population of Great Britain, 1842*, by Edwin Chadwick.

SKILLS BUILDER

1 Look carefully at Source D. What conclusions can you draw from it concerning life expectancy and:

   a social class
   b location?

2 Now read Source C again. Both sources are taken from the same report.

   In your judgment, does the text (Source C) or the table (Source D) give the more convincing evidence in favour of public health reform?

Source E

Public opinion was first widely awakened to the need for remedial measures in 1842, when Chadwick published his remarkable, one is tempted to say epic, *Report on the Sanitary Condition of the Labouring Population of Great Britain*. Drawing upon the evidence gathered by approximately 1,000 Poor Law Medical Officers of Health, Chadwick skilfully wove the most lurid details and evocative descriptions, damning statistics and damaging examples into a masterpiece of protest literature. The Report which covered 372 pages of text and another 85 of appendices, powerfully portrayed the inadequacy of existing systems of sewerage, water supply and drainage, and stressed the connection between these and overcrowding on the one hand, and epidemic diseases on the other. Playing down the broader underlying issue of poverty as a root cause of much ill-health, Chadwick stressed the environmental, miasmic causes of disease and resultant pauperism, and maintained that these causes could be removed.

From Anthony Wohl, *Endangered Lives*, published in 1983.

Chadwick's report was a significant document. In it he:

- attacked the inadequacy of existing water supplies, drainage and sewerage systems
- linked public health and the Poor Law
- pointed the finger at vested interests that stood in the way of improvement
- stressed the connection between these, overcrowding, epidemics and death.

It was the latter point that had the greatest impact. Chadwick had demonstrated, beyond reasonable doubt, that there was a connection between disease and the environment.

What was the reaction to Chadwick's report?

The reaction to Chadwick's report ranged from anger to wholehearted acceptance, passing through disbelief and derision on the way. Home secretary Sir James Graham was reluctant to act on the findings and conclusions of what was, officially at least, a purely private and largely personal report. He set up a royal commission on the health of towns with the purpose, not of questioning Chadwick's findings or even his conclusions, but to investigate more fully the legislative and financial side of his recommendations. Chadwick, meanwhile, busied himself, at Graham's request, with a report on burial practices and with giving official and unofficial briefings to the members of the royal commission.

Report of the Royal Commission for Inquiry into the State of Large Towns and Populous Districts, 1844

The members of the royal commission were drawn from those who could be expected to know something about the subject they were investigating. Led by the Duke of Buccleuch, they included a geologist, a chemist, an expert on land drainage who was also a cotton-mill manager and at least two engineers. Questionnaires were sent to the 50 towns with the highest annual death rates, and the returns studied by the commissioners themselves, who also made official visits to the worst areas.

When the first report was published in 1844, it upheld Chadwick's findings. Of the 50 towns investigated, 42 were found to have bad drainage and 30 poor water supplies. The second report in 1845 contained proposals for future legislation, and included a long memorandum from Chadwick explaining the recommendations on sewerage, drainage and water supply. It recommended that:

- central government be given extensive powers to inspect and supervise local sanitary work
- local sanitary districts be set up, with authority over drainage, sewerage, paving and water supplies
- local sanitary districts be given powers to raise money for sanitary schemes through local rates.

Source F

In 1844 the Royal Commission on the Sanitary State of Large Towns had discovered that no public baths cost less than 6d, and that there were no municipally owned washhouses. Even worse, most large industrial towns banned public bathing in rivers, pools and canals. Two years after the royal commission presented its report, the Association for the Establishment of Baths and Washhouses for the Labouring Poor was founded. The association was not without its critics, for it was argued that washhouses would remain empty since the poor liked dirt; their clothes would wear out if washed and subsidised baths would rob the poor of their independence.

From Anthony Wohl, *Endangered Lives*, published in 1983.

Why was the Health of Towns Association established?

All the published reports did not seem to move the public, and so Chadwick embarked on a propaganda campaign to raise public awareness. The Health of Towns Association, formed in 1844 and organised mainly by Southwood Smith, was part of this. It had a central committee in London and branches in most main provincial towns. Its aim was simple: to mount a propaganda campaign for public-health legislation. Members gave public lectures, published and distributed informative pamphlets and produced a 'Weekly Sheet of Facts and Figures'. It wasn't always met with support.

Source G

'Could it be supposed,' observed Mr Lawence, 'that the wives and mothers who were to be subjected to such contamination would long continue pure and virtuous?' The washhouses, he contended, would not be merely 'gossip shops' but veritable 'sinks of corruption.' Moreover, bathing was not, as some imagined, 'an article of necessity' to good health.

Gathering confidence from the cries of approval and the good humour of his audience, Mr Lawrence went on to assert that 'many a poor woman was there who would not be seen within a gin-shop, but if washhouses were to be established, the objection would soon be destroyed by the gossip of three or four companions of the washhouse, who, upon their return from work, would say to each other "Wouldn't a drop of gin be comfortable after our labour?" What would it be if the mother of a family were to go to trouble to obtain the gin, and so not be able to provide her husband's dinner?'

From *The Times*, 20 December 1844. The newspaper was reporting a meeting of the City of London's Coal, Corn and Finance Committee, who were debating a request from the Health of Towns Association for £400 to be put towards establishing public baths. The request was opposed but finally agreed at £200.

Source H

No. 111 – Petticoat Lane, Whitechapel

It is not without misgiving I address myself to the task of picturing the wretchedness and misery in this notorious pestilence-breathing lane, and the incredibly numerous alleys, courts and yards diverging from each other on either side (extending into Spitalfields) teeming with pollution to an extent which beggars all description.

Thousands of human beings are here cooped up, filthy in habits, debased in morals, oppressed with want, abandoned and reckless – because without hope of relief – the proper subjects of disease and death engendered by the foulness which taints the air they breathe, the food they eat, the water they drink, covers the ground they walk on, ever clinging to them in close companionship with their persons, their clothing, their bed and their board.

Part of a report submitted in 1844 to the Health of Towns Association by one of its members.

SKILLS BUILDER

1 Read Sources F and G. Why were public health improvements opposed?

2 Now read Source H. This is a report made by a member of a pressure group, the Health of Towns Association. Does this mean that it is not a reliable source of evidence?

Chadwick, although not officially a member of the Health of Towns Association, was its virtual leader, directing operations, finding material for the association to use in propaganda and writing many of the association's reports. Meanwhile, all those working for change in public health waited for the government to act.

Unit summary

What have you learned in this unit?

You have learned that this was a period of enquiries and reports, and that it was mainly the prevalence of disease that initiated these enquiries. Indeed, it was the cholera outbreak in Manchester in 1832 that inspired Dr James Kay to write his report *The Moral and Physical Condition of the Working Classes Employed in the Cotton Manufacture of Manchester.* This report demonstrated the connection between dirt and disease. This connection was reinforced by Edwin Chadwick's 1842 *Report on the Sanitary Condition of the Labouring Population of Great Britain,* which went further in that it linked the expense of the Poor Law with the need for public health reform. Alarmed at the lack of action on the part of Parliament, Chadwick and Southwood Smith set up a Health of Towns Association to act as a pressure group and develop a propaganda campaign. In 1844, a royal commission was established in order to confirm Chadwick's findings and to make recommendations for future legislation. Everything was in place for Parliament to act.

What skills have you used in this unit?

You have used your skills of analysis and cross-referencing to draw inferences from the source material, and have investigated their implications insofar as the connections between dirt, disease and the Poor Law are concerned.

Exam style question

This is the sort of question you will find appearing on the examination paper as an (a) question.

Read Sources B, C and G.

How far does Source G challenge Sources B and C about the benefits that would result from public health reform?

Exam tips

You tackled an (a) type question at the end of Units 1, 4, 6 and 7. Look back at the exam tips you were given there before developing and building on them here. Follow these tips to write a successful answer to an (a) question.

- Don't see this as an opportunity to display your own knowledge. All (a) questions focus on the analysis, cross-referencing and evaluation of source material. Your own knowledge won't be credited by the examiner, and you will waste valuable time writing it out.
- Do remember that the only own knowledge you should introduce will be to put the sources into context. This means, for example, that you might explain that Source B was a report written by a Manchester doctor in response to a cholera outbreak, but you should not go on to detail Dr James Kay's career, even where it impacts on public health.
- Do get 'underneath' the sources and make inferences from them.
- Compare the sources by analysing their similarities and differences, but don't rely on surface features only.
- Contextualise the sources, giving weight to the significance of their origin, nature and purpose.
- Reach a judgment on 'How far' by using the sources as a set.

Remember, there is an Exam zone section at the end of the book to help you further.

Now plan an answer to this question and write up your response.

RESEARCH TOPIC

We have focused here on Manchester and London, but enquiries were conducted at this time into living conditions in many other large towns, for example Leeds and Nottingham. Locate one such report and compare its findings with those of Manchester and London.

9 Legislation: the government gets involved

What is this unit about?

In the nineteenth century, as now, the effectiveness of legislation depended on many factors. The effectiveness depended, for example, on the acceptance by the general public that the legislation was necessary and/or desirable; on the lack of legal loopholes in it; on the existence of an infrastructure to implement the legislation and on the existence of personnel to implement it. In the mid- to late nineteenth century, not all of these factors were present all of the time for all of the legislation connected with public health reform. Nevertheless, as the century progressed, more of these factors came together, and came together more strongly, as government became more and more involved in the public health of the people. This unit explores the ways in which these factors came together, the elements that helped and hindered government involvement, culminating in the prescriptive Public Health Act of 1875.

Key questions

- What prompted the government to intervene in public health?
- How effective was government intervention?

Timeline

1835   **Municipal Corporations Act**
Created one standard system of borough government where councillors, aldermen and mayor were elected and answerable to their electors for such things as housing and sanitation.

1837   **Civil registration of births, deaths and marriages introduced**
Registrar-general, William Farr, begins collating data.

1846   **Liverpool Sanitary Act**
Made the city corporation a health authority.

          Removal of Nuisances and Prevention of Epidemic Diseases Act
Enables justices in petty sessions to prosecute those responsible for 'nuisances'.

          Baths and Washhouses Act
Enables local authorities to use public money to provide baths and washhouses.

1847   **Towns Improvement Clauses Act**
Defines the rights of towns to lay water supplies and drainage schemes.

1848 **Public Health Act**
A permissive act enabling local authorities to take responsibility for public health if they wished to do so.
Sets up General Board of Health run by three commissioners: Lord Shaftesbury, Lord Morpeth and Edwin Chadwick.

1854 **Edwin Chadwick dismissed as commissioner of the General Board of Health**

1855 **John Simon appointed medical officer to the General Board of Health**

1858 **Local Government Act and Public Health Act**
Powers of the General Board of Health split between Local Government Act office and the Privy Council.
Local boards of health given powers to take preventative action and appoint officials.
John Simon becomes the first medical officer to the medical department of the Privy Council.

1866 **Sanitary Act**
Local authorities made responsible for removal of 'nuisances' with sanction that central government could compel them to act.
Local authorities given power to improve or demolish slums.

1872 **Public Health Act**
Ensures that the whole country is covered by sanitary authorities and their duties made compulsory.

1875 **Public Health Act**
A **mandatory act**, codifying and consolidating previous acts.

> **Definition**
>
> **Mandatory act**
> An act of Parliament that had to apply to everyone, everywhere.

Source A

Whenever the adult population of a physically depressed district, such as Manchester, is brought out on any public occasion, the preponderance of youth in the crowd and the small proportion of aged, or even middle-aged, amongst them is apt to strike those who have seen assemblies of the working population of more favourably situated districts.

In the Metropolis [London] the experience is similar. The mobs from such districts as Bethnal Green are proportionately conspicuous for a deficiency of bodily strength.

The facts indicated will suffice to show the importance of moral and political considerations, namely, that a noxious physical environment depresses the health and bodily condition of the population, and hinders education and moral culture. In cutting short the duration of adult life among the working classes, it checks the growth of productive skill, social experience and steady moral habits in the community. Instead of a population that preserves instruction and is steadily progressive, it creates a population that is young, inexperienced, ignorant, credulous, irritable, passionate and dangerous, having a perpetual tendency to moral as well as physical deterioration.

From Edwin Chadwick, *Report on the Sanitary Condition of the Labouring Population of Great Britain*, published in 1842.

SKILLS BUILDER

Read Source A.

1 What arguments does Chadwick make in support of public health reforms?

2 Which of Chadwick's arguments would be most likely to appeal to well-to-do people? Remember that at this time they were the ones who dominated Parliament, which had to pass any public health legislation.

Definition

Municipal Corporations Act, 1835

This act of Parliament laid down that councillors were to be elected for three years and aldermen elected by the councillors for six years. The act applied to 178 boroughs. Additional corporations, including Manchester and Birmingham, were established later.

Sanitary legislation, 1846–8

There were a number of significant developments in the years before 1848. Some cities, for example Leeds and Manchester, took advantage of their new status under the 1835 **Municipal Corporations Act** and assumed control of paving, sewerage, street cleaning and draining. Even so, they still needed a private act of Parliament to enable them to do so, and this was by no means a cheap undertaking. What is important to recognise here is that central government showed little interest in public health. If town councils wanted to tackle the problem, then that was their affair.

The 1844 report of the Royal Commission for Inquiry into the State of Large Towns and Populous Districts (see page 120) marked a mid-century appraisal of the sanitary condition of Britain. Almost immediately it was followed by some minor legislation designed to hold the situation until the main Public Health Act could be prepared:

- **The Liverpool Sanitary Act was passed in 1846**. This was an act limited to Liverpool. It made the corporation a health authority and empowered it to appoint a medical officer of health. The town council was given powers to carry out sewerage, drainage and water-supply improvements – and it appointed W. H. Duncan as the first medical officer of health in Britain.

- **1846** saw the first of a series of **Acts for the Removal of Nuisances and Prevention of Epidemic Diseases**. These were designed to enable justices in petty sessions courts to prosecute those responsible for 'nuisances'. Nuisances were generally defined as being 'unwholesome' houses, accumulations of filth and foul drains and cesspools.

- The **1846 Baths and Washhouses Act** enabled local authorities to provide baths and washhouses out of public money.

- In **1847** the **Towns Improvement Clauses Act** defined the rights of towns to lay water supplies and drainage schemes and to control nuisances.

These acts shared a common characteristic: they only applied if the authorities wanted them to. Obviously, the Liverpool act is different from the others, but the Liverpool authorities specifically asked for the act so it is reasonable to assume that they wanted to enforce its provisions. All the other acts were there if any local authority wanted to take advantage of them. Was this to be the shape of things to come?

What were the objections to public health reform?

That something had to be done was clear to all but a small handful of people. One of the main problems lay in who was to do it: national or local government. Should the aim be to set up a national system of public health, or should public health reform be left to local initiatives? A further, but important, problem was whether people could, or should, be compelled to follow directives that were intended to be for their own good. To do this would be to move a very long way from the *laissez-faire* attitudes that dominated domestic politics in the earlier years of the century.

Health of Towns bills were introduced in 1845 and 1847 but were withdrawn; an attempt to introduce a Public Health bill in 1847 was defeated by MPs who became known as the 'Dirty Party'.

Source B

Suffering and evil are nature's rebukes; they cannot be got rid of, and impatient attempts of benevolence to banish them from the world by legislation, has always produced more evil than good.

From a journal, *The Economist*, published in 1848.

Source C

A new authority was proposed that was totally foreign to every principle of the English Constitution. It is a departure from the free principles of the Constitution and a gradual usurpation, behind the backs of the people, of the power which ought to belong to the representatives of the people. It is one more step towards the adoption of the continental system of **centralisation**.

From a report of the parliamentary debate on the 1847 Public Health bill. Here, one opponent's view is given.

Definition

Centralisation

Running services from a central, rather than a local, authority.

Source D

All they want is to expend other people's money and get popularity by letting what they may call poor have the water for nothing. I have property worth £1,000 and have been to considerable expense getting water piped to it. My neighbour has the same, but no water, and his property will be considerably benefited by having water brought to it. Is it just that I should be made to contribute a yearly sum towards furnishing his estate with water and increasing its value by 15–20 per cent?

From the proceedings of the Thoresby Society, Leeds, where a proposed municipal water supply was being discussed.

SKILLS BUILDER

Read Sources B, C and D.

1 What different reasons are given in these sources for opposing public health reform?

2 How convincing do you find these reasons?

Source E

In Manchester, gas has for some years been supplied from works erected and conducted by a body appointed (under a local Act) by an elected committee of ratepayers. The supplies of gas are of a better quality, and cheaper than those obtained from private companies in adjacent towns. Improvements are more speedily adopted than through private agreements, and the profits are kept in a public fund. Out of this fund a fine town hall has been erected, streets widened, and various large improvements made.

A proposal was made in Manchester to obtain supplies of water in the same manner as the supplies of gas, but the owners of the private pumps, who have the monopoly of the convenient springs, exact double the charge for which even private companies are ready to convey supplies to the houses. And so the proposal was defeated.

From Edwin Chadwick, *Report on the Sanitary Condition of the Labouring Population of Great Britain*, published in 1842.

Source F

The utter failure of the system of self-government for sanitary purposes is notorious to all who have taken any pains to inquire into the subject. Even if the parochial system were perfect for all other purposes of administration, it must necessarily fail when applied to some of the chief measures of sanitary improvement. Drainage, especially, which is of vast importance to health cannot be carried out by parishes. It presupposes an extensive area selected for that special object, surveyed and laid out with a scientific skill and judgement which few parishes have in their command and which popular election is extremely unlikely to ensure.

From W. A. Gay, 'The Sanitary Question', an article published in *Fraser's Magazine* in 1847.

Source G

John Bull's heart is only reached through his pocket when in a state of alarm. Cry 'Cholera!' and he bestirs himself. To cholera we owe the few sanitary measures now in force, but they were passed by the House in its agonies of fright. The moment, however, cholera bulletins ceased to be issued, John buttoned up his pockets and Parliament was dumb regarding public health.

From Charles Dickens, *Household Words,* published in 1850. 'John Bull' represents England.

Question

How likely was it that Charles Dickens' explanation (Source G) was the correct one?

SKILLS BUILDER

Read Sources E and F.

1 a What advantages had Manchester gained by having a municipal gas supply?

  b Why doesn't Manchester have a municipal water supply?

2 On what grounds is the author of Source F criticising local provision of public health?

3 How far does the author of Source F agree with the views about the provision of public health given by Chadwick in Source E?

It would seem that there was very clearly expressed and strong opposition to public health reform in the country as well as in Parliament. So why, in the autumn of 1848 was a Public Health Act rushed through Parliament? Charles Dickens (Source G) provided an explanation.

The Public Health Act, 1848

- A General Board of Health was set up, which reported to Parliament. It was based in London. The three original members were Lord Morpeth (who was behind the unsuccessful 1847 bill and the successful 1848 act), Lord Shaftesbury and Edwin Chadwick.

- Local authorities were empowered to set up local boards of health. These could be set up where:
  - ten per cent of the ratepayers asked for one, *or*
  - where the death rate was greater than 23 per 1000.

- Local boards of health were permitted to appoint a medical officer of health and pay his wages out of the rates.

- Local boards of health were to manage sewers and drains, wells and slaughterhouses, refuse and sewerage systems, burial grounds and public baths, recreation areas and public parks.
- Local boards of health could finance projects by levying local rates and buying land.

But this act was **permissive legislation**: it did not apply to all local authorities throughout the country. This was at once a great strength and a great weakness. It could be argued that its strengths were that:

- because it applied where local people wanted it, there was little or no opposition to it and so implementation, unlike that of the Poor Law Amendment Act, was relatively smooth
- because it had to apply where conditions were very poor, people were desperate for any remedy and were unlikely to put up any serious opposition
- piecemeal implementation meant that those who were suspicious or wary could see for themselves how the act worked to improve public health and would push for its introduction in their own towns and cities.

Definition

Permissive legislation
This is legislation that did not apply automatically to everyone, everywhere. A permissive act was an act that only applied if certain conditions were met: for example, if a certain number of people in a town or city wanted it to apply or if conditions reached certain specified criteria and it had to apply.

Source H

A meeting of the Board of Health, Gwydir Street, Whitehall, London, in 1849.

SKILLS BUILDER

What inferences about the Board of Health can you draw from Source H?

On the other hand, many would argue that its weaknesses were that:

- it did not apply to London – which had its own act in 1848 to establish the Metropolitan Commissioners of Sewers – or the City of London with its own City Sewers Act
- it did not apply to Scotland
- before a local authority could adopt the act, at least ten per cent of those rated for poor relief had to petition to have it applied. The General Board of Health then sent an inspector who could, if he thought it appropriate, authorise the town council to carry out the duties laid down by the act. Where there was no town council, the General Board of Health could set up a local board.

Question

On balance, do you think the advantages of the 1848 Public Health Act outweighed the disadvantages?

- The act had to apply only where the death rate in a district was more than 23 per 1000 living (the national average was 21 per 1000). Then the General Board of Health could force a local authority to set up a local board of health.

- Local boards of health were to have considerable powers over basic public health requirements: drainage, building regulation, nuisance removal and water supply. But no local board of health was required to take on the wider public health considerations that included such things as parks and baths.

- The power to appoint a medical officer of health did not become obligatory until 1875.

How effective was the 1848 Public Health Act?

It is immediately obvious that there were so many ways in which the act could be avoided or undermined that its impact, and therefore effectiveness, was almost bound to be patchy. It got off to a bad start, too, in that the immediate effects of the act were overshadowed by the second cholera outbreak to hit Britain. The General Board of Health was almost totally caught up in coping with this, and only when the epidemic had died down could it focus its whole attention on more general public health issues.

There were some clear successes:

- By the beginning of 1850, 192 towns had asked for the new public health regulations to be applied and the act had been applied to 32 of them.

- By 1853 this had risen to 284 petitions and there were 182 towns where the act had been applied.

However, this has to be put in context and set against the strength of vested interests and the reluctance of many local authorities to pay for something they considered unnecessary. For example:

- In Lancashire only 400,000 of its 2.5 million people were living under some sort of public health board.

- Of the 187 major towns (those with a mayor and corporation) in England and Wales, only 29 had the powers of draining and cleansing in the hands of one board; 30 had absolutely no powers over public health because they were in the hands of independent commissioners; 62 had no public health authority whatsoever.

- Local boards of health, where they were set up, were frequently simply the existing town corporation under a different guise. Consequently, they were governed by the same vested interests and moved in the same slow and cautious way. Sometimes this was because they were constrained by pre-1848 **private improvement acts**; more often, hesitancy was due to a reluctance to spend money and a general ignorance of sanitary engineering and of the need for it. Frequently, for example, lavatories flushed into sewers that emptied into the nearest watercourse from which drinking water was taken.

Definition

Private improvement acts
Private acts of Parliament applying to one town or city that intended to improve, for example, paving or lighting, that would make life better for its citizens.

Clearly, the 1848 Public Health Act did not have the same impact as the 1834 Poor Law Amendment Act. The reasons for this were many:

- The public and government were not convinced that order had to be brought from the confusing mix of private acts relating to public health.
- There was no existing structure that could be reformed.
- Medical knowledge was not giving clear messages.
- Vested interests in, for example, water companies, remained strong.
- Local improvement commissioners, where they existed, feared the loss of their powers.
- Sanitary engineering was expensive.

Despite all its failings, however, the 1848 Public Health Act does demonstrate that the government was prepared to do something. It was prepared to provide a solution for towns and cities trying to fight their way through the morass of private and local legislation to achieve some sort of standard of public health. It was prepared, too, to intervene on behalf of the most vulnerable members of society to nudge their local authorities in the general direction of providing for their care.

The 1858 Local Government Act and the 1858 Public Health Act

- The General Board of Health was abolished.
- The powers of the General Board of Health were given to a new Local Government Act Office.
- A medical department of the Privy Council was set up.
- Local boards of health were given powers to take preventative action and appoint officials.

Why were these two linked acts of Parliament needed, so soon after the 1848 Public Health Act? The ten years in between had shown a gradual acceptance by local authorities of the need for more powerful local public health bodies. But there was considerable hostility towards the General Board of Health and its commissioner Edwin Chadwick. He had to go, and a more acceptable way of centralising and controlling public health provision had to be found.

Splitting the powers and functions of the old General Board of Health between the Local Government Act Office and the Privy Council medical department was the solution. It was a clever one, too.

One of the main functions of the old General Board of Health had been to approve loans to local authorities for public health projects. This function was continued, although slightly differently. The permission of the Local Government Act Office was needed for all loans that local authorities wanted to raise in order to carry out public works. It was just a short step for the Privy Council medical department to carry out the relevant inspections where public health projects were involved. In other words, it was central government direct (as in the Privy Council) that for the first time became involved in the administration of public health in the localities. In the ten years up to 1868, 568 towns set up boards of health and began implementing public health reforms.

Why was there continued opposition to public health provision in the 1850s and 1860s?

Opposition to public health reforms was not so much opposition to the reforms themselves as to a variety of issues that were highlighted by the pressure for reform. These issues varied in their importance from place to place and local priorities changed over time. This is why some areas embraced reform wholeheartedly, others dragged their feet and some refused point-blank to have anything to do with it.

- Improvement schemes of any kind cost money. Property-owners spent money to have clean water piped to large cisterns in their own houses, and for sewers or cesspits to hold waste from their inside lavatories. They were loath to pay out again, via local taxes, to have similar facilities provided for their neighbours when, they argued, there would be no benefit to themselves.

- Many people felt that government was encroaching on their individual liberties by requiring them to, for example, remove dung heaps from their properties or whitewash a slaughterhouse.

- Vested interests – for example, directors of local water companies – were usually represented in local government and often on local boards of health. They were unlikely to vote for measures that would reduce their company profits.

- The civil-engineering problems posed by sewerage and water-supply schemes were barely understood by lay people on local boards of health; this caused delay and, occasionally, the implementation of inappropriate systems.

- Chadwick himself – one of the three commissioners on the General Board of Health set up by the 1848 Public Health Act – irritated, annoyed and angered many because of his bullying tactics.

SKILLS BUILDER

Read Sources I, J and K.

1 Sources I and J are both from the same newspaper and printed in the same month and year.

  a Are they saying the same thing?

  b Which is the more effective criticism, Source I or Source J?

2 How far does Source K challenge the views of the Board of Health and Chadwick in particular as expressed by *The Times* newspaper?

Source I

The first and undoubtedly greatest objection to the Board of Health is the deserved unpopularity of two of its members; the second, the vice of its constitution by which those members are empowered to carry out their perverse will, their petty intrigues and their wrong-headed dogmatism without restraint and without responsibility. Mr Chadwick and Dr Southwood Smith are just such men as always arise when a dynasty, a Ministry, or a Board is accumulating those elements of destruction of which it alone is unconscious.

Firmly persuaded of their own infallibility, intolerant of all opposition, utterly careless of the feelings and wishes of the local bodies with whom they are brought into contact, determined not only to have their own way, and using the powers delegated to them to exercise influence over matters which Parliament has placed beyond their control, these gentlemen have contrived to overwhelm a good object with obliquy and hatred and to make the cholera itself a less dreaded visitation than their own.

The Times leader article, 11 July 1854.

Source J

We prefer to take our chance with cholera and the rest than be bullied into health. There is nothing a man hates so much as being cleansed against his will, or having his floors swept, his walls whitewashed, his pet dung heaps cleared away, or his thatch forced to give way to slate, all at the command of a sort of sanitary bombaliff [official]. It is a positive fact that many have died of a good washing. All this shows the extreme tenderness with which the work of purification should advance. Not so, thought Mr Chadwick. New mops wash clean, thought he, and he set to work, everywhere washing and splashing, and twirling and rinsing, and sponging and sopping, and soaping and mopping, till mankind began to fear a deluge of soap and water. Mr Chadwick has very great powers, but it is not so easy to say what they can be applied to. Perhaps a retiring pension, with nothing to do.

From *The Times* newspaper, July 1854.

Source K

Chadwick's dismissal in 1854 and the winding up of the Board of Health in 1858 have been presented as a great triumph for the forces of localism, although the truth is more complex. Chadwick by this time openly admitted that his philosophy had centralizing, collectivizing tendencies, though he continued to urge that the powers he sought were essential to prevent waste through frequent illness and premature death.

The mantle of collectivism in public health activity was taken up by Sir John Simon, Medical Officer of the newly established medical department of the Privy Council. He had no Benthamite or Chadwickian associations, but his pragmatic assessment of the dimensions of the problem led him to remarkably similar conclusions.

From Eric J. Evans, *The Forging of the Modern State 1783–1870*, published in 1983.

The 1866 Sanitary Act

The work of John Simon

A key mover behind this new Sanitary Act was John Simon. He had been London's first medical officer of health in 1848 and medical officer to the General Board of Health in 1855. In 1858, when the General Board of Health was wound up, he became the first medical officer to the medical department of the Privy Council.

Simon worked within the permissive framework set up by the 1848 act, seeking to persuade local authorities to accept public health systems.

Biography

John Simon (1816–1904)

Born in London, he received his medical training by being first apprenticed to a surgeon at St Thomas' Hospital, and then completed his formal medical studies at King's College, London. Between 1840 and 1847 he worked as a surgeon at King's College Hospital, and later lectured in pathology. A founder member of the Health of Towns Association in 1844, in 1848 he became medical officer of health for the City of London and chief medical officer for health to the Privy Council in 1858. Like Chadwick, he was initially a firm supporter of the miasma theory of the spread of disease but, unlike Chadwick, changed his mind as evidence supporting the germ theory gradually became available. Simon helped transform the issue of public health from a political issue to one founded in scientific investigation and analysis, and his detailed reports helped bring about both the 1866 Sanitary Act and the 1875 Public Health Act. He stepped down from office in 1876, and in 1887 received a knighthood for his contribution to public health.

Throughout his career he was a superb administrator, finding ways round seemingly insurmountable problems:

- When, for example, the City of London refused to supply him with disease and mortality returns, Simon invoked the Nuisances and Disease Prevention Act of 1846 and got the data he wanted. He built up a system of house inspection by City police and Poor Law medical officers, and published weekly reports on their findings that shocked the City authorities into action.

- He promoted an act that made the adulteration of food illegal (see page 150) and which permitted local authorities to employ public analysts to check food.

- He supported vaccination and trained vaccinators, supporting a law that prosecuted parents for refusing to have their children vaccinated against smallpox.

- He implemented a programme of building inspection.

- He developed a system for making the water supply cleaner and sewers more effective, and abolished cesspools.

- He created a set of procedures to follow in the event of epidemics of contagious diseases.

By working with the current of local opinion, and walking away where he could do no good, he achieved more than Chadwick had done by bullying and outright opposition. Indeed, Simon's contemporaries regarded him as the greatest exponent of public health reform. Much pressure for progress, however, came from the local authorities themselves, although too often lack of specific powers was used as an excuse for inaction.

Simon gradually became convinced that the government had to be persuaded to embrace compulsion.

Source L

There was no power to compel the owners of property to sewer land before building human habitations on it; no power to compel the sewering and paving of the multitudinous new streets; no power to forbid cellar dwellings; no power whatever to compel the owners of old property to connect their dwelling houses with the drains.

From the *Leeds Mercury*, 3 February 1865.

Source M

I venture to submit that the time has now arrived when it ought not any longer to be discretional whether a place is kept filthy or not.

From John Simon's *Annual Report to the General Board of Health*, published in 1865.

Source N

Progress between 1848 and 1875 appears to have been limited, judged by the number of laws passed extending the range of central control over public health matters. Despite all his ability, energy and drive, John Simon, as Medical Officer of Health for the Privy Council could offer little central direction and control.

From Jane Jenkins with Eric Evans, *Victorian Social Life, British Social History 1815–1914*, published in 2002.

As a direct consequence of the sort of advice given by John Simon in his 1865 annual report, in 1866 Parliament passed a new Sanitary Act. Under this act:

- Sanitary powers that had been granted to individual local boards of health under the 1848 Act were made available to all local boards.

- Local authorities were made responsible for the removal of 'nuisances' to public health. If local authorities failed to act, central government could do the work of improvement and charge the local authorities.

- The definition of 'nuisance' was extended to domestic properties and included overcrowding.

- Local authorities were given the power to improve or demolish slum dwellings.

For the first time, compulsion was a significant element of an act of Parliament dealing with public health. No longer did the state direct and advise local authorities: it could now compel them to act. In this sense, the state was, from this point on, directing public health reform.

What were the pressures for further change?

- From 1 July 1837, all births, deaths and marriages had to be registered with the Office of the Registrar-General. Until 1879, William Farr was the chief statistician and he provided a mass of statistical data regarding, for example, causes and ages of death, city by city, area by area.

- In 1861 Louis Pasteur (1822–95) published the results of his experiments on fermentation, showing that there was a link between germs in the air and matter going bad. Decaying matter did not produce germs: it was the other way round!

- In 1867 the Reform Act effectively gave the vote to working men in towns. Politicians had to pay attention to their problems, which included public health issues.

- There was a third cholera epidemic in 1865–6, in which 20,000 people died.

- In 1869 a royal commission on public health was set up which revealed that conditions in towns were little better than when Chadwick had been masterminding investigations some 30 years earlier.

- In 1871 a Local Government Board was set up. This consolidated the functions of the Local Government Act Office, the Registrar-General's Office, the medical department of the Privy Council and the Poor Law Board. The president was usually a member of the cabinet.

- The 1872 Public Health Act ensured that the whole country was covered by sanitary authorities (town councils and local boards in urban areas and guardians in rural ones); their sanitary duties were made compulsory and they each had to appoint a medical officer of health.

SKILLS BUILDER

1 Read Source L. Does this mean that the 1848 and 1858 Public Health Acts were failures?

2 Read Source M and look back to Source J.

   How far does Source M challenge the view given in Source J?

Questions

1 Which, in your view, was the most important of the pressures for change after 1866?

2 How are these different pressures linked?

Biography

William Farr (1807–83)

A qualified doctor, he started a medical practice in Fitzroy Square, London, in 1833. Fascinated by medical statistics, William Farr was appointed chief statistician to the newly set up Office of the Registrar-General, a post he held until 1879. From 1 July 1837, all births, deaths and marriages in England and Wales had to be registered there. By insisting that doctors certified the cause, and not simply the fact, of death, Farr was able to produce statistics that were invaluable to public health reformers. He used his position to advocate public health reform, drawing attention to the wide variations in mortality between different areas of the country. A supporter of the miasma theory of disease, the 1866 cholera outbreak finally convinced him that cholera had to be water-borne.

The 1875 Public Health Act

The culmination of all these pressures was a great Public Health Act of 1875 that was to remain the foundation of all public health work until 1936.

This act broke no new ground: it was primarily a consolidation and codification of about 30 previous laws. It established that:

- Every part of the country had to have a public health authority.
- Every public health authority had to have at least one medical officer and one sanitary inspector to ensure that the laws on food adulteration, housing, water supplies and cleansing were enforced.
- Local authorities had wide powers to lay sewers and drains, build reservoirs, parks, public baths and public conveniences.

The government was now completely committed to the provision of public health for the people it governed.

Source O

An engraving by Gustav Doré, made in 1872, of a London street scene.

SKILLS BUILDER

Does Source O indicate that the public health reforms of 1848–75 had failed?

Unit summary

What have you learned in this unit?

You have learned that the years from 1830 to 1875 were the years where central government gradually became more and more involved in public health matters. In the early years, legislation was piecemeal. Various local authorities applied for private acts that applied to them only, enabling them to take responsibility for such matters as gas and water supplies, paving and the removal of nuisances. Where there were government-generated acts, these were narrowly focused and permissive. You have seen how the 1848 Public Health Act, rushed through Parliament partly in response to the threat (later the reality) of the second cholera epidemic, broke new ground insofar as government involvement in public health issues was concerned, and that the fact it was a permissive act was both a strength and a weakness. You have considered the roles of Edwin Chadwick and John Simon in trying to create a comprehensive public health system and you have considered the reasons for the opposition to what was proposed. You have understood the mounting pressures on the government to get further involved in public health that culminated in the compulsory Public Health Act of 1875.

What skills have you used in this unit?

You have worked with a range of primary, secondary and contemporary source material, evaluating and analysing them in order to understand the need for public health reforms, the reasons for opposition to them, and the gradual involvement of central government. This has enabled you to understand why the government was gradually drawn in to legislating for public health, and moved from a position of *laissez-faire*, with permissive acts, to the compulsion of the 1875 Public Health Act.

Exam style question

This is the sort of question you will find appearing on the exam paper as a (b) question.

Study Sources J, N and O, and use your own knowledge.

Do you agree with the view, expressed in Source N, that 'progress between 1848 and 1875 appears to have been limited'?

RESEARCH TOPIC

Not all the initiatives in public health reform were taken by central and local authorities. Some were taken by individuals.

You will explore the work of one such individual, Titus Salt, in the case study that ends this book (pages 154–58). He was not the only individual concerned with improving the living conditions of the poor.

Research the work of Octavia Hill in the years up to 1875 and find out what she did to try to improve public health.

Exam tips

You tackled (b) questions at the end of Units 2, 3 and 5. Look back to the exam tips you were given there because you will need them to answer this question. Above all, remember to plan and to use whichever style of plan suits you best.

- Be very sure you know what view is being expressed in Source N, and think about the importance of 'appears'.
- Analyse and interpret Sources J and O so as to establish points that challenge and points that support the view given in Source N.
- Cross-reference between the sources by focusing on support and challenge.
- Use your wider knowledge both to reinforce and challenge the points derived from the sources.
- Combine the points into arguments for and against the view given in Source N.
- Evaluate the conflicting arguments by considering the quality of the evidence used, involving a consideration of provenance (where appropriate) and the weight of evidence and range of knowledge you can find in support.
- Present a supported judgment as to the validity of the stated view and/or any alternatives.

10 Public health: persistent problems

What is this unit about?

Cholera and sewerage tend to dominate any study of nineteenth-century public health. This is inevitable because of the drama of the four killer epidemics, and the struggle to establish the need for clean water and the separation of drinking water from sewage. However, there were persistent problems that daily affected thousands of people throughout Britain. Among these were endemic diseases, such as typhoid, typhus, tuberculosis, diphtheria and scarlet fever, and the slum housing that enabled these diseases to prey upon the population. For the poor and working classes, life was a daily struggle to find clean water and unadulterated food, coupled with hazards over which they had no control, such as factory effluent and raw sewage. This unit identifies these persistent problems, and the measures taken to improve them.

Key questions

- How far, by 1874, had public health improvements eliminated the 'killer' diseases?
- To what extent had the lives of the poor and working classes been made better by public health improvements?

Timeline

1834	**Smallpox vaccine made available to Poor Law officials** Its use was voluntary.
1840	**Vaccination Act** A permissive act, allowing anyone who wished to be vaccinated by Poor Law vaccinators.
1844	**Metropolitan Buildings Act** London has specific controls over new builds. Other cities gave themselves the same control in individual improvement acts.
1851	**Common Lodging Houses Act** All lodging houses to be registered and inspected by police. Reinforced in 1853.
1853	**Vaccination Act** Made it compulsory for parents to have their children vaccinated within three months of birth. Administered haphazardly.
1855	**Nuisances Removal Act** Local authorities could fine and prosecute for overcrowding.

1858	**The 'Great Stink'**
	The River Thames becomes a sewer during a heatwave.
	The building of Joseph Bazalgette's comprehensive sewerage system begins.
	Local Government Act
	Sets out model by-laws for towns to adopt.
1860	**Adulteration of Food and Drink Act**
	Local authorities can appoint analysts to investigate complaints.
1861	**Death of Prince Albert, husband of Queen Victoria**
	The cause of death was given on the death certificate as typhoid.
1868	**Artisans' and Labourers' Dwellings Act (Torren's Act)**
	Local authorities given the power to force landlords to make repairs.
1871	**Vaccination Act**
	Makes it compulsory for local health boards to appoint vaccination officers; fines for parents failing to have their children vaccinated.
1872	**Adulteration of Food, Drink and Drugs Act**
	Local authorities enabled to investigate specific foodstuffs.
1875	**Artisans' and Labourers' Dwellings Improvement Act (Cross's Act)**
	Local councils given the power to clear whole areas.
	Sale of Food and Drugs Act
	Defined 'purity', increased powers of prosecution and punishment, enhanced status of analysis and so established a more adequate legal framework for the suppression of adulteration.

In December 1861, Prince Albert, husband to Queen Victoria, lay gravely ill. You read on page 84 that disease was no respecter of persons. Here, a member of one of the richest families in the land and treasured husband of the reigning monarch, was dying, apparently from a disease that was endemic in the slum areas of all the large cities.

SKILLS BUILDER

Read Source A.

1 What inferences can you draw from Source A about the problems involved in diagnosing typhoid as a cause of death?

2 How do these problems highlight the difficulties in preventing such diseases in the population as a whole?

Source A

Dr Jenner filed a death certificate on 21 December [1861] fixing the cause as typhoid fever; duration 21 days, the first time that the label was publicly applied; and although questions were raised in the *Lancet* and the *British Medical Journal*, about the discrepancies between the medical bulletins and the belated diagnosis, there was no autopsy. Instead, Jenner suggested to the Queen that death was 'due to the heart being over-strained by the Prince's heavy frame'. Clark added that three things had proved fatal – overwork, worry about his son the Prince of Wales' love affair, and 'exposure to chill when already sick'. In 1877, Jenner added further that '. . . no one can diagnose typhoid at first.' Victoria underlined 'no one' in her memo of the conversation. Clark's 'when already sick' spoke volumes.

From Stanley Weintraub, *Albert: Uncrowned King*, published in 1997. Here the author is considering the cause of death of Prince Albert. Dr Jenner and Sir James Clark were two of the royal medical team attending Prince Albert.

Disease: a personal or a public health problem?

Disease affected people in all walks of life. To the well-to-do, it meant tragedy and disruption. To the poor it meant tragedy and the threat of pauperism. So, for thousands, disease was inexorably linked to poverty and the fear of the workhouse. The control of endemic killer diseases was not completely dependent on the discovery of a cure, but on preventative measures such as personal and domestic cleanliness, adequate domestic living arrangements, clean water and effective sewerage systems. And so the prevention of disease was inextricably linked to effective public health.

Typhoid was only separately identified from typhus in 1869 and, indeed, it had very similar symptoms. But typhus was spread mainly by body lice; typhoid mainly by infected water. Thus typhoid hit people in all social classes and all manner of lifestyles. Prince Albert, as you have seen, probably died of it in 1861. Ten years later, his eldest son was a guest of the Countess of Londesborough at her country house outside Scarborough where many guests contracted the disease. He survived a severe attack, but his groom and the Earl of Chesterfield died. The most likely cause of typhoid was the contamination of water by human waste.

Typhus, sometimes known as Irish fever or gaol fever, was endemic in nineteenth-century Britain. It hit the country in epidemic proportions in 1837 and 1839, and again in 1847 when 10,000 died in the north-west alone. From the middle of the century, however, the disease was in decline: in 1869 there were 4,281 deaths from typhus in England and Wales and in the 1870s they averaged 1,400 a year. While there is some evidence that the disease-carrying micro-organism was itself weakening as the century progressed, it is certain that the progressive removal of heaps of excrement and the cleansing of polluted wells and repair of leaking cesspits hastened its decline.

Definitions

Typhoid

Typhoid is a bacterial infection carried in contaminated milk, water or food. It thrives in situations where human waste can contaminate water. The most common symptoms are headaches, coughs, watery diarrhoea and high fever. Some people do not display the symptoms, but are carriers and can transmit it to others.

Typhus

Typhus is usually spread from infected rodents to people by the bites or faeces of body lice, fleas, mites or ticks. It thrives in unsanitary, crowded conditions. The most common symptoms are headaches, chills and fever. Typhus and typhoid were frequently confused in the first half of the nineteenth century.

Questions

1 To what extent did the 'ash-pan method' of dealing with human excrement help to improve public health?

2 What were the drawbacks of this method?

Source B

This diagram, which shows the 'ash-pan method', was published in the Supplementary Report to the Local Government Board in 1874. This 'dry conservancy' method of dealing with human waste was used by many cities until well into the twentieth century.

The increasing use of cotton bedding and clothing – which was much more easily washed than woollen items – helped too. It must be remembered that not all lavatories were connected to cesspits or sewers. Many working-class homes used dry-ash pans supplied by their local council. This method of disposing of human waste was certainly an improvement on the earlier uncertain and unreliable efforts of night-soil men. Flushing lavatories – the ideal – were not effective until running water was laid on to all houses, which were then connected to a sewerage system which discharged safely.

Source C

The miasma theory could work as much against the building of sewers as for it, for while it was argued by some that drains were an effective and safe way of getting miasma underground and effluvia flushed out of residential areas, others maintained that defective pipes brought sewer gases, and hence diseases, right into the house. In a period when drains were often laid with no sound knowledge of how to trap them to prevent the flow-back of gases, one can well understand why some householders would be reluctant to take advantage of the opportunity to connect to main sewers, and why they would not wish to extend the sewers into working-class districts, where the quality of connecting pipes would be lower.

As in so many areas of public health, so in the treatment of sewage the Victorians were pioneers and they had to approach their work cautiously, watching each other's experiments and learning by trial and error. The scope for error was enormous and it is little wonder that sanitary authorities moved cautiously on the adoption of sewer systems. In 1874 alone, some thirty-two patents were taken out for sewage treatment systems, but how was a local authority to know which was the best? The technical difficulties involved, the scale and cost of sewering, the fear of failure, the uncertainty about their effectiveness (the Local Government Board claimed in 1876 that even after treatment the typical town's sewage smelled of cabbage water, except in warm weather when it took on the stench of rotten eggs), all combined to serve as a deterrent to the amateur local governments of the day. To add to their fears was the fact that a system of water-borne sewage (unless a town was fortunately situated on an estuary or on the coast) would pollute the local river and might give rise to law-suits.

From Anthony Wohl, *Endangered Lives*, published in 1983.

Typhus, typhoid and cholera were all so-called 'dirty' diseases, intimately connected with rotting waste matter, intestinal, and producing high fevers and diarrhoea. They were killers. But there was another raft of diseases that were respiratory and pulmonary; less dramatic, but killers nonetheless.

Tuberculosis, called the 'white plague', probably accounted for one-third of all deaths from disease in the nineteenth century. 'Probably', because it was sometimes confused with other diseases and it did not have to be notified to the authorities until 1912. Tuberculosis affected all classes, but hit hardest those who:

- had poor nutrition
- lived or worked in overcrowded, badly ventilated conditions.

Definition

Tuberculosis
Tuberculosis (TB) can be an airborne infection spread by inhaling droplets infected by the tuberculosis bacterium, or it can be caught by drinking milk from cows that have bovine TB.

Source D

From the magazine *Punch*, January 1872.

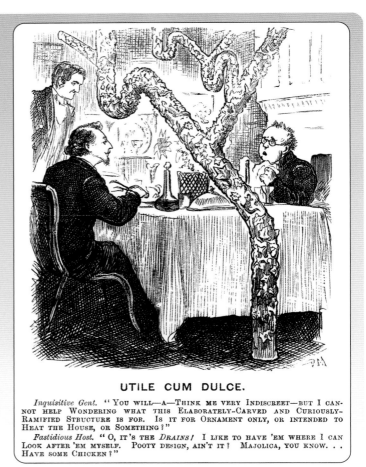

UTILE CUM DULCE.

Inquisitive Gent. "You will—a—think me very indiscreet—but I cannot help wondering what this elaborately-carved and curiously-ramified structure is for. Is it for ornament only, or intended to heat the house, or something?"

Fastidious Host. "O, it's the drains! I like to have 'em where I can look after 'em myself. Pooty design, ain't it? Majolica, you know... Have some chicken?"

SKILLS BUILDER

1 Read Source C. What reasons does Anthony Wohl give for the apparent slowness on the part of local authorities in introducing public health systems?

  Explain which you think is the most compelling reason, and show how all the reasons are linked.

2 Study Source D. This doesn't represent a real situation! What point is the cartoonist making?

  Does this cartoon support or challenge Source C?

More than any other disease, the incidence of tuberculosis charts the public health of a community: to be controlled it requires adequate housing, diet and clean milk. Deaths from tuberculosis, for example, were 50 per cent higher in back-to-back houses than in other kinds. An improved housing stock and better diet resulted in the death rate from the disease being halved by the end of the century. Moves by local authorities to, for example, prevent spitting in public places, helped too.

Scarlet fever killed children: 95 per cent of all cases were in children under 10 years old, and most died. In 1863 scarlet fever killed 34,000 and in 1874, over 26,000. Children, playing with siblings and friends, readily transmitted the disease, both inside and outside the home. In 1869 John Simon, chief medical officer to the Privy Council, called for strict quarantine to be enforced and local authorities responded slowly. Where quarantine was enforced, the death rate fell dramatically.

Diphtheria, often appearing on death certificates as 'croup' or 'throat fever', was a killer too, and was closely linked by the registrar-general with scarlet fever. A highly contagious disease, it spread rapidly, particularly among children, in crowded and poorly ventilated living conditions. About 25 per cent of those contracting the disease died.

Not all diseases, however, waited upon the physical improvements of sewerage systems and better housing for their control, nor upon the acceptance of the germ theory of disease.

Smallpox had been a controllable disease since Edward Jenner's discovery of a vaccine in 1798, but until the mid-1830s the vaccine was intermittently used by the well-to-do and comfortably off. After 1834, the smallpox vaccine was made available, free, to Poor Law vaccinators but vaccination was voluntary. The dangers of this were highlighted by the epidemic of 1837–40 in which around 42,000 people died and thousands more were disfigured for life.

What was to be done? A safe vaccine was readily available but people were reluctant to use it. The government began a gentle move towards compulsion:

- The permissive 1840 Vaccination Act meant that anybody could be vaccinated free of charge by the Poor Law vaccinators.
- The compulsory 1853 Vaccination Act made it obligatory for parents to have their children vaccinated within three months of birth. This made vaccination more common, but it was administered in a haphazard way.

In 1870–3 a second smallpox epidemic, in which 44,000 people died, resulted in a draconian act. The compulsory 1871 Vaccination Act made it obligatory for local health boards to appoint vaccination officers and imposed fines of 25 shillings on parents who refused to have their children vaccinated, with imprisonment for those who did not pay the fine.

In theory, all should have been well. But this emphasis on compulsion resulted in a groundswell of opposition and a strong anti-vaccination movement. Their arguments ranged from fear of central government interference in local government affairs, through the rights of the individual to choose to take a chance with death, to religious objections against the injection of impurities into the blood. These fears were ameliorated in 1898 by the insertion of a 'conscience clause' in the Smallpox Act.

Environmental pollution: a necessary evil?

Human effluent

In June 1858, as you read on page 110, MPs fled the Houses of Parliament. They left the corridors and libraries, tea-rooms and the chamber of the House of Commons itself. This was no bomb scare or fire: this was the summer of the Great Stink, when soaring temperatures turned the Thames into a stinking sewer. The reasons for this are not hard to find.

Definition

Smallpox

A highly contagious, and sometimes fatal, disease caused by a virus. People who catch smallpox usually have a high fever and a rash. The spots turn into pustules that can scar a person for life. Human beings are the only carriers of smallpox and so vaccination is very effective; so effective, in fact, that there have been no recorded cases of smallpox anywhere in the world for many years.

Question

Many diseases were killers in the nineteenth century. Why, then, was it cholera that provided the impetus for public health reforms and not any of the others?

Several factors combined to make the situation worse:

- The flushing water-closet – invented in the sixteenth century by Sir John Harington and refined and sold by Joseph Bramah and Thomas Crapper in the nineteenth century – removed human waste very effectively from houses and into sewers. The sewers, however, led directly to rivers and other water courses from which people took their drinking water.

- As towns grew, farms became more remote and the cost of transporting human waste to them to manure the fields increased. For poorer families, the cost became prohibitive and they allowed the waste to accumulate until it became a hazard.

- Edwin Chadwick's plan of using canal barges to spray human waste on the fields alongside the canals was impractical when put into effect.

- The market in human waste to be used as fertiliser in agriculture virtually collapsed due to the importation of guano (solidified bird droppings) that was cheaper, easier and more pleasant to handle.

- There was a lack of co-ordination and standardisation between the different commissions operating in any one town.

Fortunately, help was at hand. In 1856 Joseph Bazalgette was appointed chief engineer to the Metropolitan Board of Works (see pages 108–11) and submitted his plan for a complete sewerage system for London to the board. The protracted disputes that followed were abruptly ended by the Great Stink and Disraeli's Metropolis Management Amendment Act, which allowed Bazalgette to begin work. By 1864 London's sewage was taken by barge to the Maplin Sands; dumping sewage at sea continued until 1998. Although these events describe what happened in London, the pattern and sequence was followed throughout Britain.

Source E

Fifty years ago nearly all London had every house cleansed into a large cess-pool. Now sewers have been very much improved, scarcely any person thinks of making a cess-pool, but [the sewage] is carried off at once into the river. The Thames is now made a great cess-pool instead of each person having one of his own.

From the evidence given by Thomas Cubitt, builder and developer of most of fashionable Victorian London, to the Select Committee on the Health of Towns in 1840.

Source F

Constructing sewers in 1862.

Industrial effluent

Increasing industrialisation meant that Britain was a dirty, smelly place that polluted the atmosphere and the earth. It also produced enormous wealth. 'Where there's muck, there's brass,' was not said lightly in the industrial towns of the north. And herein lies the paradox. The Lancashire mills that belched smoke over the squalid rows of back-to-back houses produced cotton goods that were essential to personal hygiene; the potteries that led to the Black Country being so named produced lavatory pans and sewerage pipes; and the alkali works that poured hydrochloric acid into the air produced cheap soap and washing powders.

Source H

The view from Blackfriars Bridge, Manchester, over the River Irwell. It was printed in *The Graphic*, a weekly magazine dealing with social issues, in the 1870s.

London fogs were known as 'London particulars' and were really heavy smog: a blend of smoke and fog with a high sulphur and hydrocarbon content that was lethal to anyone with respiratory troubles. By 1875 over 150 tons of fine soot were being discharged into the atmosphere every day from London's domestic fires. A city the size of Glasgow could burn up to a million tons of coal a year on domestic fires and in gas-production and manufacturing industries. The sheer amount of pollution produced in this way was enormous.

In order to control, or attempt to control, industrial pollution, it was necessary to show that what was clearly unpleasant was also poisonous. This required sophisticated chemistry and record-keeping, as well as the will to change. Too frequently, industrial pollution and prosperity were seen as necessary partners, as you can see from Source I.

Source G

[In Manchester] nearly 500 chimneys discharge masses of the densest smoke; the nuisance has risen to an intolerable pitch, and is annually increasing, the air is rendered visibly impure, and no doubt unhealthy, abounding in soot, soiling the clothing and furniture of the inhabitants, and destroying the beauty and fertility of the garden as well as the foiliage and verdure of the country.

From the minutes of the Parliamentary Select Committee on Smoke Prevention, 1843.

SKILLS BUILDER

1 Study Sources E and F. Use your own knowledge to explain how far the work shown in Source F would solve the problems described in Source E.

2 Study Sources G and H. There is a gap of about 30 years between these sources. Are you surprised that nothing seems to have been done to improve industrial pollution in Manchester during these years?

Source I

The question as I look at it is whether Darlington is to be a manufacturing town or not. If I go to Middlesborough I see large works there sending out thousands and thousands of cubic feet of gas and smoke close to private residences. I ask the individuals who live there if they do not suffer in their health. They say 'No, it is all good for trade, we want more of it, we find no fault with smoke.'

An argument presented by a member of the Board of Health for Darlington in 1866.

Question

How would Edwin Chadwick or John Simon have replied to the member of the Darlington Board of Health (Source I)?

Domestic pollution was slightly different. To attempt to put controls on the domestic hearth was seen by most people as being a gross interference in the 'Englishman's castle' – his home. Furthermore, any attempt to control discharges from the domestic hearth would involve inspection, another invasion of the domestic citadel. The 1875 Public Health Act (see page 136) did consolidate restrictions against 'nuisances', but there was a 'get-out' clause for industries: 'No offence of creating excessive smoke can be construed if fireplaces and furnaces are constructed in such a manner as to consume as far as practicable, having regard to the nature of the manufacture or trade.' Proper and effective control of smoke pollution had to wait until the last decades of the twentieth century.

Scarce water and adulterated food: the acceptable face of industrial Britain?

Water

A ready supply of clean water is an essential part of a decent public health system. Yet, for most people living in Victorian Britain, the supply was hardly 'ready' and rarely clean. The East London Waterworks, for example, did not supply water on Sundays; a Staffordshire waterworks turned off supplies every night in order to build up pressure in the mains; and in many parts of the country the supply of water was, at best, erratic, and not always of good or even reasonable quality.

The well-to-do had water piped to their houses and stored in huge cisterns in attics and cellars. For them, water did, usually, come at the turn of a tap. In the 1840s, 20 per cent of Birmingham's and ten per cent of Newcastle's homes had water piped in. Household accounts for the country houses of the rich, through to the comfortable villas of the middle classes, reveal no lack of water for washing clothes, cooking and personal hygiene.

It was different for those who were less well off. The poor, in the middle of the nineteenth century, had to queue for their water at standpipes and street plugs, and carry it back home through dirty streets and courtyards. This must have been an arduous, back-breaking business, and one frequently undertaken by children. For the poor – living in crowded, bug- and rat-infested rooms, sometimes below the level of the street, off fetid alleys and courtyards – trying to keep clean must have been a dispiriting business. It was no wonder that many gave up the attempt. Most of the poor, quite simply, stank.

Source J

They merely pass dirty linen through very dirty water.* The smell of the linen itself, when so washed, is very offensive, and must have an injurious effect upon the health of the occupants. The filth of their dwellings is excessive, so is their personal filth. When they attend my surgery, I am always obliged to have the door open. When I am coming downstairs from the parlour, I know at a distance of a flight of stairs whether there are any poor patients in the surgery.

* It is likely that this 'dirty water' was urine. The poor frequently stored their urine in stone bottles until it was very strong and then used it to wash their clothes, believing it to be an effective cleansing agent.

From Edwin Chadwick, *Report on the Sanitary Condition of the Labouring Population of Great Britain*, published in 1842. Here he is quoting the observations of John Liddle, who was the medical officer for health for Whitechapel, London.

Source K

An engraving showing people queuing for water, dated 1862.

SKILLS BUILDER

Study Sources J and K. How far does Source K challenge the opinions regarding the state of the poor described in Source J?

The objection of railway managers to workmen's trains and of Church of England congregations and clergy to the attendance of the poor in their midst was based as much on their smell and the offence this gave to 'respectable' people as on anything else. While the smell itself did not produce disease (except in the minds of those adhering to the miasma theory) it was indicative of conditions in which disease flourished. Typhus and TB were common and diphtheria, scarlet fever and measles were regular child-killers. For the poor, body lice and nits were commonplace; bedbugs, living in straw-filled mattresses, were constant companions. In 1871 the Parliamentary Select Committee on the Protection of Infant Life heard evidence from all over the country. It was told that at a Manchester day-nursery every single child was infested with lice and they all had to be de-bugged every day.

By 1875 the situation had improved for many people, but the situation was patchy. In Edinburgh, for example, over 50 per cent of those with houses of a rateable value less than £35 had piped water, whereas in West Bromwich the figure was 16 per cent. An investigation into urban water supplies by the Local Government Board found that there were huge areas without easy access to cheap, clean water.

Food

Large-scale adulteration of food was only possible in industrial, or industrialising, societies. In earlier times, there had always been cheats and liars who passed off lightweight loaves of bread and watered beer, for example, as the genuine article. But the deliberate, widespread adulteration of food for profit needed a consuming public, divorced from the producers of the food. In nineteenth-century Britain, food adulteration became a widespread and highly remunerative commercial fraud. It affected the health of the people by not giving them the nutrients they thought they were purchasing; it frequently made them ill and sometimes it killed them.

One of the first people to highlight the problem was analytical chemist Frederick Accum, who published his *Treatise on Adulterations of Food and Culinary Poisons* in 1820. He found that nearly all foods and drinks were adulterated to some extent, and he exposed methods and named names. Some of the most common adulterations Accum found were:

- bakers using alum to whiten cheap flour in order to pass off their loaves as being of high quality

- brewers putting a dangerous poison containing picrotoxin into ale and porter, along with hartshorn shavings, orange powder, caraway seeds and ginger

- tea being mixed with ash, sloe and elder leaves that had been curled and coloured on copper plates

- pickles given their green colour from copper shavings

- cheese rind being coloured with red lead.

Initially acclaimed, Accum was forced to flee the country on what appears to have been a trumped-up charge of mutilating books. As well as drawing people's attention to the nature of the food they were eating, his meticulous descriptions instructed a whole new generation of food adulterers.

In 1830 an anonymous publication again alerted people to the dangers of adulteration. Called *Deadly Adulteration and Slow Poisoning Unmasked: or Disease and Death in the Pot and Bottle*, it aimed at sensationalism:

- oil of vitriol in gin

- opium in beer

- burned bones in bread

- ground stone in flour.

Public interest in food adulteration was revived and kept alive by *A Treatise on the Falsifications of Food,* written in 1848 by John Mitchell, an analytical chemist who had studied food adulteration for some years. He found that food adulteration had increased since Accum's findings were made public:

- Every sample of bread he looked at contained alum and sometimes potato as well.

- Samples of flour contained chalk, pipe-clay and powdered flints.

- Beer contained sulphate of iron, which gave it a good 'head'.

- Eight factories in London dried used tea leaves and supplied them to fraudulent dealers who sold them on as 'fresh'.

Of course, the rich and comfortably off could afford to buy their food and drink from high-class, reputable suppliers. It was the poor, already debilitated by poor living and working conditions, who had to bear the brunt of food adulteration. Evidence for food adulteration can be found in reports of various government departments and select committees, but it wasn't until Dr Arthur Hassell published his *Food and Its Adulterations* in 1855 that a government committee on the subject was appointed.

Source L

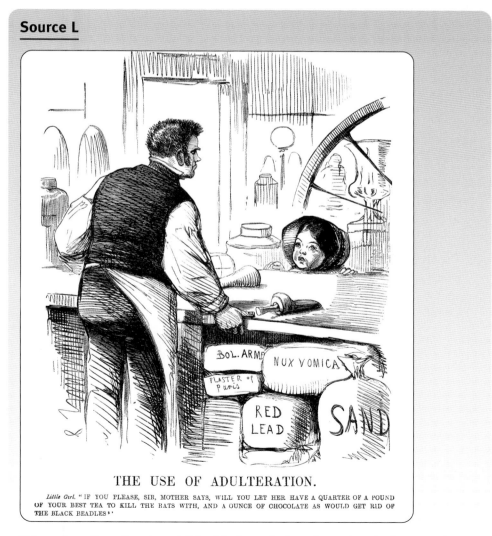

THE USE OF ADULTERATION.

Little Girl. "IF YOU PLEASE, SIR, MOTHER SAYS, WILL YOU LET HER HAVE A QUARTER OF A POUND OF YOUR BEST TEA TO KILL THE RATS WITH, AND A OUNCE OF CHOCOLATE AS WOULD GET RID OF THE BLACK BEADLES'."

This cartoon from *Punch*, published in August 1855, formed part of a campaign the magazine waged against food adulteration.

SKILLS BUILDER

Read Sources M, N and O.

1 What reasons can you find for improvements in public health being slow?

2 Create a spider diagram to show how all these reasons are linked.

Source M

Frequently, interested parties are seated as Boards of Guardians who are ready to stop anything which may lead to expenditure for the proper repair of dwellings of the labouring classes.

Where additional supplies of water are called for, one cry raised is 'Oh the interest of the companies is too powerful to be touched.'

From a letter written by Edwin Chadwick to the Earl of Shaftesbury in April 1844.

This resulted in a sequence of acts of varying effectiveness:

- The 1860 Food and Drugs Act enabled local authorities to appoint analysts who could investigate food if a complaint was received.
- The 1872 Adulteration of Food, Drink and Drugs Act enabled local authorities to order an investigation of specific foodstuffs even if no complaint had been received.
- The 1875 Sale of Food and Drugs Act tried to define unadulterated food.

In general, implementation of the Food and Drugs acts was patchy, and any prosecutions resulted in ridiculously small fines being levied. However, a start had been made and the state was moving inexorably to protect its most vulnerable members.

Housing: a public health issue?

The pressures of a growing population upon the existing housing stock during the first half of the nineteenth century have been described and explained on pages 87–92. The health of the poorer and most vulnerable people in Britain was dependent to a large extent upon the provision of good-quality housing. But that housing had to be cheap if the poor were to afford it, and herein lies the problem. No speculative builder was going to build good-quality housing that was also cheap. No landlord was going to charge lower rents for his properties than he could obtain on the open market.

Source N

(i) The Boot and Shoe Yard cottages are said to pay the best annual interest of any cottage property in the borough.

From Edwin Chadwick, *The Sanitary Conditions of the Labouring Population – Local Reports*, published in 1842.

(ii) The property proposed to be purchased consists of the Boot and Shoe Yard, which is a disgrace to the town and from which locality the number of cases sent to the Infirmary, the Dispensary and the House of Recovery are of fearful extent.

From the Committee Report Book, Leeds, when, under the authority of the 1842 Leeds Improvement Act, permission was sought to demolish the cottages.

Source O

Opposing views impeded substantial working-class housing progress until the last quarter of the nineteenth century. One view was that until urban drainage and water systems were improved, then the effects of insanitary housing would continue to imperil inhabitants' lives. Factors external to the house – paving, street cleansing, sewers, drainage, water supply – were stressed as indispensable to environmental improvement and indissolubly linked to housing conditions, poverty and health. This view was contaminated by association with Chadwick. But it also foundered on its requirement for a quantum leap in public expenditure during the infancy of reformed local government sensitive to electors' unwillingness to spend money.

From Richard Rodger, *Housing in Urban Britain 1780–1914*, published in 1989.

Was the way forward to be one of compulsion or of state-built housing to the required standard that would be cheap enough to house the poorest in the community? There was no clearly defined government housing policy until the last two decades of the nineteenth century. Some towns and cities had inserted clauses in their own private improvement acts that empowered them to have some control over new building, sewerage connections and cellar dwellings. These were:

- Leeds and Liverpool in 1842
- Manchester in 1844–5
- Nottingham and St Helens in 1845
- Burnley and Newcastle in 1846.

The 1844 Metropolitan Buildings Act gave the London authorities similar powers. However, to give controls to an authority was not the same as that authority actually acting upon them. Hundreds of new buildings did not conform to the regulations that were supposed to govern them.

It was the Local Government Act of 1858 (see page 131) that set out model by-laws, and ten years later some 568 towns were using them. However, although building regulations were generally available in the 1860s, their impact was less than it could have been. Vested interests fought them through the local courts; localities developed their own variants; and there was always the problem of enforcement. The Public Health Act of 1875 (see page 136) set out very clearly what the powers of local authorities were with regard to building regulations, and it was because of the firmness and clarity of this act that standard local government by-laws were laid down in 1877. These sought to regulate such things as the width of streets, the height of buildings and systems of drainage.

However, all these measures were primarily concerned with new buildings. It was going to take years before these building regulations had any sort of cumulative effect on public health. Faced with cholera epidemics and endemic 'dirty' diseases, the authorities had to fall back on the expedient:

- The Common Lodging Houses Acts of 1851 and 1853 laid down that all lodging houses were to be registered and inspected by the police. However, the act was badly drafted and rarely enforced.
- The Nuisances Removal Act of 1855 (see page 138) empowered local authorities to combat overcrowding, as a nuisance, with fines and prosecution.
- The Sanitary Act of 1866 (see page 133) placed limitations on the use of cellars for occupation.
- The Artisans' and Labourers' Dwellings Act of 1868 (sometimes called Torren's Act) gave local councils the power to force a landlord to repair an insanitary house. If they did not, the council could buy it and pull it down.
- The Artisans' and Labourers' Dwellings Improvement Act of 1875 (sometimes called Cross's Act) gave local councils the power to clear whole districts, not just individual houses.

Manchester street, 1848

Question

Changes to the treatment of the poor were brought in quickly. Why were changes to public health so slow?

These last two acts were permissive. Some councils adopted them with alacrity. Birmingham, for example, began a huge slum-clearance programme under the direction of its progressive mayor **Joseph Chamberlain**. He organised the clearance of several acres of slums in the city centre and the redevelopment of the site. However, the people who had lived there had to make do as best they could. This highlights the main problem with the Artisans' and Labourers' Dwellings Acts: that they made no provision for the compulsory housing of those made homeless by slum clearance. So the dispossessed simply moved on, to create a slum somewhere else. It was not until 1890 (for London) and 1909 (for the rest of the country) that councils were obliged to rehouse at least half of the people evicted in their slum-clearance programmes.

Biography

Joseph Chamberlain (1836–1914)

Born in London, Joseph was educated at University College School and went to work in Nettleford's screw factory in Birmingham. He retired when he was 38 years old, having made a fortune. He entered politics and in 1868 was elected a Birmingham town councillor, then became the city's mayor in 1873. He became MP for Birmingham in 1876; four years later he was in the Cabinet as president of the Board of Trade. A radical social reformer, he embarked on a massive slum-clearance programme in Birmingham, built housing for the poor, set up free public libraries and art galleries, and took gas, water and sewerage systems into the control of the city council. He had little regard for the aristocracy, believing they should pay for their privileges. Queen Victoria was not amused. He broke with the Liberal Party in 1886 because he distrusted Gladstone and opposed his Home Rule policies. In 1895 he became colonial secretary in Salisbury's Conservative–Unionist government, where he supported expansion in Africa. He resigned in 1903 so that he could promote his own policy of tariff reform, which was based on giving preferential treatment to imports from the colonies and protection for colonial industries. In 1906 he left public life because of a stroke and he died on the eve of the First World War.

Elsewhere, men of substance took a different attitude and were not dependent on acts of Parliament before they could act. Titus Salt, a wealthy Bradford mill-owner, moved his factory and its workers out of a filthy, polluted environment to the purpose-built village of Saltaire (see pages 154–58). He first built a new mill, and then houses, a school, park, almshouses and a hospital for his workers. This benevolent paternalism was resented by some, derided by others, but accepted with speed and enthusiasm by those who willingly swapped some individual freedoms for fresh air, clean water and decent housing.

Unit summary

What have you learned in this unit?

You have learned that there were persistent problems that affected the lives of thousands of people in the British Isles and that the resolution of these would significantly improve the public health of the population as a whole. Endemic 'dirty' diseases (typhus, typhoid and cholera) were killers, but then so were respiratory and pulmonary diseases such as TB, scarlet fever and diphtheria; however, the impact of these lessened throughout

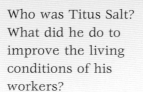

RESEARCH TOPIC

Who was Titus Salt? What did he do to improve the living conditions of his workers?

This task will provide you with background to the case study with which this book ends.

the period. An improvement in the living conditions of all, and working-class people in particular, would have a considerable impact on these killer diseases. The health of the poorest and most vulnerable people was to a very large extent dependent on the provision of good-quality housing, but that there was little incentive to provide this until the end of the period when the government stepped in with the two Artisans' and Labourers' Dwellings Acts. A ready supply of clean water is an essential part of a good public health system, but in many parts of the country in the years to 1875 a supply of water was at best erratic and not always of a good or even reasonable quality. This particularly hit the poor, as did the sale of adulterated food and drink. The discharge of industrial effluent was rife and remained a problem throughout the period.

What skills have you used in this unit?

You have worked with a range of primary, contemporary and secondary sources to explore the impact of persistent problems on the population, and particularly on the most vulnerable members of society. You have seen how the poor suffered from poor housing, indifferent water supplies, adulterated food and drink, and industrial effluent. You have explored the reactions of those in a position to bring about change to working-class people's living conditions that could impact on public health provision, and by using your skills of cross-referencing and analysis you have understood the reasons why progress to public health reforms in these areas was slow.

Exam style question

This is the sort of question you will find on the examination paper as a (b) question.

Read Sources M, N and O and use your own knowledge.

Do you agree with the view that there was no will, in the years before 1875, to contribute to public health reforms by improving the living conditions of working-class people?

Exam tips

This is a slightly different question from the (b) style questions you have worked on so far, in that the 'view' is in the question, not the source.

You have worked on (b) questions at the end of Units 2, 3, 5 and 9, so you should have a good idea of the sort of plan you prefer. As you draw it up, remember the following points:

- Be very clear about the view being put forward. In this case, the view refers to the supposed lack of will on the part of central and local government to tackle the living conditions of working people and so improve public health. You will need to use your knowledge of exactly what was, and what was not, done and the reasons why.
- Analyse the three sources for points that support and points that challenge the view.
- Cross-reference between the sources for points of agreement and points of disagreement.
- Combine these points with your own wider knowledge into an argument for or against the view given in the question.
- Reach a balanced, supported conclusion.

Case study

Titus Salt: hard-headed businessman or generous philanthropist?

This case study brings together the work you have done on poverty and public health by looking at the impact one person had on both. Titus Salt made a fortune as a mill-owner in Bradford, west Yorkshire. He then moved his workforce, lock stock and barrel, to a model village and mill that he had had built for them between 1851 and 1872, in the countryside by the River Aire, where the air was good and the water clean. He called the village Saltaire. And he made another fortune! And therein lies the paradox. Was he motivated by the desire to make money, or to improve the lives of his workforce? Robert Owen (see page 18) was motivated in his radical attitude to his workforce by the belief that capitalism created poverty. What was Titus Salt's motivation? Profit or philanthropy? He certainly gave away a lot of money, but he ruled the daily lives of his workers with a rod of iron. Indeed, does it matter what his motivation was, as long as the lives of people were improved? How far, in fact, had their lives been improved? It is clear that a lot had been gained by the move to Saltaire, but what had been lost in the process?

In this case study you will explore the impact Titus Salt had on the lives of his workforce, and you will investigate the extent to which their lives had been improved by the move to Saltaire. You will do this by using the sources that are provided here, and, if these aren't wholly appropriate for the investigation you are pursuing, by finding other, alternative resources in libraries or via the internet. There are quite a few references to Bradford already in this book, and you should start with those (see the Index).

Remember that you will need to interrogate the sources you select in order to gain evidence from them. You will need, for example, not just to consider the content of a source and make inferences from it, but you will need to make decisions about its reliability and about how much weight you can give to the evidence it provides. You will need, too, to explore the context of the sources, and answer questions such as 'What was Bradford like at this time?' 'What did Salt's mills produce?' 'What was public health like in Bradford and then in Saltaire?' 'What was the extent of poverty in Bradford and Saltaire?'

First, however, you need to plan. Working individually or in small groups, decide on your overall 'big' question.

This can be:

(i)   What impact did Titus Salt have on the lives of his workforce?

(ii) To what extent did the move to Saltaire improve the lives of Titus Salt's workforce?

(iii) 'The profit motive, not the desire to improve the lives of his workers, was Titus Salt's driving force.' How far do you agree with this view?

(iv) Write your own enquiry title, providing it focuses on poverty, public health, Titus Salt, Bradford and Saltaire.

Now break down the 'big' question into smaller, sub-questions that will lead you to an answer to the 'big' question. Divide the work up between you and agree a timescale for completion. Good luck!

Source A

Bradford in the 1840s. The first spinning mill was built there in 1803. By 1851, over 129 steam powered mills had been built, and the population had grown from around 13,000 to about 70,000 people.

Source B

The two waterways that ran through the town – Bradford Beck and Bradford canal – were open sewers, overloaded with domestic and industrial effluent. In the 1840s the canal was popularly known as 'River Stink'. The town was notorious for the smoke that poured from its ever multiplying factory chimneys, irritating throats and lungs, and soiling clothes and buildings.

Housing conditions for the poorest inhabitants were appalling. A survey in 1845 among hand woolcombers, one of the most impoverished trades, revealed cases of eight or twelve people living and working in just two rooms. Not all the town's working population had to endure such degraded housing, but it was the lot of thousands. Those fortunate enough to enjoy better accommodation still had to put up with impure water, rudimentary sewage disposal and atmospheric pollution. The result, in an age before antibiotics, was an extremely high death rate from infectious diseases like smallpox and tuberculosis. Average expectation of life in the town in the 1840s was barely twenty years, the lowest in Yorkshire. The rate of infant mortality was the fifth highest in the country. A cholera epidemic killed 426 people 1848–9.

From John Styles, *Titus Salt and Saltaire*, published in 1990.

Source C

The cholera most forcibly teaches us our mutual connection. Nothing shows more powerfully the duty of every man to look after the needs of others. Cholera is God's voice to his people.

> Part of a speech made by Titus Salt, who was mayor of Bradford, in 1848.

Source D

The life of Mr. Titus Salt was one of intense devotedness to business: his brain was ever busy and his hands ever occupied in the management of the various manufactories now in full working order. The demand for alpaca goods increased with remarkable rapidity, so that within the short space of three years the import of the staple had risen to 2,186,480lbs., and now the yearly consumption, with other kindred fibres, in the Bradford trade alone, amounts to about 4,000,000lbs.

But it was not so much the immediate profit that accrued to himself that rendered his present achievements so remarkable, but the stimulus it gave to trade generally. A new mine, as it were, was opened in Bradford, which invited many toilers to work it, for the treasures it possessed. Employment was thus created for thousands of workpeople, who were attracted from all parts of the country by the high remuneration offered. Whole streets of dwellings soon sprung up in the vicinity of the mills. Merchants, who had hitherto transacted business through local agents, found it necessary to remove their residence from the metropolis and other places, to this thriving centre of industry. Even foreigners regarded it their interest to leave their fatherland, to become naturalised citizens of this country and dwellers in this community. Indeed, the indirect results of Mr. Titus Salt's achievements are so interwoven with the growth of Bradford, in population, in building, in trade and commerce, in moral and intellectual improvement, that it is impossible to separate the one from the other.

> From Reverend R. Balgarnie, *Sir Titus Salt, Baronet: His Life and Its Lessons*, published in 1877.

Source E

In 1847, the year of the Charter of Incorporation, Mr Salt, who had already been appointed Chief Constable, was made an alderman, and in the following year became Mayor and one of the town's leading magistrates.

A political opponent accused him for working for the incorporation of the town, and then removing his plant to Saltaire in order to avoid the heavy taxation which he knew must follow.

> From Joseph Fieldhouse, *Bradford*, published in 1978.

Source F

An illustration, dated 1862, showing fashionable dresses made from alpaca.

Source G

Expansion and prosperity had at last in 1846 brought Bradford its railway link with London, via Leeds. The route lay through Shipley, at one point converging on the Leeds–Liverpool canal and the river Aire. Manufacturing in overcrowded, unhealthy and dangerous surroundings was no longer necessary; all the separate processes could be gathered together in one place, out in the country.

Although Salt could have packed his money-bags and retired to a green spa or blue coast, merely to die a millionaire was not an end in itself in his scale of values. A down-to-earth realist in business, Salt had a dream which he believed was his God-given duty to turn into reality.

From Jim Greenhalf, *Salt and Silver*, published in 1997.

Source H

Between 1851 and 1871 Salt spent £170,000 building homes for his workers, and sundry amenities which he considered essential for a healthy and civilised life. These included a row of 14 shops on Victoria Road (the village had 40 by 1871), a public baths and washhouse on Caroline Street (the former had 24 baths for men and women, the latter contained six washing machines, wringers and a heated drying closet). Salt spent nearly as much again building 45 almshouses, a three-ward hospital, a school for boys and girls, a multi-purpose club and institute. After 1870 he added 11 acres of landscaped park on the side of the river Aire, where his workers might stroll, play cricket, tennis, bowls or even practise archery.

From Jim Greenhalf, *Salt and Silver*, published in 1997.

Source I

An illustration of the mill at Saltaire, made just after it was opened in 1853.

Source J

Lord Harwood: How is it, Mr Salt, that you do not invest your capital in landed property and enjoy the remainder of your life free from the strain of business?

Titus Salt: In the first place, I thought that by the concentration of my works in one locality I might provide occupation for my sons. Moreover, as a landed proprietor I felt I should be out of my element. Outside of my business I am nothing. In it, I have considerable influence. By the opening of Saltaire I also hope to do good to my fellow men.

A reported conversation between Titus Salt and Lord Harwood at a dinner to mark the opening of Salts Mill in 1853.

Source K

Titus Salt was a severe critic of the 1834 Poor Law. He also supported the move to reduce working hours and was the first employer in the Bradford area to introduce the ten-hour day. However, Salt held conservative views on some issues. He refused permission for his workers to join trade unions and disagreed with men like Richard Oastler and John Fielden who wanted Parliament to pass legislation on child labour. Salt employed young children in his factories and was totally opposed to the 1833 Factory Act that attempted to prevent children under the age of nine working in textile mills.

From www.spartacus.schoolnet.co.uk/IRsalt.htm.

Source L

Titus was perhaps the greatest captain of industry in England, not only because he gathered thousands under him but also because, according to the light that was in him, he tried to care for all those thousands. We do not say that he succeeded in realising all his views or that it is possible to harmonise at present all relations between capital and labour. Upright in business, admirable in his private relations, he came, without seeking the honour, to be admittedly the best representative of the employer class in this part of the country, if not the whole kingdom.

From an article written by the editor of the *Bradford Observer* on the death of Titus Salt on 29 December 1876.

These sources, and others you have worked with in this book, should have given you some ideas as to where you could look to expand your understanding of the impact Titus Salt had on public health and poverty. Was he the only factor influencing the changes that happened and the differences between Bradford and Saltaire? You could, for example, look for workhouse records, at the differences made by the 1848 and 1875 Public Health Acts, and at whether there were any reports or investigations written about the state of the two places.

Use the knowledge and understanding you have gained through working with this book, and the skills you have developed, in creating your case study.

Thematic review: source-based debate and evaluation

It is important, especially when dealing with a topic that addresses change over time, to stand back and review the period you have been studying. You need to ask yourself not only what happened, but why it happened and why it happened then and not, say, 100 years earlier or 20 years later. What had driven change? Which factors were significant and which were not? Were there any events that were critical turning points? Thematic review questions, spanning the whole time period, will help to focus your thinking.

These are the thematic review questions that relate to 'Poverty, Public Health and the Growth of Government 1830–75'. You can probably think of more, but for the moment these are the ones with which you will be working:

- In considering the changes that had been brought about to poverty and public health, to what extent had the doctrine of *'laissez-faire'* been overturned by 1875?

- How far were reforms in the treatment of poverty easier to implement than those in public health?

- To what extent was the work of individuals the key to change in the treatment of poverty and reforms in public health in the period 1830–75?

- How far had changes to the treatment of poverty and public health reforms improved the lives of the poorest and most vulnerable members of society during this period?

Choose one of these thematic review questions that you plan to answer. Working through this section will make much more sense if you have an actual question in mind.

Answering a thematic review question

There are two keys to answering a thematic review question: *select* and *deploy*.

Select   You need to select appropriate source material. You need to select appropriate knowledge.

Deploy   You need to deploy what you have selected so that you answer the question in as direct a way as possible.

Unpacking 'select'

You will see that all the thematic review questions are asking for an evaluation. They ask 'How far. . .' and 'To what extent. . .' which means that you will have to weigh up the evidence given by the sources you have selected. You will, therefore, have to select sources that will give you a range of evidence. Six diary entries, for example, will not give you the range you want. You will also need to select sources that seem to provide evidence that pulls in different directions. Eight sources saying more or less the same thing but in different ways will not help you weigh up the significance of different sorts of evidence and reach a reasoned, supported conclusion.

So now go ahead.

1 Look back through this book and select the sources, primary and secondary, that you think will give you the appropriate range, balance and evidence.

2 Make notes of the knowledge you will need to use to contextualise the sources and create an argument.

You can't, of course, simply put some sources into an answer and hope that whoever is reading what you have written can sort things out for themselves. You need to evaluate the sources you have selected and use that evaluation to create the argument you will be making when you answer the question. You have already had practice of doing this, but here is a reminder of some of the questions you will need to ask of a source before you can turn it into evidence:

- Is the *content* appropriate for the question I am answering?
- Can I supply the appropriate *context* for the source?
- How *reliable* is the source as evidence? Was the author or artist *in a position to know* what he or she was talking/painting about?
- What was the intended *audience* of the source? What was the *purpose* of the source?
- If the source is a photograph, did the photographer *pose* the people in the picture? Was the photographer *selective* in what he or she chose to photograph?
- If the source is a *painting*, why did the artist choose to spend time on that particular view?
- If the source is a *cartoon*, what point was the cartoonist making and how far did that *reflect* current attitudes in society?
- How *useful* is this source in developing an answer to the question? Remember that a source that is unreliable can still be useful.

Now that you have your selection of source material, you need to think about it as a package. Does it do the job you want it to do? Does it supply you with enough evidence to argue your case, while at the same time providing you with enough evidence of different points of view so that you can show you have considered what weight the evidence will bear in reaching a reasoned, supported conclusion? In other words, can you effectively *cross-reference* between the sources, showing where they support and where they challenge each other?

Unpacking 'deploy'

The key to successful deployment of evidence and knowledge in answering a question like the one you have selected is always to keep the question in the forefront of your mind, Keep focused! Don't be tempted to go off into interesting by-ways. Make every paragraph count as you build your argument.

You have already had a lot of practice in essay planning and writing, so this is just a reminder of the main things you need to bear in mind.

Plan carefully how you are going to construct your answer and make out your case.

Structure your answer, and you could use this framework as a guide:

- **Introduction:** Here you 'set out your stall', briefly outlining your argument and approach.
- **Paragraphs:** These should develop your argument, using the evidence you have created by questioning the sources. As you create the case you are making, remember to cross-reference between the sources you are using so as to weigh the evidence, showing on which you place the greater weight.
- **Conclusion:** Here you should pull your case together, giving a supported summary of the arguments you have made and coming to a reasoned, supported judgment.

In other words, say what you are going to do, do it, and show that you have done it.

You do not, of course, have to respond to these thematic review questions by writing an essay all by yourself. You could work collaboratively in a small group, or you could use one or more of the questions to prepare for a class debate. In whatever way you are going to use these thematic review questions, the approach will be the same: select, deploy and keep to the point.

Good luck!

Exam zone

Relax and prepare

Hot tips: What other students have said

From GCSE to AS level

- I really enjoyed studying Modern World History at GCSE but I am glad that I had the chance to look at some nineteenth- and twentieth-century English history at AS level. It has been challenging but enjoyable to study a different period.

- Many of the skills that I learned at GCSE were built upon at AS level, especially in Unit 2 where the skills of source evaluation and analysis are very important.

- AS level History seems like a big step up at first with more demands made on independent reading and more complex source passages to cope with. However, by the end of the first term I felt as if my written work had improved considerably.

- The more practice source-based questions I attempted, the more confident I became and quite quickly I picked up the necessary style and techniques required for success.

- I found it really helpful to look at the mark schemes in the textbook. It was reassuring to see what the examiners were looking for and how I could gain top marks.

What I wish I had known at the start of the year

- I used the textbook a lot during the revision period to learn the key facts and practise key skills. I really wished that I had used it from the beginning of the course in order to consolidate my class notes.

- I wish I had taken more time reading and noting other material such as the handouts my teacher gave us. Reading around the subject and undertaking independent research would have made my understanding more complete and made the whole topic more interesting.

- AS History is not just about learning the relevant material but also developing the skills to use it effectively. I wish that I had spent more time throughout the year practising source questions to improve my style and technique.

- I wish I had paid more attention to the advice and comments made by my teacher on the written work I had done. This would have helped me to improve my scores throughout the year.

How to revise

- I started my revision by buying a new folder and some dividers. I put all my revision work into this folder and used the dividers to separate the different topics. I really took pride in my revision notes and made them as thorough and effective as I could manage.

- Before I started the revision process, I found it helpful to plan out my history revision. I used the Edexcel specification given to me by my teacher as a guideline of which topics to revise and I ticked off each one as I covered it.

- I found it useful to revise in short, sharp bursts. I would set myself a target of revising one particular topic in an hour and a half. I would spend one hour taking revision notes and then half an hour testing myself with a short practice question or a facts test.

- I found it useful to always include some practice work in my revision. If I could get that work to my teacher to mark, all the better, but just attempting questions to time helped me improve my technique.

- Sometimes I found it helpful to revise with a friend. We might spend 45 minutes revising by ourselves and then half an hour testing each other. Often we were able to sort out any problems between us and it was reassuring to see that someone else had the same worries and pressures at that time.

Refresh your memory

Revision checklist

Unit 1: How effective was the old Poor Law?

- What was the significance of the Elizabethan Poor Law?
- The role of the parish and the importance of settlement
- Poorhouses, workhouses and houses of correction
- Outdoor relief: Speenhamland, the Labour Rate and the Roundsman system

Unit 2: The old Poor Law attacked: why was change necessary?

- Theories: Malthus, Ricardo, Paine, Owen and Bentham
- Practical pressures: Napoleonic wars, Swing Riots, expense
- Poor Law Commission: its composition and powers
- Recommendations of the Poor Law Commission, and the reasons for them

Unit 3: Implementing the Poor Law Amendment Act

- Passage of the bill through Parliament and the main provisions of the act
- The Poor Law Commission: its composition and powers
- Problems faced by commissioners in implementing the government's Poor Law policy

- Reactions to the Poor Law Amendment Act from different sections of society

Unit 4: Union workhouses: pauper palaces or bastilles?

- The principle of 'less eligibility' and the operation of the 'workhouse test'
- Who were the new paupers?
- The continuation and operation of outdoor relief
- Workhouse design, routine and staff

Unit 5: How did the Poor Law develop between 1847 and 1875?

- The greater involvement of government: the replacement of the Poor Law Commission by the Poor Law Board (1847) and by the Local Government Board (1871)
- The changing cost of maintaining the poor
- The balance achieved between indoor and outdoor relief
- The changing treatment of the poor

Unit 6: Dirt, disease and public health: the nature of the problem

- The rate of urban growth and its impact on living conditions
- Urban sanitation: dirt, disease and death
- Theories of disease
- The adequacy of public health provision before 1848

Unit 7: Cholera: the impetus for reform?

- Epidemics and treatments
- The reaction of local and national government
- Case study: John Snow and the Broad Street pump
- The work of John Simon and Joseph Bazalgette

Unit 8: Reports, investigations and enquiries: what was their impact on public health reform?

- The importance of Dr James Kay's report on the cotton workers of Manchester, 1832
- The impact of Edwin Chadwick and his *Report on the Sanitary Conditions of the Labouring Population of Great Britain*, 1842

- The significance of the *Report of the Royal Commission for Inquiry into the State of Large Towns and Populous Districts*, 1844

- The importance of the Health of Towns Association, 1844

Unit 9: Legislation: the government gets involved

- The importance of early sanitary legislation 1846–8

- The significance of the 1848 Public Health Act

- Why were further acts needed in 1858, 1866 and 1875?

- Why was there opposition to public health provision?

Unit 10: Public health: persistent problems

- Disease: a personal or public health problem?

- Housing: a public health issue?

- Environmental pollution: human and industrial effluent

- Scarce water and adulterated food

This revision checklist looks very knowledge-based. The examination, however, will test your source-based skills as well. So remember that, when dealing with sources, you must be able to do the following:

- Comprehend a source and break it down into key points.

- Interpret a source, drawing inferences and deductions from it rather than treating it as a source of information. This may involve considering the language and tone used as well.

- Cross-reference points of evidence between sources to reinforce and challenge.

- Evaluate the evidence by assessing its quality and its reliability in terms of how much weight it will bear and how secure are the conclusions that can be drawn from it. This may include considering the provenance of the source.

- Deal with the sources as a set to build a body of evidence.

Result

You have spent a lot of time working on plans and constructing answers to the (a) and (b) questions. In Units 1, 4, 6, 7 and 8 you worked with (a) questions; in Units 2, 3, 5, 9 and 10 you worked with (b) questions. So you now have a pretty good idea about how to plan an answer and write a response to the question on the examination paper. But what are the examiners looking for? And what marks will you get?

What will the exam paper look like?

There will be three questions on the paper.

(a) Compulsory: everyone has to do this.

(b) (i) and *(b) (ii)* You will have a choice here and will only have to answer one (b) question.

Sources: there will be nine sources on the examination paper. But don't worry: you won't have to deal with them all! You'll only need to deal with six sources – three for each of the questions you will be answering. And here is the good news. So far, you have worked with very long sources, some of which were complicated. In the examination, because you will only have 1 hour and 20 minutes to answer the two questions, the sources will be much shorter. You'll probably be dealing with no more than around 550 words altogether.

Question (a)

What will you have to do, and what marks will you get for doing it?

You will have to focus on reaching a judgment by analysis, cross-referencing and evaluation of source material. The maximum number of marks you can get is 20. You will be working at any one of four levels. Try to get as high up in the levels as you can. Remember that the only relevant knowledge, outside of that which you can find in the sources, is what examiners call 'contextual' knowledge. This means you can write enough to enable you to interpret the source, but no more. For example, if one of the three sources is by Edwin Chadwick you will need to show the examiners that you know about his work in producing reports on the Poor

Law and public health, but you do not need to go into detail about his experiences with the various commissions and boards with which he was involved, unless this information helps the understanding of a particular source.

Level 1 Have you shown that you understand the surface features of the sources, and have you shown that you have selected material relevant to the question? Does your response consist mainly of direct quotations from the sources?

1–5 marks This is what you will score.

Level 2 Have you identified points of similarity and difference in the sources in relation to the question asked? Have you made at least one developed comparison or a range of undeveloped ones? Have you summarised the information you have found in the sources? Have you noted the provenance of at least one of the sources?

6–10 marks This is what you will score.

Level 3 Have you cross-referenced between the sources, making detailed comparisons supported by evidence from the sources? Have you shown that you understand you have to weigh the evidence by looking at the nature, origins, purpose and audience of the sources? Have you shown you have thought about considering 'How far' by trying to use the sources as a set?

11–15 marks This is what you will score.

Level 4 Have you reached a judgment in relation to the issue posed by the question? Is this judgment supported by careful examination of the evidence of the sources? Have you cross-referenced between the sources and analysed the points of similarity and disagreement? Have you taken account of the different qualities of the sources in order to establish what weight the evidence will bear? Have you used the sources as a set when addressing 'How far' in the question?

16–20 marks This is what you will score.

Now try this (a) question.

Study Sources A, B and C. How far do the sources suggest that the main aim of those who supported changes to the Poor Law in 1834 was to reduce the cost of providing for the poor?

Source A

Compulsory provision for the poor in this country has produced the natural result of encouraging population growth in the lower orders of society, and therefore the numbers of the poor. Much stress has been laid on the financial concerns arising from the rapid increase in rates in recent years, but I do not consider this of the greatest importance. The worst consequence is the increasing proportion of dependent poor encouraged by the existing poor laws. These burden the working labourer and lower the real price of labour, while the whole business of Settlement is a tyranny that binds them in dependency. These arrangements destroy all honourable feeling and spirit among the lower ranks of society and will make more and more of the community dependent.

From a letter written by Thomas Malthus to Samuel Whitbread MP in 1807. Whitbread had sought his advice on reforming the Poor Laws.

Source B

The first and most essential of all conditions is that the situation of the pauper in relief shall not be made really, or apparently, so eligible as the situation of the independent labourer of the lowest class.

From the report compiled by the 1832 Commission of Enquiry into the Operation of the Poor Laws, published in 1834.

Source C

Years	Average expenditure per year	Cost per head of the population
1814–18	£6,437,000	11s 7d (58p)
1819–23	£6,788,000	11s 2d (56p)
1824–28	£6,039,000	9s 2d (46p)
1829–33	£6,758,000	9s 8d (49p)
1834–38	£4,946,000	6s 7d (33p)

Poor Law expenditure in England and Wales 1814–38.

Now use the marking criteria to assess your response.

How did you do?

What could you have done to have achieved a better mark?

Question (b)

What will you have to do and what marks will you get for doing it?

You will have to analyse and evaluate a historical view or claim using three sources and your own knowledge. There are 40 marks for this question. You will get 24 marks for your own knowledge and 16 marks for your source evaluation. You can be working at any one of four levels. Try to get as high up in the levels as you can. The examiners will be marking your answer twice: once for knowledge and a second time for source evaluation.

This is what the examiners will be looking for as they mark the ways in which you have selected and used your knowledge to answer the question:

Level 1   Have you written in simple sentences without making any links between them? Have you provided only limited support for the points you are making? Have you written what you know separately from the sources? Is what you have written mostly generalised and not really directed at the focus of the question? Have you made a lot of spelling mistakes and is your answer disorganised?

1–6 marks   This is what you will score.

Level 2   Have you produced a series of statements that are supported by mostly accurate and relevant factual material? Have you made some limited links between the statements you have written? Is your answer mainly 'telling the story' and not really analysing what happened? Have you kept your own knowledge and the sources separate? Have you made a judgment that isn't supported by facts? Is your answer a bit disorganised with some spelling and grammatical mistakes?

7–12 marks   This is what you will score.

Level 3   Is your answer focused on the question? Have you shown that you understand the key issues involved? Have you included a lot of descriptive material along with your analysis of the issues? Is your material factually accurate but a bit lacking in depth and/or relevance? Have you begun to integrate your own knowledge with the source material? Have you made a few spelling and grammatical mistakes? Is your work mostly well organised?

13–18 marks   This is what you will score.

Level 4   Does your answer relate well to the question focus? Have you shown that you understand the issues involved? Have you analysed the key issues? Is the material you have used relevant to the question and factually accurate? Have you begun to integrate what you know with the evidence you have gleaned from the source material? Is the material you have selected balanced? Is the way you have expressed your answer clear and coherent? Are your spelling and grammar mostly accurate?

19–24 marks   This is what you will score.

This is what the examiners are looking for as they mark your source evaluation skills:

Level 1   Have you shown that you understand the sources? Is the material you have selected from them relevant to the question? Is your answer mostly direct quotations from the sources or re-writes of them in your own words?

1–4 marks   This is what you will score.

Level 2   Have you shown that you understand the sources? Have you selected from them in order to support or challenge the view given in the question? Have you used the sources mainly as sources of information?

5–8 marks   This is what you will score.

Level 3   Have you analysed the sources, drawing from them points of challenge and/or support for the view contained in the question? Have you developed these points, using the source material? Have you shown that you realise you are dealing with just one viewpoint and that the sources point to other, perhaps equally valid ones? Have you reached a judgment? Have you supported that judgment with evidence from the sources?

9–12 marks   This is what you will score.

Level 4   Have you analysed the sources, raising issues from them? Have you discussed the viewpoint in the question by relating it to the issues raised by your analysis of the source material? Have you weighed the evidence in order to reach a judgment? Is your judgment fully explained and supported by carefully selected evidence?

13–16 marks   This is what you will score.

Now try this (b) question.

Read Sources D, E and F and use your own knowledge.

Do you agree with the view that the main factor encouraging the improvement in public health was fear of cholera?

Explain your answer, using the evidence of Sources D, E and F and your own knowledge.

Source D

Everywhere cholera was much less fatal than pre-conceived notions had anticipated. The alarm was infinitely greater than the danger. When the disease gradually disappeared almost everyone was surprised that so much apprehension had been entertained.

Report from the Annual Register, 1832.

Source E

Not only is it now certain that the faulty water supply of a town may be the essential cause of the most terrible epidemic outbreaks of cholera, typhoid fever, dysentery and other allied disorders; but even doubts are widely entertained whether these diseases, or some of them, can possibly obtain general prevalence in a town except where the faulty water supply develop them. Dr Snow was not able to furnish proofs of his theory, but afterwards (and happily before his death in 1858) distinct experiments, as well as much new collateral information, established as almost certain that his bold conjecture had been substantially right.

From the annual report by John Simon, chief medical officer of health, to the Privy Council in 1870.

Source F

Although cholera had a dramatic impact unequalled by any other diseases it was 'fever' which throughout the nineteenth century stimulated the most action from both central and local authorities. Cholera came and went, but, as the Privy Council noted in 1864, 'typhus fever appears never to be wholly absent.' Frequently rising to epidemic proportions, the various fevers were always endemic, always lurking as a threat to the nation's health. Fever drew attention to filth and to poverty and so forced authorities to come to terms with public health, that is, with social and environmental conditions.

From Anthony Wohl, Endangered Lives, published in 1983.

Now use the marking criteria to assess your response.

How did you do?

What could you have done to have achieved higher marks?

The examiners will not be nit-picking their way through your answer, ticking things off as they go. Rather, they will be looking to see which levels best fit the response you have written to the question, and you should do the same when assessing your own responses.

How will I time my responses?

You have 1 hour 20 minutes to answer two questions. Remember that the (a) question is compulsory and that you will have a choice of one from two (b) questions. Take time, say, five minutes, to read through the paper and think about your choice of (b) question. The (a) question is worth half the marks of the (b) question, so you should aim to spend twice the time on the (b) question. This means that, including planning time, you should spend about 25 minutes on the (a) question and about 50 minutes (again, including planning) on the (b) question.

You have now had a lot of practice in planning, writing and assessing your responses to the sort of questions you can expect to find on the examination paper. You are well prepared and you should be able to tackle the examination with confidence. Good luck!

Glossary

Adulterate Spoiling food or drink by adding something to it, for example, adding chalk to bread to make it look white (to mislead as to its quality).

Apprenticeship Originally a medieval system whereby young people (usually boys) were apprenticed to a master craft worker for a certain number of years to learn a specific trade. It continued, with variations, into the twenty-first century, where young people could obtain apprenticeships in shipbuilding and vehicle engineering, for example. In the nineteenth century, youngsters could be apprenticed to the many mills and factories in the industrial north and midlands, in order to learn skills that would make them self-supporting.

Bashaw A haughty, proud, imperious man; a grandee.

Benthamite A follower of the teachings of Jeremy Bentham (see page 19).

Board of Guardians Under the old Poor Law, unelected 'overseers of the poor' were responsible for the local administration of the Poor Law. They were severely criticised by the Poor Law Commission of 1832–4. Under the Poor Law Amendment Act, Poor Law guardians were similarly responsible for the local administration of the Poor Law, but they were elected by local ratepayers. The more property a ratepayer had, the more votes that ratepayer had to use in these elections. In practice, many of the old overseers were returned as guardians, thereby enabling not simply continuity between old and new ways, but also continuity of the old corrupt practices and attitudes to paupers. It was not until 1894 that the property qualification was abolished and women were thus able to become guardians.

Bubonic plague A highly infectious epidemic disease. It was carried by fleas that lived on rats, and transmitted to people via flea bites. Bubonic plague first appeared in Europe as the Black Death in around 1348–9 and returned at regular intervals, disappearing from England in the 1660s. Mortality rates were very high.

Centralisation Running services from a central, rather than a local, authority.

Chartism Chartism was a radical movement that began in the 1830s, after the 1832 Reform Act had failed to give the vote to working people. Chartists supported the six points of the People's Charter: annual elections, equal electoral districts, payment of MPs, universal manhood suffrage, the secret ballot and the abolition of a property qualification for MPs. Chartism as a movement died out in the 1850s, but by 1920 all its demands (except for annual parliaments) had been realised.

Civil registration In 1538 Thomas Cromwell instructed every parish to keep books in which the vicar should enter every baptism, marriage and burial at which he officiated. This entry should be made after the service on Sunday with a churchwarden as a witness. This practice continued, with more or less efficiency and accuracy, until the nineteenth century. The rise of non-conformity, the fall in church attendance and the increasing mobility of the population made parish registers increasingly unreliable. In 1837 the system of civil registration was introduced, which meant that national, civil certificates of births, marriages and deaths were issued as legal documents and records kept, initially, at Somerset House.

Cyclical unemployment Unemployment that would only be short term and was related to trade cycles. For example, the failure of one season's cotton crop in the USA could mean unemployment for workers in Manchester's cotton mills, but a good crop next time would lead to full employment.

Elementary Education Act (Forster's Act), 1870 This Act provided for local elementary schools to be set up where there were gaps in the church provision of schools. These 'Board' schools were to be financed from the locally levied rates. Many workhouses sent their children to Board schools rather than try to provide education within the workhouse walls.

Germ theory of disease By the beginning of the nineteenth century, most scientists and doctors knew of the existence of micro-organisms. Many believed that they were caused by disease, not that they were the cause of disease. Some people believed that disease was caused by miasma, or gases in the air. In the 1860s Louis Pasteur (1822–95) made the link between micro-organisms (commonly called germs) and disease. It was Robert Koch (1843–1910) who took the next step of linking specific diseases with certain microbes.

Habeas Corpus   Literally, 'you have the body'. In 1679 the Habeas Corpus Act was passed by Parliament to prevent people being imprisoned in secret and without trial. It was suspended in 1817 (and in other times of crisis), which meant that people could be imprisoned without trial for an indefinite period.

Impotent poor   People, such as the sick, disabled and old, who could not look after themselves.

Indigence   A frequently used nineteenth-century term meaning a person's inability to support themselves, and so they became **indigent**.

Laissez-faire   Literally, 'let be' or 'leave alone'. The belief that the government should involve itself as little as possible in the affairs of its people. In the context of poverty, this did not mean that the poor should be neglected, simply that it was not the government's responsibility to look after them.

Less eligibility   One of the definitions of 'eligibility' is 'the ability to choose'. When applied to the Poor Law, 'less eligibility' meant 'less worthy of choice'. In other words, the poor would not choose to become paupers if they could support themselves otherwise. It followed that conditions inside a workhouse had to be worse than those of the poorest individual who was existing on his or her own wages.

Mandatory act   An act of Parliament that had to apply to everyone, everywhere.

Miasma   People who believed in the miasma theory of disease said that a miasma was a poisonous vapour characterised by a bad smell created by decaying matter. The existence of a miasma in the air, they said, caused disease.

Micro-organism   Tiny organisms, such as a virus or a bacterium, which can only be seen under a microscope.

Municipal Corporations Act, 1835   This act of Parliament laid down that councillors were to be elected for three years and aldermen elected by the councillors for six years. The act applied to 178 boroughs. Additional corporations, including Manchester and Birmingham, were established later.

Napoleonic Wars   A series of wars fought by different combinations of European states against revolutionary France and the armies led by Napoleon. The wars were fought during 1792–7, 1798–1801, 1805–7 and 1813–14. British involvement was during 1793–1802 and 1803–1815. The wars ended with the Battle of Waterloo on 18 June 1815, when the forces of Prussia under Blucher, and Britain under Wellington, defeated the armies of Napoleon.

Oligarchy   Strictly speaking, this means 'government by a small group of people'. A self-perpetuating oligarchy would be a group of people who kept themselves in office, year after year.

Overseer of the poor   Each year, every parish appointed one or two overseers of the poor who were approved by the local magistrates. These people were usually churchwardens or landowners. Overseers were responsible for administering poor relief in their parish. They levied a poor rate and supervised its distribution. Under the 1834 Poor Law Amendment Act, boards of guardians took over the work of the overseers and, where overseers did remain, their job was usually one of simply assessing and collecting the poor rate.

Parish   Originally an area served by a vicar and a parish church. However, acts of Parliament from the sixteenth century used the parish as an area for secular administration.

Parliamentary Reform Act, 1867   This increased the number of voters to over two million men, and included the 'respectable' working classes by allowing occupiers of dwelling houses who had lived there for 12 months to have the vote.

Pauper   A person in receipt of poor relief.

Pauperism   The situation when the poor could no longer feed and clothe themselves, even at subsistence level, and had to turn to the authorities for help.

Permissive legislation   This is legislation that did not apply automatically to everyone, everywhere. A permissive act was an act that only applied if certain conditions were met: for example, if a certain number of people in a town or city wanted it to apply or if conditions reached certain specified criteria and it had to apply.

Poor rate   A tax on property levied at parish level and used to provide relief for the parish poor.

Private improvement acts   Private acts of Parliament applying to one town or city that intended to improve, for example, paving or lighting, that would make life better for its citizens.

Proletariat   Originally the name given to the lowest class of citizen in ancient Rome. By the nineteenth century it had come to mean the lowest class in any community and was usually used derogatively. The term usually referred to wage-earners with little or no property of their own, who depended for their income on the sale of their labour.

Radicals   Radicals are people who seek a fundamental change in political structures. In nineteenth-century Britain, radicals looked for reform within the existing constitutional framework: they did not look to overthrow the existing system, simply to change it legally and legitimately. There was never a single radical party. Radicals grouped differently under different causes: free speech, factory reform and free trade, for example.

Relief Support given to paupers to enable them to maintain a basic standard of living. This relief could be 'outdoor' (in their own homes) or 'indoor' (in a workhouse or poorhouse).

Six Acts, 1819 The Six Acts together prohibited meetings of more than 50 people, increased stamp duties on newspapers, made the publication of blasphemous and seditious material a transportable offence, forbade military training by civilians, limited the right of an accused person to adjourn his or her trial to prepare a defence and gave magistrates powers to search private houses for arms.

Smallpox A highly contagious, and sometimes fatal, disease caused by a virus. People who catch smallpox usually have a high fever and a rash. The spots turn into pustules that can scar a person for life. Human beings are the only carriers of smallpox and so vaccination is very effective; so effective, in fact, that there have been no recorded cases of smallpox anywhere in the world for many years.

Ten Hours Movement A sustained campaign in the 1830s for the reduction of hours worked in textile mills to ten per day. The campaign was led inside Parliament by Lord Shaftesbury and John Fielden, and outside by Richard Oastler. In 1847 the Ten Hours Act limited the work of women and young persons (aged 13–18) in textile mills to ten hours a day for five days a week and eight hours on Saturday.

Tolpuddle Martyrs In 1834 six agricultural labourers from Tolpuddle, Dorset, led by George Loveless, were sentenced to seven years' transportation for swearing illegal oaths. The oath-swearing was part of a loyalty ceremony that bound the men into a trade union. Although trade unions were not banned at this time, the government feared that unions of agricultural workers would heighten the general rural unrest and so used this device to nip such unions in the bud. After a series of mass campaigns, the men were pardoned and returned home in 1838.

Tories One of the two main political parties in Britain between the late seventeenth and mid-nineteenth centuries, they were traditionally associated with the belief that the Crown and the Anglican Church were the mainstays of political, religious and social order. The Tory groupings of the 1830s resulted in the emergence of the Conservative Party.

Tuberculosis Tuberculosis (TB) can be an airborne infection spread by inhaling droplets infected by the tuberculosis bacterium, or it can be caught by drinking milk from cows that have bovine TB.

Typhoid Typhoid is a bacterial infection carried in contaminated milk, water or food. It thrives in situations where human waste can contaminate water. The most common symptoms are headaches, coughs, watery diarrhoea and high fever. Some people do not display the symptoms, but are carriers and can transmit it to others.

Typhus Typhus is usually spread from infected rodents to people by the bites or faeces of body lice, fleas, mites or ticks. It thrives in unsanitary, crowded conditions. The most common symptoms are headaches, chills and fever. Typhus and typhoid were frequently confused in the first half of the nineteenth century.

Utilitarianism A theory that society should be organised so as to secure the greatest happiness for the greatest number of people. Actions and institutions should be judged according to whether or not they added to this sum total of happiness. Utilitarianism underpinned the reforms of the first half of the nineteenth century, in particular the Poor Law Amendment Act of 1834 and sanitary reform. Jeremy Bentham was one of the thinkers who developed this theory and it had a profound influence on his secretary, Edwin Chadwick.

Vagrancy Roaming from place to place with no settled home, work or obvious means of support.

Vested interest This phrase is used to suggest that people are more likely to support a measure if they, their families or social group will benefit from the measure. People with power – whether that power rests in land, money, trade or industry – will look very carefully at measures that might damage that power.

Vestry minutes A vestry is a room in an Anglican church where meetings are held. Vestry minutes would therefore be a written account of such meetings – in this case, meetings of churchwardens or overseers of the poor.

Whigs One of the two main political parties in Britain between the late seventeenth and mid-nineteenth centuries, they were traditionally associated with political, religious and social reform. By the middle of the nineteenth century, Whigs had been absorbed into the new Liberal Party.

Woolcombers Woolcombers combed fleeces to straighten the fibres and remove lanolin from the wool. This entailed heating huge iron combs in open fires and pulling the hot combs through the fleeces, which were hung up close to the fire. Most woolcombers lived and worked in the same dwellings and were desperately poor.

Workhouse test That all those seeking relief had to apply to their union workhouse.

Index